Human Resources
for the Non-HR Manager

Human Resources
for the Non-HR Manager

Carol T. Kulik
University of Melbourne

Psychology Press
Taylor & Francis Group

New York   London

Psychology Press
Taylor & Francis Group
711 Third Avenue
New York, NY 10017

Psychology Press
Taylor & Francis Group
27 Church Road
Hove, East Sussex BN3 2FA

© 2004 by Taylor & Francis Group, LLC
Psychology Press is an imprint of Taylor & Francis Group
Originally published by Lawrence Erlbaum Associates

International Standard Book Number-13: 978-0-8058-4296-8 (Softcover)

Cover design by Sean Trane Sciarrone

Library of Congress Cataloging-in-Publication Data

Kulik, Carol T.
    Human resources for the non-HR manager / Carol T. Kulik.
        p. cm.
    Includes bibliographical references and index.
    ISBN 0-8058-4295-0 (cloth : alk. paper) ISBN 0-8058-4296-9 (pbk. : alk. paper)
    1. Personnel management. 2. Personnel management—United States. I. Title.
HF5549.K775   2004
658.3—dc22
                                                                2003060016

Visit the Taylor & Francis Web site at
http://www.taylorandfrancis.com

and the Psychology Press Web site at
http://www.psypress.com

To Gaylord,
whose bottomless reservoirs of patience,
loyalty, and optimism are a daily inspiration

Contents

Preface

We tend to think of the human resource function as being confined to the human resources department and its legions of equal employment opportunity officers, recruiters, and human resource (HR) managers. But, in fact, the day-to-day activities of hiring, motivating, and retaining employees fall heavily on the shoulders of the frontline managers in marketing, finance, and other functional specializations. Managers, unfortunately, are often poorly prepared for these activities. Business education and technical training programs generally give little attention to the interpersonal aspects of management. The business press frequently describes managers who are frustrated trying to hire employees in a tight labor market, who suffer sweaty palms when they need to give an employee a less-than-stellar performance review, and who spend sleepless nights agonizing over layoff decisions.

A basic understanding of the human resource function can be beneficial to all managers, regardless of their particular line function or area of expertise. Competency in the human resource area has perhaps never been more critical. Changes in the U.S. economy are affecting the daily operation of local and international businesses. Newspapers report on the latest waves of layoffs sweeping through the business world and hint at a shifting balance of power between employees and employers. While yesterday's manager was desperate for workers and offered prospective job applicants a high starting salary and innovative benefits (including daily massages and the opportunity to bring pets to work), tomorrow's manager may have the opportunity to be far more selective in choosing among potential hires.

This book is designed for non-HR managers who find themselves engaged in HR activities on a regular basis, despite having little training (or perhaps, even interest!) in HR. Who are these managers? What are the challenges they face? Here are a few examples, all people I met while I was developing and writing this book:

- A fine arts undergraduate plans to open an art gallery after graduation. Knowing she will need exposure to basic managerial skills, she enrolls in a "management for nonmanagement majors" class that devotes less than a week to human resources. How can she fill in the gaps in her knowledge?
- An MBA graduate is promoted into his first managerial position. He finds that his MBA concentration in finance gives him little information about how to conduct the performance appraisals of the financial assistants assigned to him. How can he learn to evaluate performance and communicate performance ratings to his assistants and ensure a smooth working relationship?
- The small business owner finds that her business is expanding to the point that she needs to hire additional help. She places a help-wanted ad and hires the first five employees who apply. Unfortunately, she eventually fires all five employees. How can she avoid hiring mistakes in the future?
- The "insanely great" computer programmer has reached the top of his pay grade. The only way to advance in the organization is to become a team leader in his workgroup. How can he prepare himself for the human resource activities that will now be a part of his work responsibilities?

In all of these examples, the manager's main interest and primary expertise is in a field other than human resource management. Yet, the manager's success ultimately depends on his or her ability to enact human resource activities effectively. *Human Resources for the Non-HR Manager* is designed as an accessible resource for anyone who faces a similar challenge. This book presents HR material using nontechnical language and offers practical guidelines for the manager in coping with the day-to-day issues inherent in managing people at work.

ORGANIZATION OF THE BOOK

The book is organized into five major parts. Part I contains introductory material. Chapter 1 provides an overview of the many activities that fall under the umbrella term *human resource management* and explains why these activities are increasingly the responsibility of frontline managers.

Chapter 2 summarizes the federal laws governing the recruiting, selecting, managing, and disciplining of employees.

The next three parts (Parts II, III, and IV) trace a manager's human resource activities from the initial recruitment and selection of new employees, through compensation and performance appraisal decisions, and ultimately to the unpleasant but sometimes necessary disciplinary and termination actions. Part II focuses on the front end of the manager–employee relationship and addresses topics related to finding and hiring new employees. Chapter 3 focuses on the activities of the non-HR manager in making job opportunities known to prospective applicants and discusses the relative advantages and disadvantages of external and internal recruiting methods. Chapter 4 can help managers avoid hiring mistakes. This chapter describes the range of selection techniques available to the frontline manager (including ability tests, personality tests, and integrity tests) with special attention to their relative costs, ability to predict on-the-job performance, and applicant reactions. Chapter 5 focuses on the most popular, but also the most flawed, selection technique used by frontline managers. This chapter describes the problems associated with traditional selection interviews and explains how managers can improve their interviewing effectiveness.

The chapters in Part III cover the critical management issues that come into play after a new employee is hired. Chapter 6 describes the most common performance appraisal techniques and provides advice to frontline managers about how to provide employee feedback. Chapter 7 is intended to help managers design a compensation system that will motivate employee performance, be perceived as fair, and still control costs. This chapter describes the basic components of traditional compensation systems (base salary, short- and long-term incentives, and benefits) and their implications for employee attraction, motivation, and retention. Chapter 8 uses a career stage model to contrast traditional and "new" careers. Special emphasis is placed on describing ways that managers can meet their employees' career needs even when promotions are not available.

Part IV covers the final stages of the employment relationship, including disciplinary actions and terminations. Chapter 9 tackles the difficult task managers face in correcting the behavior of the employees they supervise. The chapter includes a discussion of organizational grievance procedures and conflict resolution techniques. Chapter 10 discusses alternative reasons for termination (performance, discipline, downsizing) and their implications for communicating the termination decision to affected employees. This chapter prepares frontline managers to make legally defensible termination decisions and to manage morale among termination "survivors."

Finally, Part V addresses some day-to-day concerns in human resource management associated with employee demographics (gender, age, and disabilities). Chapter 11 presents an explanation of sexual harassment law and its implications for managerial activities. Special attention is given to the particular responsibilities of the frontline manager in preventing and managing sexual harassment in the workplace. Chapter 12 addresses the legal and social challenges associated with managing members of different age groups. Chapter 13 introduces frontline managers to the challenges and rewards associated with employing workers with disabilities. The chapter describes the implications of the Americans with Disabilities Act for hiring new employees and managing existing employees.

SPECIAL FEATURES

There are a number of special features in *Human Resources for the Non-HR Manager* designed to make the material more accessible and personally relevant. First, starting with chapter 2, each chapter includes several Manager's Checkpoints. These checkpoints are a series of questions that help the reader apply the material to his or her own organizational context. Second, the chapters also include Boxes that describe real-life examples of how companies are responding to HR challenges. Third, for the reader who wants more information about a particular HR topic, each chapter contains several suggestions under the heading "For Further Reading." These are references to articles published in outlets that bridge the academic–practitioner divide (e.g., the *Harvard Business Review*, the *Academy of Management Executive*). Finally, each chapter concludes with a series of Manager's Knots. The knots describe typical managerial problems, presented in a question-and-answer format. The knots take the reader into some of the gray, ambiguous areas of HR and suggest ways to apply the chapter material to real-life managerial dilemmas.

FOR THE INSTRUCTOR

An Instructor's Manual (written by Molly Pepper and Carol Kulik) is available to instructors who adopt *Human Resources for the Non-HR Manager* for classroom use. The manual contains chapter outlines, supplementary materials, and recommended activities. The manual also includes additional Manager's Knots that might be used for classroom discussion.

ACKNOWLEDGMENTS

Like any major project, writing a book requires two distinct forms of motivation—the motivation to begin and the motivation to finish. Many people in my life believed that this book was needed, and believed that I was the person to write it. Included in this group are Christina Shalley, Alison Davis-Blake, Blake Ashforth, Maureen Ambrose, Greg Northcraft, Annette Paciga, Jennifer Rhodes, and Peter Hom. Thank you for giving me that initial push. However, I am particularly indebted to two people who made it possible for me to finish the book: Elissa Perry and Loriann Roberson. They read every chapter multiple times, offered valuable suggestions, and were endlessly encouraging and supporting. Thank you for pulling me and my draft across the finish line. I a also grateful to Anne Duffy, my editor at Lawrence Erlbaum Associates, for her continuing efforts to support the project and see it through.

ABOUT THE AUTHOR

Carol T. Kulik has taught courses in human resource management at Carnegie Mellon University, the University of Illinois, and Arizona State University. She is now a Professor of Human Resource Management at the University of Melbourne, Australia. Carol received her bachelor's degree in psychology and her PhD in business administration from the University of Illinois at Urbana–Champaign. Her interests encompass cognitive processes, demographic diversity, and fairness, and her research focuses on how human resource management interventions influence the fair treatment of people in organizational settings. Recent projects have examined the effectiveness of organizational diversity training, the role of demographic characteristics in mentoring relationships, and the ways organizational insiders and outsiders "gripe" on the Internet. Carol's main interest, however, is the HR–non-HR interface, and the way that both HR *and* non-HR managers "do HR" in today's organizations. Carol is currently a senior associate editor at the *Journal of Management* and is an active member of the Academy of Management, the Society of Industrial/Organizational Psychology, and the Society for Human Resource Management.

I

Human Resources
for the
Non-HR Manager

1

What's It All About?

This is a book about human resource management (HRM)—the overall process of managing people in organizations. HRM encompasses the vast array of decisions frontline managers make about the people they supervise: Who should I hire? How can I reward good performance (and motivate even better performance)? Who should I promote into positions of higher responsibility (and who needs more training to do the jobs they are already occupying)?

This book was written for people just like you: people who either are, or soon will be, in positions where they are managing other people. You may not see yourself as an HR manager. Your primary interests may lie elsewhere—in finance, in marketing, or in accountancy—but your managerial responsibilities will no doubt include HR activities. This book will introduce you to the basics of HRM. It covers the fundamentals of hiring, performance appraisal, compensation systems, and other HR functions so that you can approach these parts of your job with confidence.

ISN'T HR THE HR MANAGER'S JOB?

Well, the answer depends on what you mean by HR! There's been a major shift in the responsibilities of the professional HR manager. Managers whose *primary* responsibility is HR, and who are housed in an HR department, are increasingly focusing on the broader strategic issues associated with managing people in organizations. HR managers, for example, may be predicting the organization's long-term hiring needs based on projections of company growth and competency requirements. Or they may be developing organization-wide human resource information systems that track all of the information about employees that used to be stored on paper in file drawers. Or they may be benchmarking company HR practices against industry competitors. All of these are big, time-consuming jobs, and they don't leave HR managers much resource slack to deal with the basic tasks (hiring, firing, and the like) that used to be the exclusive domain of the HR department. Fundamental HR activities are increasingly being decentralized and handed off to managers like you—line managers working front-and-center.[1] And that's a good thing, for the most part. After all, you're the one who is working with your employees day in and day out. You're the one spending time with them, getting to know them, listening to them, challenging them, rewarding them—aren't you in the best position to assess their needs and make the managerial decisions that directly affect them?

ISN'T HR JUST COMMON SENSE?

The answer is no! If good HR practices were that easy to implement, we'd have a lot more satisfied employees out there! What makes the *Dilbert* cartoon strip so funny? It's the fact that we've all had (or at least observed) a pointy-haired manager who doesn't know the first thing about managing people. Employees tell us, using a variety of electronic and nonelectronic forums, that their managers are *not* doing a good job of managing them. In anonymous surveys, exiting employees say that the number one reason they are leaving organizations is their relationship with their immediate supervisors—even though they may give other reasons (e.g., better salaries) to the boss to avoid burning any bridges.[2] Electronic forums like Boss from Hell (http://home.netscape.com/business/packages/hellboss/) are full of horror stories of bad management. Most definitely, there's a lot of bad HR going on out there! The question is, why?

Most managers have not been trained in HR. A lot of people are what I call *accidental managers*. Take Diane, for example. Diane designs flight decks for commercial airplanes. She loves the technical work. But the longer she's been with her employer, the more she has found herself taking on supervisory responsibilities for her group and making HR decisions—activities she didn't anticipate when she was taking all those engineering classes in graduate school. But even graduates of professional management programs get very little exposure to HR material. Given the rapid-fire pace of MBA programs and executive education programs, technical skills are usually given a lot more attention than the interpersonal aspects of management. Take Phil. His management program gave him a choice of second-year tracks, and he decided to focus on finance. In an effort to be as competitive as possible when he went out on the job market, he arranged his schedule to take as many specialty finance electives as he could—squeezing out the one or two HR electives that were available.

And once they're on the job, managers often find themselves too busy putting out fires to worry about the "soft" stuff like HR. Let's face it, it's tough out there. You're managing in an environment where you have a smaller budget, less job security, and generally fewer resources than the generations of managers who have gone before you.[3] But here's an inside secret: It's exactly these troublesome conditions that make HR so important today. You probably wouldn't be surprised to know that effective HR practices are linked to higher employee productivity and lower turnover.[4] But you might be surprised to learn that effective HR practices also impact on long-term company financial performance.[5] In short, good HR makes you a better manager, and makes your organization more competitive in today's marketplace.

SO, WHY THIS BOOK?

A basic understanding of the human resource function can be beneficial to all managers, regardless of their functional specialization or area of expertise. But it can be hard to get that basic understanding on your own. Academics tend to publish HR research in journals targeted to other academics—it can make for some pretty dense reading. And trying to follow the legal developments that affect HR decisions can be even more challenging. Even HR professionals have a hard time keeping up to date on HR issues—and knowing this stuff is a direct part of their job responsibilities.[6]

This book summarizes the material that a non-HR manager needs to know about HR. I review the research (the classics as well as the latest developments) and present it using nontechnical language. HR isn't rocket science, but it does have its own unique vocabulary—I'll explain those HR terms, and show you what they mean in practice.

The overall organization of the book follows a manager's human resource activities from the initial recruitment and selection of new employees, through compensation and performance appraisal decisions, and ultimately to the unpleasant but sometimes necessary disciplinary and termination actions. And once I've covered the basics, I'll get into a little more depth on some particularly challenging management issues: controlling sexual harassment, managing people of different ages, and managing people with disabilities. For each topic, the focus is always on *your* responsibilities as a *non-HR* manager. That means the distribution of material in this book is a little bit different from what you'd find in a standard HR text-book targeting HR professionals. For example, I won't spend a lot of time telling you *how* to validate a selection test—that's an activity you're likely to leave to an HR professional. However, I will help you to understand why va-lidity matters—and what you should be asking that HR professional before you agree to adopt the test (chap. 4). And, in comparison to the standard HR textbook, I've spent more time on the face-to-face interactions that characterize a non-HR manager's HR activities. Your responsibilities don't end once the HR decision is made—you also have to communicate that decision in performance appraisal meetings (chap. 6), disciplinary discus-sions (chap. 9), and termination meetings (chap. 10).

The book contains several unique features that I think you'll find helpful. First, starting with chapter 2, each chapter includes several Manager's Checkpoints. These checkpoints are a series of questions that will help you to apply the material to your own organizational context. Second, the chap-ters also include Boxes that describe examples of how companies are re-sponding to HR challenges. These examples may or may not be transferable to your own organization—but they'll definitely stimulate your thinking about how to creatively apply the material in your own context. Third, each chapter contains several suggestions under the heading, For Further Reading. These are references to articles published in outlets that bridge the aca-demic–practitioner divide (e.g., the *Harvard Business Review*, the *Academy of Management Executive*). They are a good source of more detailed infor-mation about the chapter topic. Finally, each chapter concludes with a series of Manager's Knots. The knots describe typical managerial problems, pre-sented in a question-and-answer format. The knots will take you into some of the gray, ambiguous areas of HR and help you to apply the chapter mate-rial to real-life managerial dilemmas.

WHAT'S NEXT?

If you're ready, let's go on and get started. We'll start with the "big picture." The next chapter focuses on the fundamentals of equal employment op-portunity law. It describes the legal environment that guides (and con-strains) managers' HR activities.

FOR FURTHER READING

Caudron, S. (1999, August). HR vs. managers. *Workforce*, 32–38.
Humphrey, B., & Stokes, J. (2000, May). The 21st century supervisor. *HRMagazine*, 185–192.
Rynes, S. L., Brown, K., & Colbert, A. E. (2002). Seven common misconceptions about human resource practices: Research findings versus practitioner beliefs. *Academy of Management Executive, 16*(3), 92–102.

Ulrich, D. (1998, January/February). A new mandate for human resource. *Harvard Business Review*, 124–134.

ENDNOTES

1. Evans, T. (2002, July). Feeding the line. *HR Monthly*, 12–13.
2. Dixon-Kheir, C. (2001, January). Supervisors are key to keeping young talent. *HRMagazine*, 139–142.
3. Conlin, M. (2002, May 13). The big squeeze on workers. *Business Week*, 96–97.
4. Huselid, M. A. (1995). The impact of human resource management practices on turnover, productivity, and corporate financial performance. *Academy of Management Journal, 38*, 635–672.
5. Huselid, M. A. (1995). The impact of human resource management practices on turnover, productivity, and corporate financial performance. *Academy of Management Journal, 38*, 635–672; Huselid, M. A., Jackson, S. E., & Schuler, R. S. (1997). Technical and strategic human resource management effectiveness as determinants of firm performance. *Academy of Management Journal, 40*, 171–188.
6. Rynes, S. L., Colbert, A. E., & Brown, K. G. (2002). HR professionals' beliefs about effective human resource practices: Correspondence between research and practice. *Human Resource Management, 41*(2), 149–174.

2

Understanding Equal Employment Opportunity Law

In this chapter, we'll be talking about federal laws that govern the employer–employee relationship. You need to understand the basics of federal equal employment opportunity (EEO) law so that you can develop HR systems that are consistent with legal requirements and make HR decisions that are legally defensible. Violating EEO law can be very costly. Employees who claim that they've been discriminated against are winning many of their cases, and the financial awards they're receiving are making employers gasp. In November 2000, Coca-Cola agreed to pay $192 million to settle charges of racial discrimination brought by a group of African American employees, and we're seeing multimillion-dollar verdicts even in cases involving a single employee.[1] And that's just the financial cost—imagine the cost to your company's reputation that can result from discrimination charges.

As you read this chapter and learn about EEO law, you'll see that employment laws generally emphasize what you *cannot* do as a manager. As long as an organization's practices don't violate EEO law, it's left up to the organization's management to decide how to best recruit, select, and just generally manage employees. In other words, a legally defensible HR system is only the foundation of an effective HR system, not the endpoint. That's why this chapter on EEO law is one of the first chapters in the book!

Once you've got the basics of EEO law, we can build on that and discuss HR practices that are legally defensible *and* effective.

The legal environment in the United States operates on multiple levels. At the highest level are federal laws. But there are also laws operating at the state and local levels. These state and local laws are generally consistent with the federal laws. However, many states and localities have passed EEO legislation that offers employees greater protection than federal law. For example, while federal EEO legislation does not protect employees from discrimination based on sexual orientation, many states and localities do offer that protection. I'm going to focus on federal level legislation, but you'll also want to get familiar with the state and local laws that operate in your area.

FEDERAL EEO LEGISLATION: THE BIG THREE

I'm going to start by describing three important federal laws governing equal opportunity. Why these three? These laws have wide-reaching scope. They apply to every human resource management decision you can think of: hiring, firing, compensation, work hours, you name it. And only the smallest private employers are exempt from this legislation. Firms operating in the United States, regardless of their country of incorporation, must comply with federal EEO laws. U.S. companies with offices or plants in foreign locations must comply with both U.S. and host-country requirements in their overseas locations.[2] Table 2.1 provides a brief summary of these three laws.

All three of these laws are administered by the *Equal Employment Opportunity Commission* (EEOC). The EEOC is the federal agency responsi-

TABLE 2.1

The Primary Federal Equal Employment Opportunity Laws

Federal Law	Who Is Affected	What the Law Says
Civil Rights Act (1964, 1991)	Employers with 15 or more employees	Prohibits discrimination on the basis of race, color, religion, national origin, or gender
Age Discrimination in Employment Act (1967)	Employers with 20 or more employees	Prohibits discrimination on the basis of age for people age 40 or over
Americans with Disabilities Act (1990)	Employers with 15 or more employees	Prohibits discrimination on the basis of physical and mental disabilities; requires "reasonable accommodation" of qualified applicants with disabilities

ble for enforcing EEO law and hearing employee complaints. A person who thinks that he or she has been discriminated against, and wants to file a formal claim against the offending company, first has to go to the EEOC. If the EEOC thinks the claim has some merit, the agency will try to help the two parties (the individual claimant and the company) to reach a mutually agreeable settlement. If a settlement cannot be reached, the EEOC can pursue the case in court on behalf of the claimant, or can give the claimant permission to pursue the case on his or her own.[3] During the 2001 fiscal year, the EEOC received 80,840 charges of discrimination.[4] With that many claims to investigate, there's no way that the EEOC could possibly shepherd each of those individual claims through the legal system. Instead, the EEOC emphasizes out-of-court agreements and only takes direct legal action in cases that are likely to have a major impact—class action suits that affect a large number of people or are likely to set a legal precedent for future cases.[5]

The agency's role in investigating discrimination claims can lead some managers to think of their relationship with the EEOC as primarily adversarial—especially if they've found themselves facing the agency's representatives in a courtroom. However, a key part of the EEOC's mission is preventing discrimination claims from occurring in the first place.[6] Therefore, the EEOC plays a huge educational role in helping businesses to understand the law and avoid claims of discrimination. The EEOC helps businesses to interpret the law by developing guidelines and recommendations about how to develop human resource management systems that stay inside the law. The EEOC holds training programs that help employers to understand how to stay within the law.[7] In addition, the EEOC's Web site (eeoc.gov) is a gold mine of resources for the manager who wants to understand EEO law.

Civil Rights Act (1964, 1991)

The Civil Rights Act (CRA) is a broad, sweeping piece of legislation that prohibits discrimination on the basis of race, color, religion, sex, and national origin. Title VII is the part of the CRA that applies to employment situations, and it prohibits discrimination based on those five characteristics in all human resource decisions—including hiring, firing, and all of the day-to-day conditions of employment (e.g., work hours, training opportunities). There are, however, a few exceptions to this blanket prohibition that I'll address a little later in this chapter. The CRA is also the law that is applied to sexual harassment. We'll talk more about the CRA and how to manage sexual harassment in chapter 11.

Under the CRA of 1964, employees who had been discriminated against could be awarded back pay and some attorney's fees, and be reinstated to jobs they had been denied because of discrimination. These remedies were intended to reposition the employee in the circumstances they would have been in had discrimination not occurred. However, the CRA of 1991 significantly extended the remedies available to discriminated employees. Now employees can also be awarded compensatory and punitive damages (e.g., for emotional suffering) in cases involving intentional discrimination, making it more lucrative for aggrieved employees to pursue their claims in court.[8] The CRA of 1991 also permits cases to be heard by juries rather than by judges.[9]

Notice that the wording of the CRA does not limit its protection to members of specific groups. By prohibiting discrimination based on sex, Title VII of the CRA protects both men *and* women from sex discrimination. By prohibiting discrimination based on race, Title VII of the CRA protects both Whites *and* members of racial minorities from race discrimination. The bulk of discrimination claims received by the EEOC are filed by women and racial minorities—but the law protects everyone. Take the situation at Jenny Craig. Jenny Craig is a weight loss company with a predominantly female workforce. A group of men working at Jenny Craig complained that they received poor treatment at the company, such as unfavorable sales assignments, orders to perform demeaning tasks (carrying trash, shoveling snow, fixing the boss's car), and a constant barrage of humiliating remarks. In other words, the men believed that they had been discriminated against because of their sex. Because the CRA prohibits sex discrimination, the men were able to file a claim against their employer.[10]

Under Title VII of the CRA, organizations are required to make a reasonable effort to accommodate employees' religious obligations. The religious protection afforded by the CRA encompasses "sincerely held" moral or ethical beliefs—an employee does not have to be affiliated with an organized religion to be protected against discrimination.[11] Employers are expected to make an effort to accommodate employees' religious holidays and to allow workers to dress in ways mandated by their religious beliefs.[12] For example, some factories have changed production schedules to accommodate Muslim employees' prayers, which are performed five times a day.[13] However, employers do not have to make accommodations that create an undue hardship (e.g., accommodations that involve monetary cost or result in a loss of productivity).[14] For example, an employee whose religious obligations make it impossible for him to work a Saturday shift might be accommodated by allowing him to switch shifts with a coworker. However, if a volunteer is not available to switch shifts, the employer is not required to pay a premium to a coworker or a supervisor to get the shift covered.[15]

Recently, the CRA's prohibition against discrimination based on national origin has been applied to English-only rules in the workplace. As racial and ethnic diversity in the workforce has increased, employees have brought a diversity of languages into the workplace. Some employers established policies prohibiting employees from using any language other than English at work, arguing that when employees use non-English languages it segregates the workplace, alienates English-speaking customers, and interferes with workplace efficiency. However, the EEOC's position is that these English-only rules constitute a form of national origin discrimination.[16] Only a handful of cases have directly addressed the legality of English-only rules, but a consistent picture is beginning to emerge. An English-only rule is most likely to be acceptable if the employer can establish a legitimate business justification for its policy. For example, English-only rules might be appropriate in manufacturing or construction contexts, where miscommuni- cation can result in mistakes that are costly not only in financial terms but in terms of employee health and safety. However, rules that require employees to speak English on their breaks or in private areas (e.g., employee cafeterias, rest rooms) would be hard to justify.[17]

Age Discrimination in Employment Act (1967)

A few years after the CRA of 1964 was passed, Congress passed the Age Discrimination in Employment Act (ADEA). This law prohibits discrimination against people 40 years of age and older. Like the CRA, the ADEA applies to all employment decisions. But unlike the CRA, the ADEA protects only older people—a person under age 40 is not protected. We'll talk more about the ADEA (and managing employees of different ages) in chapter 12.

Americans With Disabilities Act (1990)

Then, many years later, the Americans with Disabilities Act (ADA) was passed. This law prohibits discrimination against people with physical or mental disabilities. "Disability" is defined as a physical or mental impairment that substantially limits one or more major life activities, such as walking, talking, seeing, hearing, or working. That means the disabilities category includes physical disabilities like paraplegia and blindness, and also encompasses "invisible" disabilities like a heart condition or depression. Employers are required to make a "reasonable accommodation" for those applicants or employees capable of performing essential functions of the job. Depending on the nature and severity of the disability, reasonable accommodation might include restructuring the work to redistribute tasks across coworkers, allowing modified work schedules, or installing equipment to assist the disabled employee in his or her job.[18] We'll talk more about the ADA (and about managing people with disabilities) in chapter 13.

Manager's Checkpoint

Now that you've read about the Big Three EEO laws, use the following questions to make sure you understand their scope and application:

- Is my business affected by the CRA, ADEA, and/or ADA? (Unless you are a very small private employer, you probably are affected by these laws.)
- Which of my employees are protected by these laws? (All employees are protected against discrimination based on race, religion, national origin, and gender. However, only employees 40 or older are protected against age discrimination. And the ADA applies only to people with a disability otherwise qualified to do the work.)
- What human resource decisions are affected by these laws? (All of them, all the time. These laws apply to every human resource decision you make about your employees—including whether they get hired in the first place, how you manage their employment on a daily basis, and how the employment relationship is terminated.)

WHAT'S DISCRIMINATION, ANYWAY?

You've probably noticed that the three laws (CRA, ADEA, and ADA) provide surprisingly little detail about how to recognize or prevent discrimination. The law leaves managers with a responsibility to "not discriminate," but offers little guidance about how to avoid discrimination in day-to-day management practices. We have two sources available to help us to apply the law to management practice. First, we can look at the case law. We can look at cases in which judges or juries have been asked to make a decision about one organization's HR practices. By looking at these judicial decisions, we can see how judges are applying the law and see what practices they think are allowable under the law. Second, the EEOC provides guidelines to businesses explaining how they interpret the law. The guidelines issued by the EEOC are not themselves law—but these guidelines are treated with "great deference" and respect by the legal system.[19] You can find these guidelines on the EEOC's Web site, eeoc.gov.

Since the EEOC guidelines are not law, there are times when the EEOC's recommendations and judicial decisions conflict. I'll give you an example. In 1998 Blockbuster Video, like many organizations, had grooming requirements for its employees. These requirements banned long hair for male employees, but placed no restriction on hair length for female employees. The EEOC's interpretation of the CRA was that these grooming regulations were discriminatory on the basis of sex. But the judge disagreed and let Blockbuster off the hook.[20]

Managers sometimes find this kind of ambiguity frustrating—how are you supposed to understand the law if even the people enforcing the law disagree on what's discriminatory and what isn't? It helps to remember the purpose of EEO law and the EEOC's role in administering it. EEO law is intentionally general. Congress writes laws so that they can be applied in a very wide range of circumstances—many of those circumstances can't even be imagined yet. It was impossible for the people drafting the CRA and including religion as a protected characteristic in 1964 to anticipate the large number of cases being filed by Muslim employees who claimed they were discriminated against during a post-September 11 backlash—and yet the CRA is flexible enough to accommodate these employees' concerns.[21] The EEOC's job is to make sure that businesses stay within the law—so their interpretation of the law is always the less risky alternative. A manager who stays within the EEOC guidelines is certain to be operating within the law.

Disparate Treatment and Adverse Impact

Two types of discrimination are recognized in EEO law. The first type is called *disparate treatment*. Disparate treatment discrimination occurs when members of different groups receive unequal treatment or are evaluated by different standards. Suppose, for example, a business took out a classified ad soliciting applicants for a clerical position and specified at the bottom of the ad "no Catholics will be considered." That's an example of disparate treatment because non-Catholics are considered for the position, but Catholics are not (unequal treatment). Another example of disparate treatment would be if an organization used an intelligence test to decide who would be hired, but changed the cutoff score depending on the employee's national origin—Non-Asians were hired with a passing score of 80%, but Asians had to score 95% before they were hired (different standards for different groups).

Disparate treatment cases often involve direct, intentional forms of discrimination. You might think that today's organizations would be unlikely to engage in the kind of blatant discrimination associated with disparate treatment, but cases of disparate treatment still make their way to the light of day. One recent case involved a company called Rent-A-Center. Rent-A-Center treated men and women very differently on the job and during the hiring process. Witnesses testified that Rent-A-Center's store managers and company executives had repeatedly articulated an anti-female hiring policy ("Women don't belong in rent-to-own" and "get rid of women any way you can") and destroyed women's job applications.[22] The percentage of women in Rent-A-Center's workforce dropped from 22% to 2% over just a few years.[23] Rent-A-Center and the EEOC eventually reached a settlement in this case. The company agreed to pay a cash settlement of $47 million and to begin making wide-ranging institutional changes.[24]

The second type of discrimination can be a little trickier to recognize. *Adverse impact* discrimination occurs when groups are unequally affected by the same treatment or standards. For example, if I insist that all the accountants in my office meet a 6-foot height requirement, I'm not likely to hire Hispanic or female applicants (because, in general, Hispanics and women tend to be shorter than non-Hispanics and men in the population). In adverse impact discrimination, the organization is using a procedure or strategy that looks like a perfectly innocent nondiscriminatory practice— but the procedure has a disproportionate effect on members of a particular group. For example, a Domino's Pizza franchise required that all of its delivery employees be clean-shaven. Why is that a problem? About half of the Black male population in the U.S. suffers from a skin condition (pseudo-folliculitis barbae) that makes facial shaving painful—about 25% of Black males can't shave at all. So by establishing "clean-shaven" as a requirement for the job, Domino's was more likely to hire White males than Black males—in other words, the shaving requirement had an adverse impact on Black applicants.[25]

Adverse impact discrimination can apply to other human resource decisions besides hiring standards. For example, we'll be talking about downsizing decisions in chapter 10. When an organization decides to downsize, it applies certain criteria (e.g., seniority, performance appraisals, skills) to decide which employees will stay and which will be terminated. These downsizing decisions may also have adverse impact on members of certain groups.[26] For example, a male-dominated organization that has been proactively hiring women over the last few years is likely to terminate a disproportionate number of women if a strict seniority rule is applied.

The Shifting Burden of Proof

Now that we've clarified the two types of discrimination, let's see how the legal standards get applied. Suppose you have a job applicant who didn't get hired by your organization. This applicant believes that his or her rights have been violated. The applicant contacts the EEOC and files a claim. What happens next?

First, the EEOC investigates the applicant's claim to see if a *prima facie* case can be established. Prima facie means, literally, "on the face of it." The

EEOC will screen out cases that are clearly nondiscriminatory, keeping trivial or nuisance cases out of the court system. Prima facie cases are the ones that remain—cases in which the EEOC finds sufficient evidence of discrimination to require you, the employer, to defend your actions. Once a prima facie case is established, it becomes your responsibility to demonstrate that your organizational practices did not violate the law. This exchange is called the *shifting burden of proof.* However, the particular kind of evidence presented by each side depends on whether the applicant's claim to the EEOC is one of disparate treatment or adverse impact.

Applicants making a disparate treatment case must show that they were treated differently because of their race, national origin, sex, or one of the other dimensions protected by EEO law. For example, an applicant who didn't get hired would need to show that he or she was treated differently in the hiring process as a function of one or more of those dimensions. As the employer, you would then need to show that there was a *non*discriminatory reason why you didn't hire the applicant. For example, you might provide evidence that the applicant was not qualified for the job, or you might show that the person who did get the job had better qualifications than the applicant.[27]

For adverse impact cases, a prima facie case is usually established through statistical comparisons—I'll tell you more about these comparisons in just a minute. Then, as the employer, you need to provide evidence that your hiring procedures are valid, despite the adverse impact that they create against a particular group. In other words, you would demonstrate that the procedures you used to make the hiring decision (e.g., the selection tests, the job interviews) predict performance on the job (you'll hear a lot more about validity in chap. 4).

Now, let's go back to those statistical comparisons I mentioned earlier. The challenge in establishing a prima facie case of adverse impact is figuring out how much adverse impact is enough to count as discrimination. Even with a completely valid, nondiscriminatory hiring procedure, you'd be unlikely to hire *exactly* the same number of men and women, or the same number of Whites, Blacks, Hispanics, and Asians. How much of a difference across groups is acceptable, and how much is too much? How do we decide that an "unequal effect" is large enough to qualify as adverse impact under the law? To help with these questions, the EEOC has established the four-fifths rule. The four-fifths rule is a heuristic, a rule-of-thumb, used to draw the line between nondiscriminatory and discriminatory situations.

The Four-Fifths Rule.   The four-fifths rule establishes a clear cutoff point: A human resource procedure becomes discriminatory when the selection rate of one group is less than 80% (four-fifths) of the selection rate of the group with the highest selection rate. It'll be a lot clearer with an example. Take a look at Table 2.2. Your help wanted ad has attracted 100 appli-cants—60 of these applicants are White, 30 of these applicants are Hispanic, and 10 of these applicants are Black. Based on their scores on a selection test, you hire 50 of these applicants: 40 Whites, 4 Hispanics, and 6 Blacks. The selection rate of each group is obtained by dividing the num-ber of people hired by the number of applicants—so, the White selection rate is 40/60 = .67, the Hispanic selection rate = 4/30 = .13, and the Black selection rate is 6/10 = .60. Because the selection rate of Whites is the highest, that selection rate becomes the standard. If the selection rate for Hispanics or Blacks is less than 4/5ths (or .80) of .67 (the selection rate for Whites), there is adverse impact in the procedure. In fact, the selection rate for Hispanics (.13) is only .19 of the selection rate for Whites—so we con-clude that the test does have adverse impact on Hispanics (.13/.67 = .19, and .19 < .80). However, the procedure does not have an adverse impact on Black applicants (.60/.67 = .90, and .90 > .80).

The four-fifths rule is a common procedure for establishing a prima facie case of adverse impact, but there are other possibilities too. Sometimes a prima facie case is established by demonstrating that the number of em-ployees in a company who belong to one group is not proportional to the number of people in the labor pool who are members of that group. For ex-ample, an adverse impact case might be established by demonstrating that the number of Black lawyers in your law firm is not proportional to the number of Black people in the labor market who have law degrees. The big question here is, what's the relevant labor market? Law firms often recruit on a national level, so the relevant comparison would be the number of Blacks in the national labor force with relevant law degrees. However, in a prima facie case involving Black secretaries, the relevant labor market might be restricted to Blacks having secretarial skills and living within com-muting distance of the employer.

Notice that in the shifting burden-of-proof dance, it's the EEOC who ac-tually runs the numbers on your workforce distributions. But you can run

TABLE 2.2
Applying the Four-Fifths (.80) Rule

	Whites	Hispanics	Blacks
Number of applicants	60	30	10
Number of hires	40	4	6
Selection rate	40/60 = .67	4/30 = .13	6/10 = .60
Comparison to highest selection rate		.13/.67 = .19	.60/.67 = .90
Adverse impact ?		Yes: .19 < .80	No: .90 > .80

your own internal checks to see if you are vulnerable to adverse impact claims. There's no reason why you shouldn't periodically conduct a self-audit and see if you are violating the four-fifths rule or other statistical indicators of adverse impact. These kinds of checks give you the chance to identify vulnerabilities in your human resource practices and correct them—before they turn into lawsuits.[28]

Manager's Checkpoint

Use the following questions to see whether your HR practices might be vulnerable to claims of discrimination under federal EEO legislation:

- Are all decision makers aware of the fundamentals of EEO legislation? (If not, some decision makers may be using protected characteristics as part of their hiring, managing, or firing decisions—contrary to EEO law.)
- Are all decision makers aware of the legal requirement to accommodate the needs of employees with religious obligations or employees with disabilities? (In addition to requiring nondiscrimination based on religion or disability status, EEO requires accommodation of these employees unless the accommodation imposes an undue hardship on the employer.)
- Do any of my organizational policies (on hiring, managing, or firing decisions) make distinctions between people based on protected EEO characteristics? (Look closely, for example, at grooming standards or dress codes that are gender-specific. These group-specific policies might constitute disparate treatment under EEO law.)
- Do any of my organizational practices (regarding hiring, managing, or firing) have adverse impact on members of a group (e.g., people of a particular sex, race, or age)? (Heuristics like the four-fifths rule can be helpful in identifying organizational practices that appear neutral but have an adverse impact on some groups.)

IS IT EVER OK TO DISCRIMINATE?

EEO laws prohibit discrimination on protected characteristics, but there are exceptions. There are certain limited situations in which religion, sex, national origin, or age (but usually not race or color) can be used directly in employment decisions—situations in which *only* members of a particular group (e.g., members of a particular religion or sex) are capable of performing the job. In these cases, the protected characteristic is a *bona fide occupational qualification* (a BFOQ). A BFOQ exception, for example, might be claimed by a denominational school that integrates religious teaching throughout its curriculum. Only a Baptist history teacher can serve as a Baptist role model and integrate his or her Baptist experience into the history classroom—so religion (being Baptist) is a BFOQ. A nursing home with only female residents might claim a BFOQ exception if attendants perform intimate hygiene activities that would be morally objectionable to the residents if they were performed by an attendant of the opposite sex. Only female attendants can perform those activities without offending the residents—so sex (being female) is a BFOQ.

It's not that easy to know when the BFOQ exception applies and when it doesn't. Try this one: You probably are familiar with Hooters restaurants, a national chain that features female waitstaff (Hooters Girls) who wear bright orange short shorts. Is "being female" a BFOQ for the job of waiting tables at a Hooter's restaurant? The EEOC said it wasn't—the agency said there was nothing about "being female" that made women uniquely suited for serving food in a restaurant.[29] The EEOC recommended that the chain eliminate the Hooters Girl position and make all those waitstaff jobs available to men.[30] But Hooters said that "being female" *was* a BFOQ—they claimed that the Hooters girl was an essential component of the marketing goals of the restaurant, a component that could only be fulfilled by women. The EEOC chose not to litigate this case, so we'll never know for sure how it would have been decided in court. However, in related cases, courts have generally not been persuaded by marketing arguments as a basis for establishing a BFOQ. Airlines who argued that passengers preferred female flight attendants or that their marketing strategy depended on maintaining a "sexy image" were not successful in establishing "being female" as a BFOQ for flight attendants.[31]

EQUAL OPPORTUNITY vs. AFFIRMATIVE ACTION

What's the difference between equal opportunity and affirmative action? In general, all that equal opportunity laws require of U.S. businesses is *passive nondiscrimination*—the laws specify personal characteristics (e.g., sex and race) that should *not* be used in employment decisions. In contrast, *affirmative action* involves more proactive attempts to increase the number of minorities and/or women in specific positions. Affirmative action is a very broad term encompassing a variety of recruiting and selection activities. For example, an organization might engage in affirmative action by recruiting at women's colleges as well as at coed ones, or an organization might make a special effort to place its job advertisements in magazines targeting readers associated with a particular demographic group. These forms of affirmative action are not usually controversial.[32] However, affirmative action activities may also include consciously using an applicant's sex and race in employment decisions. Many people have strong negative reactions to this type of affirmative action—even those people who might benefit from such a program.[33]

There are two situations in which American businesses are required to go beyond passive nondiscrimination and engage actively in affirmative action. First, affirmative action is required of businesses that have contracts with the U.S. government. That's because federal contractors have to abide by additional legal requirements not imposed on private employers. These requirements usually take the form of *Executive Orders*. Unlike the EEO laws we've been discussing so far, executive orders are issued directly by the President of the U.S. rather than going through Congress. Executive orders are not administered by the EEOC—instead, they are administered by the Labor Department's Office of Federal Contract Compliance Programs (OFCCP). However, the two agencies have parallel responsibilities, and their written regulations are similar as well.[34]

A series of Executive Orders prohibit federal contractors and subcontractors from discriminating based on the characteristics protected by the Big Three (race, sex, religion, national origin, age, and disability status), as well as a few others (political affiliation, marital status). But in addition, federal contractors are required to take affirmative steps to hire members of underutilized groups.

When is a group underutilized? *Underutilization* occurs when there are fewer minorities or women in a particular job group than would reasonably be expected by their availability in the local labor market. Contractors need to compare, for each job category, the percentage of that group (e.g., the proportion of female welders) with the percentage of that same group (e.g., female welders) in the relevant labor market. (Sounds a lot like the way we demonstrate adverse impact, doesn't it? Similar statistical techniques are used to demonstrate underutilization and adverse impact.) Based on the utilization analysis, the contractor should then establish goals and timetables to create a more balanced workforce. These goals and timetables are supposed to be flexible, not hard-and-fast quotas.[35] In addition, the goals should only be kept in place until the underutilization has been corrected— affirmative action should not be used to *maintain* a demographically balanced workforce.

Second, affirmative action may be required if a business is found guilty of discrimination. In these cases, a judge may order a business to engage in affirmative action for a specified length of time in an effort to make amends for earlier discrimination. Affirmative action may also be part of the terms of agreement if a case is settled out of court. For example, in that Rent-A-Center settlement I mentioned earlier, Rent-A-Center agreed to earmark 10% of future vacancies over a 15-month period to women who were victims of discrimination in the past, to actively seek qualified women to serve on its board of directors, and to publicize its desire to recruit qualified and interested women for jobs in its stores and for promotions at all levels.[36]

Notice that both of these situations are very narrowly applicable. If your organization is not a federal contractor, and if you have not been found guilty of discrimination in the past, you are not required to engage in affirmative action—you are only required to engage in passive nondiscrimination. In fact, affirmative action (explicitly considering race or sex in your hiring decisions) might be considered discriminatory under EEO law.

OTHER IMPORTANT FEDERAL LEGISLATION

In addition to the Big Three EEO laws, there are a few other pieces of federal legislation you should know about. These laws don't have the same range or scope as the Big Three—they have more limited application. I've summarized these additional laws in Table 2.3.

Pregnancy Discrimination Act (1978)

This Act is an amendment to Title VII of the CRA, and it clarifies how organizations should manage employees who are pregnant. The Act recognizes pregnancy as a temporary disability, and requires that pregnant women not be treated differently than other employees with temporary disabilities. Dates for beginning maternity leave may not be set arbitrarily, and a pregnant woman must be allowed to continue working as long as she is physically able.

Family and Medical Leave Act (1993)

This Act allows employees to take time off from work to attend to certain family responsibilities without being penalized by their employer. Employees may take 12 weeks of unpaid leave during any 12-month period to care for a newborn child, to care for an adopted child, to care for a spouse, child, or parent with a serious health condition, or to cope with their own serious health condition. Employers may require that employees use up all of their accrued vacation time or personal or sick leave before taking unpaid leave. Upon returning to work, employees are entitled to the same job or one that is equal in status and pay.[37]

TABLE 2.3

Additional Federal Employment Laws

Federal Law	Who Is Affected	What the Law Says
Pregnancy Discrimination Act (1978)	Employers with 15 or more employees	Prohibits discrimination on the basis of pregnancy or pregnancy-related condition; Pregnant employees must be treated in accordance with short-term disability policies
Family and Medical Leave Act (1993)	Employers with 50 or more employees	Requires employers to provide up to 12 weeks' unpaid leave per year for a variety of family and health issues
Equal Pay Act (1963)	Employers with 2 or more employees	Requires equal pay for men and women performing substantially equal work in the same job classifications
Immigration Reform and Control Act (1986)	All employers	Requires employers to verify applicants' eligibility to work; prohibits discrimination against noncitizens who are eligible to work in the U.S.

Equal Pay Act (1963)

This Act requires that employers provide equal pay to men and women performing substantially equal work in the same job classification. While the Act is generally consistent with the requirements of the CRA, its scope is considerably more narrow. For one thing, the Equal Pay Act only applies to pay and not to other types of human resource decisions (e.g., hiring). For another, the Equal Pay Act only applies in situations where men and women are performing essentially the same work—work that requires comparable skill, effort, and responsibility, and is performed under similar working conditions. The Equal Pay Act does permit employers to pay unequal wages to men and women if the wage differences are based on differences in education, prior experience, or seniority.[38]

Immigration Reform and Control Act (1986)

This Act requires that employers verify the citizenship status of all new employees within 3 days after they are hired. The Act also clarifies whether employers can discriminate on the basis of U.S. citizenship. It's allowable for an employer to use U.S. citizenship as a tiebreaker in making a choice between a U.S. citizen and an equally qualified noncitizen. However, employers are prohibited from using citizenship as a pretext for national origin discrimination.[39] For example, the Act would be violated if an employer was unwilling to hire Asian noncitizens, but regularly hired European noncitizens.

WHAT'S NEXT?

Now that you know the fundamentals of EEO law, let's move on. How do you develop human resource strategies that are both legal and effective? The best place to start is at the very beginning of the employment relationship. The next chapter focuses on recruiting issues.

FOR FURTHER READING

Bland, T. S. (2000, October). Sealed without a kiss. *HRMagazine*, 84–92.
Crosby, F. J., & Konrad, A. M. (2002, Winter). Affirmative action in employment. *The Diversity Factor*, 5–9.
Roffer, M. H., & Sanservino, N. J., Jr. (2000, September). Holding employees' native tongues. *HRMagazine*, 177–184.
Yakura, E. K. (1996). EEO law and managing diversity. In E. E. Kossek & S. A. Lobel (Eds.), *Managing diversity* (pp. 25–50). Cambridge, MA: Blackwell.

MANAGER'S KNOT 2.1

"I work for a company that does a large amount of business internationally, and so I regularly send my employees to other countries to meet with clients. In some of these countries, it's still unusual for women to work in managerial positions, and I'm concerned that some of my clients may not respond well if I send my female employees as representatives. Is it a problem if I take the manager's sex into consideration before deciding where I'll send them?"

Yes, it could be a problem. In general, customer preference or bias is not an adequate defense for discrimination under the CRA. By choosing to send only men to certain locations, you are establishing disparate treatment (men and women are not given equal consideration for international postings). In addition to potentially being discriminatory, your policy is limiting the career potential of the women you supervise by denying them developmental opportunities.

MANAGER'S KNOT 2.2

"I work for a toy manufacturer, and we just started recruiting employ-ees using the Internet. Our website is very playful, and we've made it very easy for interested applicants to apply online. But a significant proportion of our applications are from kids who just think it would be fun to work at a toy company—most of these kids aren't even old enough to work! Do I need to consider these kids as 'applicants' when I check our procedures for adverse impact?"

This is a great question, and it's an issue that the EEOC is grappling with right now. By lowering the physical and geographic hurdles that used to limit people's opportunities to apply for jobs, organizations are also reeling in applicants who are just curious, unqualified, or generally poorly suited for the job. The EEOC is currently drafting guidelines that will more clearly de-fine an "applicant" for the purpose of employer record-keeping. These guidelines are likely to make a distinction between "serious applicants" and nonserious ones.[40] Stay tuned.

MANAGER'S KNOT 2.3

"One of my employees asked for some time off, citing a 'serious health problem' under the Family and Medical Leave Act. I gave him the leave, but then I learned that his 'serious health problem' was a case of his ul-cers acting up. Do ulcers entitle leave under the FMLA? After all, the employee's condition was not life-threatening."

Since the FMLA took effect in 1993, employers have struggled to understand the definition of a "serious" health condition. Courts have established that a wide range of ailments can qualify as serious conditions as defined by the FMLA, including many nonlife-threatening conditions such as morning sick-ness, migraine headaches, and lumbar strains. An employee's medical condi-tion is "serious" if it (a) requires inpatient care in a hospital, or (b) requires continuing treatment by a health care provider. For example, if your employee's ulcers were a chronic condition that required periodic visits to a doctor or on-going treatment with prescription drugs, it could certainly qualify as a "serious" condition under the FMLA.[41]

ENDNOTES

1. Workers winning big awards in lawsuits. (2001, March 28). *USA Today*, p. 1B.
2. Rosse, J., & Levin, R. (1997). *High-impact hiring*. San Francisco: Jossey-Bass.
3. Bland, T. S. (2000, October). Sealed without a kiss. *HRMagazine*, 84–92.

4. Burrough, D. J. (2002, March 10). Bias claims rising in US. *Arizona Republic*, p. EC1.
5. Seligman, D. (1996, July 22). The EEOC in retreat. *Fortune*, 156.
6. Leonard, B. (2002, May). On a mission. *HRMagazine*, 38–44; Woodward, N. H. (2001, September). Help from the EEOC? *HRMagazine*, 123–128.
7. Woodward, N. H. (2001, September). Help from the EEOC? *HRMagazine*, 123–128; Work week. (2001, December 18). *Wall Street Journal*, p. A1; Montwieler, N. (2002, January). Dominguez sets EEOC agenda, redefines "job applicant." *HRNews*, 2.
8. Jones, D. (1998, April 2). Fired workers fight back … and win. *USA Today*, p. 1B; Arthur, D. (1995). *Managing human resources in small and mid-sized companies.* New York: AMACOM.
9. Arthur, D. (1995). *Managing human resources in small and mid-sized companies.* New York: AMACOM; Gutman, A. (2000). *EEO law and personnel practices.* Thousand Oaks, CA: Sage.
10. Carton, B. (1994, November 29). Muscled out? *Wall Street Journal*, pp. A1, A7; Gross, J. (1995, February 26). Now look who's taunting. Now look who's suing. *New York Times*, sect. 4, p. 1.
11. Frierson, J. G. (1988, July). Religion in the workplace. *Personnel Journal*, 60–67.
12. Lansing, P., & Feldman, M. (1997). The ethics of accommodating employees' religious needs in the workplace. *Labor Law Journal, 48,* 371–380.
13. Schellhardt, T. D. (1999). In a factory schedule, where does religion fit in? *Wall Street Journal*, pp. B1, B12.
14. Frierson, J. G. (1988, July). Religion in the workplace. *Personnel Journal*, 60–67; Levy, T. I. (2000, February). Religion in the workplace. *Management Review*, 38–40.
15. *TWA v. Hardison*. (1977). 422 U.S. 63.
16. Davis, A. (1997, January 23). English-only rules spur workers to speak legalese. *Wall Street Journal*, pp. B1, B7.
17. Roffer, M. H., & Sanservino, N. J., Jr. (2000, September). Holding employees' native tongues. *HRMagazine*, 177–184.
18. Arthur, D. (1995). *Managing human resources in small and mid-sized companies.* New York: AMACOM.
19. *Albemarle Paper Company v. Moody.* (1975). 442 U.S. 405.
20. Work week. (1998, June 16). *Wall Street Journal*, p. A1; Harper v. Blockbuster Entertainment Corp. (1998). 139 F.3d 1385 (11th Cir.).
21. Workplace bias to be addressed. (2001, December 12). *Arizona Republic*, p. A20; Leonard, B. (2002, May). On a mission. *HRMagazine*, 38–44.
22. Grimsley, K. D. (2001, December 29). 4,800 women in class to sue Rent-A-Center. *Washington Post*, p. E01; Grossman, R. J. (2002, August). Paying the price. *HRMagazine*, 28–37.
23. Chynoweth, D. (2002). 4800 seek damages for sex discrimination from Rent-a-Center. Retrieved January 14, 2002, from http://www.ucimc.org
24. U.S. Equal Employment Opportunity Commission (2002, March 8). *EEOC announces $47 million agreement in principle to settle claims of class-wide sex bias against Rent-A-Center.* Press release.
25. McEvoy, S. A. (1995–1996). A "hairy" question: Discrimination against employees who violate employers' appearance policies. *Journal of Individual Employment Rights, 4*(1), 67–79. Bradley v. Pizzaco of Nebraska, Inc. (1993). 7 F.3d 795 (CA8).
26. Dunham, K. J. (2001, November 8). Fair layoffs? *Wall Street Journal*, p. B8.
27. Rosse, J., & Levin, R. (1997). *High-impact hiring.* San Francisco: Jossey-Bass.

28. Grensing-Pophal, L. (2001, November). A balancing act on diversity audits. *HRMagazine*, 87–95.
29. Grimsley, K. D. (1995, December 18–24). Playing hardball with the EEOC. *Washington Post*, weekly ed., p. 20.
30. Millman, N. (1995, November 16). EEOC, lawsuits claim girls-only job is no hoot. *Chicago Tribune*, sect. 3, pp. 1–2.
31. *Diaz v. Pan American World Airways*. (1971). 442 F.2d 385; Wilson v. Southwest Airlines (1981). 517 F.Supp 292 (ND Texas).
32. Konrad, A. M., & Linnehan, F. (1995). Formalized HRM structures: Coordinating equal employment opportunity or concealing organizational practices? *Academy of Management Journal, 38*, 787–820.
33. Kravitz, D. A., & Platania, J. (1993). Attitudes and beliefs about affirmative action: Effects of target and of respondent sex and ethnicity. *Journal of Applied Psychology, 78*, 928–938.
34. Ledvinka, J., & Scarpello, V. G. (1991). *Federal regulation of personnel and human resource management* (2nd ed.). Boston: PWS-Kent; Leonard, B. (2002, May). On a mission. *HRMagazine*, 38–44.
35. Rosse, J., & Levin, R. (1997). *High-impact hiring*. San Francisco: Jossey-Bass.
36. Grossman, R. J. (2002, August). Paying the price. *HRMagazine*, 28–37.
37. Arthur, D. (1995). *Managing human resources in small and mid-sized companies*. New York: AMACOM.
38. Arthur, D. (1995). *Managing human resources in small and mid-sized companies*. New York: AMACOM.
39. Joel, L. G., III. (1996). *Every employee's guide to the law*. New York: Pantheon.
40. Leonard, B. (2002, May). On a mission. *HRMagazine*, 38–44.
41. Paltell, E. (1999, September). FMLA: After six years, a bit more clarity. *HRMagazine*, 144–150.

II

Organizational Entry

3

The Recruiting Process

One of the biggest challenges for a manager is recruiting new employees. You want to attract a pool of high quality applicants so that you can select those who have the best fit to your jobs and your organization. But where are these applicants? How do you find them? In this chapter, I'll present a menu of recruiting choices, and discuss the relative advantages and disadvantages of each option. In general, the best recruiting method (or combination of methods) for your hiring needs is the one that quickly delivers the highest proportion of quality applicants without breaking the bank. As I describe each of the recruiting methods, keep the following four criteria in mind:

1. Cost. Keeping costs down without sacrificing quality is always a managerial concern. The cost of recruiting varies widely across methods, ranging from inexpensive newspaper ads to costly headhunter fees. Why pay Mercedes prices if a domestic compact will do the job?

2. Speed. Recruiting new employees can sometimes move at lightning speed and sometimes at a snail's pace. So one thing you need to consider is how quickly you need new employees to be on board.

3. Diversity. As an organization grows, managers need to be sure that their recruiting practices are consistent with equal employment opportunity requirements. In addition, hiring new employees who differ from cur-

rent employees in demographics, backgrounds, and experience may bring fresh ideas and innovation into the workplace. Different recruiting methods access different subsets of the labor force, and your choice of recruiting method may have important consequences in terms of the diversity of the resulting applicant pool.

4. Efficiency. Let me introduce a concept called the *yield ratio*. For each recruiting method, a yield ratio can be calculated in the following way:

Yield ratio = number of "hirable" applicants recruited through method A
total number of applicants recruited through method A

Putting that equation into words, the yield ratio is the proportion of applicants recruited through a given method that you would seriously consider hiring. The yield ratio is a simple, but extremely powerful, tool for comparing the efficiency of various recruiting methods. Some recruiting methods (e.g., putting a want ad in the local newspaper) can result in a huge number of applications. But if very few of the applicants have the necessary qualifications, this recruiting method can be very inefficient and result in a manager spending an inordinate amount of time sifting through applicant materials and screening out those who would be a poor fit to the job. Alternatively, some recruiting methods (e.g., employee referrals) may result in only a handful of new applicants. But if all of those applicants are people who the manager would be interested in hiring, this recruiting method can save a great deal of time and energy.

Unfortunately, few organizations systematically collect the data needed to compute yield ratios, and so managers have only a vague idea of how their recruiting strategies are performing. It's a good idea to get in the habit of asking each applicant how he or she learned about your job, and to record that information for later use. It's important to collect this information from every job applicant, even the ones you aren't interested in hiring. That way, you can compare the yield ratios associated with different recruiting methods to see which are most efficient in attracting quality applicants to your organization.

RECRUITING METHODS

For ease of discussion, I've organized the recruiting methods into two broad categories. In the first set of recruiting methods (External Recruiting Methods), a manager's attention is focused outside the organization—making people outside the organization aware of available openings. In the second set of recruiting methods (Internal Recruiting Methods), a manager is more focused on advertising available positions to people already associated with the organization—current employees, current customers, or former employees. As you'll see, both internal and external recruiting methods have some clear advantages and disadvantages.

External Recruiting Methods

Advertising.   One way to let people know about your available positions is to advertise. The predominant form of job advertising is still a printed ad in newspapers or trade journals. Recent estimates suggest that as much as $2.18 billion is spent each year on help-wanted ads, but your cost will vary depending on the size of your ad, the length of time you want it to run, and the prestige and circulation of the publication outlet. As the cost of print ads has risen, outlets such as radio,[1] billboards, and aerial banners[2] have become more popular. These alternative outlets may offer more exposure at a similar price tag—for example, the cost of broadcasting a radio ad over multiple days can cost the equivalent of a single Sunday print ad.

Advertising job positions externally has certain advantages. For a fairly low cost, your job opening can be presented to large numbers of people. In addition, because help wanted ads are aimed toward the general public, they can attract a highly diverse applicant pool. The speed with which your ad appears depends on the publishing schedule of your newspaper and advertisement availability on your radio station, but job advertisements are frequently followed by job applications soon after.

That sounds good, but help-wanted ads are associated with one big disadvantage: There are very few factors limiting any individual newspaper reader or radio listener from submitting an application. For the cost of a stamp, any Tom, Dick, or Sally can submit a resume in response to your ad. As a result, unless you have written a very specific, very focused ad, you may find that your help wanted ad elicits applications from individuals who are poorly qualified for the position. In other words, help-wanted ads can be a very inefficient recruiting method.

Internet Advertising.   Many organizations are now using the Internet as an expansion of their old-style help-wanted advertising, and posting their position announcements on one or more career Web sites. You can choose from a wide range of sites that appeal to general (e.g., monster.com, hotjobs.com, or careermosaic.com) or specialized (e.g., casinocareers.com for casino workers, jobsinthemoney.com for finance types, or funeralnet.com for morticians) audiences. This strategy can have the same advantages and disadvantages of newspaper advertising, although at a more accelerated pace. The Internet can offer an inexpensive way to let potential applicants all around the world know about your position.[3] An interested applicant can forward his or her resume electronically with just a few clicks of a mouse—and it can appear in your e-mail inbox seconds later.

However, because there are few obstacles to applying, you may find yourself flooded with applications from individuals who are poorly suited to your job.[4] In fact, the application glut associated with Internet recruiting has in turn spawned an industry offering automated software products that filter resumes based on employer keywords.[5] Some companies now refuse to accept electronic resumes to reduce the flood of applications in response to online advertising.[6] In addition, there is some concern that Internet career Web sites are most likely to attract young White male applicants.[7] Computer access is not equally distributed across the population, and relying on the Internet as a source of applicants may limit the diversity of your applicant pool. Finally, the cost of advertising on the Internet is going up. A single 60-day job posting on monster.com cost $175 in 1998 and rose to $305 in 2002.[8]

Campus Recruiting, Search Firms, and Employment Agencies. One way that organizations improve the efficiency of external recruiting methods is to enlist intermediaries. For example, an organization might send recruiters to college campuses, hire an executive search firm, or enlist the help of an employment agency. The intermediary (the campus recruiter, the executive search firm, or the employment agency) prescreens job applicants using a set of criteria specified by the hiring organization and sends forward only those applicants who meet minimum requirements. Depending on the intermediary's network, this method may result in a diverse pool of applicants. And because the applicants have been prescreened for their qualifications, the time and energy demands on the hiring organization are reduced.

While intermediaries can definitely improve the yield ratio associated with external recruiting, the enhanced efficiency comes with a cost. There are the obvious costs associated with hiring recruiters to visit campuses and the fees associated with search firms—large search firms typically charge a fee of one-third of a new hire's starting salary.[9] But there can also be other costs that are more difficult to quantify. Inevitably, the hiring manager has to give up some control over the screening process. If you were doing the hiring yourself, you might be willing to seriously consider a highly motivated job applicant with less than the desired level of experience, or you might recognize that higher qualifications on one dimension could compensate for shortcomings on another. These preferences and trade-offs are difficult to translate into a straightforward list of hiring criteria to be used by an outsider. As a result, the intermediary may send you inappropriate candidates, or more likely, may miss qualified applicants who might be ideal hires. One of the biggest concerns is that the intermediary may not be sufficiently informed about the job or the organization to present an accurate picture to the job applicant. In recent years, organizations have been held liable for promises made to job applicants by recruiters who misrepresented the position's responsibilities and opportunities. These *truth-in-hiring* cases represent an emerging area of employer liability and may result in legal costs down the road.[10]

In addition, using intermediaries can result in a slower, lengthier recruiting process. Campus recruiting operates on a schedule based on the academic calendar, and even after you've identified appropriate applicants, they may not be able to start on the job until after graduation, leaving your position open for several months. Employment agencies and executive search firms serve many clients, and the speed with which your position is filled may depend less on the availability of job applicants in the labor market than on the slack resources your intermediary has available to reach them.

Internal Recruiting Methods

Job Posting. So, what's the alternative? Rather than advertising your positions to the outside world, suppose you advertised these positions to your existing employees. Chances are you've made some good hiring decisions in the past, but these employees may now be interested in different positions. Many organizations post jobs internally (either literally by thumbtacking a job announcement to a bulletin board, or virtually by posting the announcement onto an Intranet Web site). Recruiting doesn't get any cheaper than this. The speed of this method is somewhat unpredictable, and depends on your employees' motivation and interest in the posted positions. Also, because you are only reallocating existing employees across positions, you are not going to boost the diversity of your workforce. But this method is associated with an extremely high yield ratio. The applicants already know you and your company, and you already have a good deal of information about the applicants. As a result, both sides can make informed decisions about job fit.

Doesn't internal posting only postpone the recruiting problem? Yes, but internal posting can help slot qualified applicants into higher-level or more difficult-to-fill positions. Hiring new employees into the positions former employees vacate may be both easier and less risky.

Employee Referrals. Have you ever hired an employee who was so good that you wished you could clone him or her? Well, employee cloning is unlikely in the near future, but that employee may have friends or family members who would make good hires. Employee referral programs, in which current employees receive a bonus for referring successful job candidates, tend to have some of the highest yield ratios around. Your current employees know the organization very well, and can do a very accurate informal prescreening of potential hires.

Many managers are skeptical of employee referral programs, and their concerns usually revolve around the possibility that employees will refer a large number of friends or family members who are either unsuitable or who won't stick around very long. However, in practice, those kinds of problems are rare. Most employees are well aware that their own reputations are at stake when they refer friends or family for employment, and think carefully before doing so. In addition, you can design the program to require that new hires remain on the job for a fixed period of time (e.g., 90 days) before a referral bonus is paid. This can reduce the applicant pool to those referrals who are very serious in their interest in working for you.

What should you offer? Referral bonuses range widely (see Box 3.1 to get an idea of the kinds of referral bonuses companies are offering). Some organizations offer payment in an installment plan—say, $50 on the day of referral, another $100 after 60 days of employment, and another $300 after the new hire has remained on the job for 12 months. Even if your organization doesn't have a formal employee referral program, you may be able to use this method on an informal basis by encouraging your employees to refer friends and family members.

BOX 3.1
What's a Referral Worth?

Savi Technology Inc. Sunnyvale, CA	$5,000 for referring a lower-level manager or engineer; $25,000 for referring a vice president[11]
Lands' End Dodgeville, WI	$35 and a shot at Green Bay Packers' tickets for each new hire; referrals account for about 55% of applications[12]
Next Jump Inc. Somerville, MA	$200 for referring a full-time employee who stays 6 months[13]
Tyco Electronics **Federal Credit Union** Redwood City, CA	$100 post-tax the day the new hire starts; $900 pre-tax if both the hire and the employee making the referral are still employed a year later[14]
Docent Inc. Mountain View, CA	$5,000 for each referral who stays 90 days plus a shot at winning a year's worth of housing costs up to $40,000[15]
Deloitte & Touche Wilton, CT	$2,500 bonus plus a chance at winning a Chevrolet Corvette or $50,000[16]

Sound too good to be true? Well, employee referrals do have their downsides. First, the speed factor is unpredictable. In some cases, employees may be able to respond quickly to your requests for referrals. But your employees may not have a very extensive network, and even if they know suitable applicants, those referrals may already be committed to other employers. In addition, relying on employee referrals may result in a very homogeneous workforce. When your employees refer friends and family members, they are very likely to be referring applicants of the same race, nationality, or religion as themselves. Sometimes that homogeneity may be useful. For example, when Alpine Bank in Colorado needed tellers who could accommodate Spanish-speaking customers, the bank asked their Spanish-speaking Latino employees to refer family members for employment.[17] Courts have repeatedly upheld the legality of employee referral systems—organizations don't have to spend extra money on recruiting to guarantee a diverse workforce.[18] But if you are hoping that your employees will generate diverse ideas or reflect a diverse customer base, recruiting strategies that limit the employee demographic diversity may be problematic. In that case, you might still want to use employee referrals, but supplement this method with other strategies that reach a broader applicant pool (e.g., help-wanted ads).

Another disadvantage of employee referral programs can become salient if you ever need to trim your workforce. Some organizations have found that employees who are hired together also tend to "hang together" when the time comes to end the employment relationship.[19] The same personal connections that brought in the employee referrals can also lead to employees leaving "en masse" if they feel that one of their own has been unfairly treated.

By the way, customers may also be a good referral source, especially for customer service positions. Several airlines (including Southwest Airlines and American Airlines) encourage frequent fliers to refer friends and family to vacant positions.[20] These customers have had ongoing contact with the organization and have a pretty good idea of what it takes to provide successful customer service.

Former Employees. Today, many organizations are enthusiastically rehiring former employees. Employees who worked for you in a limited capacity (e.g., on a part-time basis, through an internship program, or in a consulting arrangement) may now be interested in full-time, long-term employment. Many organizations are also hiring "boomerangs" who left traditional organizations for dot-com startups and are now interested in returning to the fold.[21]

Depending on the size and history of your organization, former employees may represent a relatively small applicant pool. Therefore, this is not a method that is likely to yield a large quantity of diverse applicants in a short period. However, applicants that are drawn from this pool may have a very high probability of success. These former employees have already experienced your organization in its entirety—the good, the bad, and the ugly. As a result, both you and the applicant can make informed decisions about fit.

Choosing Between External and Internal Methods

So far, I've laid out the advantages and disadvantages of external and internal recruiting methods. These relative advantages and disadvantages are also summarized in Table 3.1. External methods such as newspaper or Internet advertising are relatively inexpensive and can identify applicants quickly, but they are associated with low yield ratios. Using intermediaries can boost the yield ratio, but this also raises costs and increases the length of time before new hires are on the job. Internal recruiting methods such as internal posting, employee referrals, and rehiring former employees have high yield ratios and lower costs, but are unpredictable in their speed and can result in a very homogeneous workforce.

So how do you choose? Well, the answer depends on your needs and your resources. If you need a lot of employees on board quickly, you may want to use newspaper and Internet recruiting, recognizing that you will have to invest considerable time and resources to sift through applications for suitability. If you anticipate a slower growth rate, and are willing to wait

TABLE 3.1

Advantages and Disadvantages of External and Internal Recruiting Methods

	Cost	Speed	Diversity	Efficiency (Yield Ratio)
External recruiting				
Advertising	Low-Moderate	Moderate-Fast	High	Poor
Internet advertising	Low-Moderate	Extremely Fast	Low-Moderate	Poor
Campus recruiting, search firms, and employment agencies	Moderate-High	Slow-Moderate	High	Moderate-High
Internal recruiting				
Job posting	Extremely Low	Slow-Fast	Low	High
Employee referrals	Low-Moderate	Slow-Fast	Low	High
Former employees	Low	Slow	Low	High

for high quality applicants to present themselves, then using intermediaries, starting an employee referral program, or posting jobs internally may be more appropriate. And remember that one option is to compensate for the disadvantages of one recruiting method by pairing it with another recruiting method. For example, an employee referral program can be initiated simultaneously with a newspaper advertising campaign, or a job announcement can be posted on both Internet and Intranet sites.

Manager's Checkpoint

Use the following questions to decide which recruiting methods are right for your hiring needs:

- How large is my recruiting budget? (If your recruiting budget is extremely small, you may be unable to hire intermediaries or offer inducements for employee referrals.)
- How many employees do I need? How long can I wait to fill open positions? (If you need to hire many employees quickly, internal recruiting methods may not produce enough applicants in time.)
- How important is it that I hire employees who are demographically diverse? (If you want to increase the diversity of your workforce, external recruiting methods may be more effective than internal methods.)
- How much time and energy am I willing to invest in applicant screening? (If you want to limit your involvement in prescreening, using intermediaries or internal recruiting methods may be more efficient.)

IMPROVING THE YIELD RATIO

You've probably noticed that in Table 3.1 the internal recruiting methods are consistently associated with higher yield ratios than the external recruiting methods. Why is that? Well, applicants hired through internal recruiting methods tend to have a much clearer picture of a job and its demands than applicants who have only read a brief job description or heard a brief summary of the job responsibilities from a recruiter.[22] Employees regularly discuss aspects of the job (the workload, the customers, the quality of supervision) with coworkers and with family or friends. Former employees, current employees, and applicants with friends or family working in the organization have accumulated a rich storehouse of information about life in your organization—warts and all. As a result, when these individuals put forward a formal application, they know what they are getting into, and they are likely to have already engaged in a thorough self-assessment of their fit to the job.

In contrast, most external recruiting efforts "accentuate the positive and eliminate the negative." Want ads extol the benefits of a position (Make good money! Set your own hours!) while omitting the downsides. Recruiters eager to "reel the candidate in" describe the job in glowing terms and conveniently neglect to mention the negatives. But let's face it: *every* job has some undesirable characteristics. For example, telemarketers put up with constant rejection and abuse.[23] Even the jobs that appear most glamorous from the outside have undesirable characteristics. While high school students may dream of traveling around the world as flight attendants, real-life flight attendants talk about difficult customers, jet lag, and other common complaints.

When a job applicant is left in the dark about a job's undesirable characteristics, both the applicant and the organization may face a reality shock down the road. If the applicant doesn't learn about the negative aspects of a job early in the recruiting process, the hiring manager may invest considerable time and effort only to learn that the applicant is poorly suited for the job. And if the applicant doesn't learn about the downsides until after the hiring decision, low performance and job dissatisfaction are likely to result.

Research suggests that applicants who receive a *realistic job preview* are more likely to be successful hires. What's a realistic job preview? In addition to telling people about all the positive things a job has to offer (e.g., high pay and benefits, good opportunities for advancement), recruiters also tell applicants about the unpleasant aspects they should be prepared for ("it's hot, dirty, and sometimes you'll have to work on the weekends"). You can also incorporate some of the negative information about your opening in the advertisements you place in newspapers or on the Internet. As a result, individuals who apply for your job do so with a balanced picture of the job's pluses and minuses.

The idea of providing negative information during the recruiting process may seem counter-intuitive. Managers who have had a hard time finding applicants may be reluctant to risk scaring them off. You're right to expect that negative information may immediately make some potential applicants unwilling to consider the job. But a realistic job preview can ultimately have the effect of boosting your long-run yield ratio. Remember, the people who are so turned off by the negative elements you present in the realistic job preview that they decide not to apply are the same people who would be likely to quit soon after being hired. A realistic job preview can help you to avoid investing time and training in applicants who ultimately are not good fits to the job.

If you are reluctant to directly present negative information to applicants, you might consider opening a communication channel so that potential applicants can gather realistic information about your organization and its job openings. For example, visitors to Cisco's Web site are invited to join the MakeFriends@Cisco program, which connects potential applicants with a real-life person from the department in which they want to work.[24] Web sites such as vault.com provide forums for potential applicants, current employees, and customers to interact and share information about life in the organization.

Manager's Checkpoint

The following questions might help you to decide whether you want to integrate realistic job previews into your recruiting process:

- Do new hires seem surprised about skill requirements, workload demands, or other aspects of the job? Are these surprises associated with employee dissatisfaction or attrition? (If your answer to both questions is yes, applicants may be receiving skewed information during the recruiting process.)
- Have I encouraged recruiters, managers, and current employees to share accurate information (both positive and negative) with applicants? (If your answer is no, organizational members may be trying to "help" in the recruiting process by overemphasizing positive elements of the job.)
- Have I given applicants access to customers and employees who can provide accurate information (both positive and negative) about the job? (If your answer is no, applicants may not be able to gather enough information to develop an accurate picture of what their day-to-day life in the organization is likely to be.)

EXPANDING THE APPLICANT POOL

You know the saying, drastic times call for drastic measures? That was the situation managers faced in the late 1990s, and Box 3.2 describes some of the strategies they used to fill positions. Will organizations face this kind of widespread recruiting challenge again? Sure—the only question is, how soon? Analysts suggest that in the years ahead a labor shortage will result from the retirement of huge numbers of baby boomers—a crunch likely to last for years or even decades.[25] But even when workers are plentiful, you may have a difficult time finding the right ones—you may be trying to fill jobs with some killer negative characteristics (6-day work weeks with low pay),[26] or your company may be located in a rural area with a small population base.[27] In these situations, you need to identify new untapped sources of job applicants. When you want to increase the applicant pool, there are three interrelated issues to consider: Who falls outside of your typical applicant pool? How can you reach them? And what would attract them to your organization?

Identifying Nontraditional Applicants

Let's start with a little exercise. Take a few moments to describe your "typical" employee in terms of demographics and lifestyle. Do you employ more men than women? Are most of your employees relatively young? Do your employees tend to be single? Where do your employees live in relation to work? Now, try "tweaking" each of those dimensions and consider the implications.

BOX 3.2
Recruiting in Lean Times

✷ In an effort to compete with larger firms offering higher pay, Controls Unlimited Inc., a small company in rural Ohio, put together a recruiting package for engineers that included twice-monthly company cookouts, free flights home for a long weekend when engineers work at remote sites (even in locations as distant as India), and an all-expense-paid weekend anywhere in the continental U.S. for an employee and spouse on the employee's 15th anniversary at the company.[28]

✷ iCube, an information technology consulting company in Cambridge, Massachusetts, offered employees a 32-inch TV for every new hire they referred. But when iCube needed 26 more consultants very quickly, they added a VCR to the package.[29]

✷ Starved for workers, Metro Plastics Technologies in Indianapolis offered 40 hours of pay for 30 hours of work with just one catch: Employees had to show up on time for their shift. The offer drew 300 applicants in 2 days.[30]

✷ Hi-tech jobs in Silicon Valley were so hard to fill in the late 1990s that recruiters were pulling business cards from restaurant fishbowls where engineers had placed them hoping to win a free lunch.[31]

✷ Shared Resources Inc.—a computer consulting company in Columbus, Ohio, with fewer than 100 employees—was so desperate for new employees in the late 1990s that the owner traveled to Chennai, India, to recruit new workers (and ultimately hired 6).[32]

Managers who go through this exercise sometimes find that their recruiting methods have attracted a particular "type" of employee—even though other types might be equally effective in the organization. Consciously identifying those employee groups who currently are not well-represented within your organization may provide useful clues about how you can change your recruiting strategies to "pull in" previously underutilized segments of the labor force. For example, when the aging workforce made it difficult to find high school students interested in jobs flipping burgers, McDonald's actively recruited retired and disabled members of their local communities. Another example of recruiting nontraditional applicants comes from the health sector. Historically, jobs associated with medical professions have had very skewed sex distributions: Nurses were usually women and pharmacists were usually men. When U.S. hospitals experienced a nursing shortage, they began to actively recruit male nurses, and when pharmacists became difficult to hire, pharmacies invested extra effort in recruiting and training female pharmacists. Employers have teamed up with groups as diverse as local prisons[33] and refugee service agencies[34] to open up new applicant pools. While prisoners and refugees aren't usually targets of organizational recruiting efforts, organizations pursuing these groups have found that they represent pools of underutilized labor resources.

Sometimes new segments of the labor pool can be identified by easing up on geographic constraints. Is your organization located in the inner city, but you would like to recruit from the suburbs? Or, is your organization located in a rural area, but you would like to recruit employees from distant towns and villages? It's becoming more and more common for organizations to offer transportation services to new employees as a way of broadening the recruiting pool. For example, an exclusive resort in the Florida Keys negotiated with the local transit system to establish a new bus route enabling them to recruit workers from 30 miles away.[35]

Another way to increase your applicant pool is to ask yourself whether you have imposed any artificial constraints on the recruiting process. For example, is there an age or skill requirement that could be lifted? Grocery store chains have been experimenting with hiring 14- and 15-year-olds as baggers.[36] Could you reallocate job responsibilities and create jobs that require less credentials (e.g., a paralegal degree rather than a J.D.) as a way of expanding the potential applicant pool?

Recruiting Channels

Now that you've identified these underutilized segments of the labor pool, the next challenge is reaching them. Your current recruiting strategies may not be attracting the attention of these nontraditional applicants. In some cases, the new strategy may simply be variations on your existing strategy. You may want to supplement your newspaper advertisements with ads in publications directed toward more specialized audiences (e.g., *Working Woman, The Advocate, Hispanic Times*).[37] Or you might want to review the list of college campuses where you recruit, and add some colleges that have significant minority or female enrollments.[38] Or you might want to investigate specialized recruiting sites, like www.BlackVoices.com, that target members of minority groups.[39] Adding these alternative outlets to your usual mix of recruiting channels can demonstrate to members of untapped applicant pools that your organization is committed to building a diverse workforce.[40]

Now, think about this. When you place a help wanted ad in a newspaper or on an Internet job board, you are only reaching people who are *actively* searching for a job. The biggest untapped part of the labor market includes those people who are not currently seeking employment. This group includes people who might be great fits to your job and your organization— but because they aren't reading the help-wanted ads, they'll never be able to consider you as an employer. How can you get your opportunity onto their radar screen?

Organizations recruit in many diverse contexts. Texas Instruments recruits employees at flea markets and sports events.[41] Cisco Systems targets art fairs, microbrewery festivals, and home and garden shows.[42] UPS sends recruiters to Metallica concerts.[43] What do all of these events have in common? They represent relaxed settings that attract plenty of people but few employers—giving the companies a chance to advertise their positions to a broad audience with little competition.

Firms are now placing their help-wanted ads on pizza boxes and restaurant place mats.[44] Provident Bank of Maryland encourages their employees to give "referral cards" to talented service providers (e.g., restaurant servers) they encounter in their daily lives.[45] The cards compliment people on their customer service skills and invite them to talk with the bank about service representative positions. Again, these methods put the position before the eyes of the *passive job seeker*—the one who doesn't yet know that he or she is interested in a new job.

We discussed Internet recruiting earlier. Organizations who use the Internet merely as an extension of their traditional recruiting strategies will only reach active job seekers, the ones who are actively monitoring career Web sites for new job opportunities. But passive job seekers surf the net too. Some high-tech firms monitor public Internet forums to find potential hires. If a poster offers a creative solution to a software user's problem on one of these forums, the firm can e-mail the poster and invite him or her to discuss employment opportunities.[46] Your own company Web site may also attract browsers or customers who aren't actively looking for a job. For example, Inacom, a former employee computer services firm in Omaha, attracted techies to its Web site by offering a flashy, graphics-enhanced game with a prize for successfully answering a series of technical questions.[47] Players were simultaneously being screened for potential employment at Inacom, and high-scorers were later contacted to discuss employment opportunities. Other organizations offer easy ways to learn about jobs on their own Web sites.[48] A customer might visit Southwest Airline's site to make a travel reservation, and invest a few minutes investigating employment opportunities before they leave. The advantage of all these recruiting methods is that your job announcement is being seen by a broader pool.

Inducements

In a tight labor market, organizations offer signing bonuses to fast food employees, full-time benefits to part-time workers, concierge services, on-site massages, and other glamorous benefits. However, it's important to recognize that while these methods of "extreme recruiting" attract a lot of attention, the goal is not just to offer more benefits. The goal, ideally, is to find the benefit that will make your organization more attractive than your competitors to a significant segment of the applicant pool. For example, in 1991, Lotus Development began offering employees with same-sex significant others the same spousal benefits available to employees in traditional marriages. Now, of course, benefits for gay partners are relatively common,[49] but as one of the first employers to offer this benefit, Lotus had a tremendous advantage. Most experts suggest that gays and lesbians represent about 10% of the overall population. Given the intense competition for high-tech employees, if a benefit like this makes Lotus just a little more attractive to that 10% than its competitors, then the value of the benefit may far exceed the costs of administering it.[50]

One option may also be tailoring your benefits to different segments of the applicant pool. For example, a Burger King franchise in Michigan offered applicants an education bonus program that allowed students to earn $1 for every hour worked up to $2,500 a year to further their education beyond high school. But older job applicants had the option of taking advantage of this bonus themselves or passing it on as a gift to a younger family member.[51] Trilogy Software Inc. in Austin, Texas, offers two different levels of health coverage and allows workers to configure their own compensation packages. Younger employees can take more risks if they want to (e.g., by designing a compensation package that emphasizes base salary), but older employees don't have to take the same risks if they choose not to (e.g., by designing a compensation package with a lower base salary but a higher level of health coverage).[52]

Manager's Checkpoint

These questions might help you to identify ways that you can expand your applicant pool:

- Have I been hiring a particular "type" of employee? (If your answer is yes, your recruiting strategies may be missing other viable segments of the labor pool.)
- Can I supplement my regular recruiting channels with alternatives that will reach these underutilized segments of the labor pool? (The answer here is almost certainly yes!)
- Am I currently offering benefits that might appeal to particular segments of the labor pool? If so, can I highlight these benefits in my recruiting practices? If not, are there benefits I would be willing to provide in order to attract additional applicants? (Again, the goal here is to match the inducements with particular segments of the labor pool.)

ALTERNATIVES TO RECRUITING

In this chapter, we've discussed a variety of ways that you can make your positions known to applicants. But, a word of caution: Recruiting new permanent employees may not always be the answer. Many businesses experience cycles in which there is high demand one week and low demand the next. During the 1990s, new workers were in short supply, and organizations recruited year-round to ensure enough workers for the peak periods.[53] But hiring for the peak periods may mean firing during the downturns. So one possibility to consider is whether peak demands can be accommodated through overtime, subcontracting, or hiring temporary help. Temporary workers no longer are limited to low-wage clerical positions; organizations can hire contingent employees at all professional levels. In addition, temporary assignments can be a great way to test fit before making a permanent hire—think of the temporary assignment as an extended realistic preview for both sides.[54]

Also, it's possible that your business cycle may differ from that of other local businesses. Some companies team up to share employees, shifting them from organization to organization depending on demand. For example, Olsten, the staffing company, created a pool of workers in Denver who are shared among eight companies.[55] Lands' End teamed up with a local cheese maker to share seasonal workers; when the cheese maker lays off workers in November, Lands End hires them to cope with the holiday rush.[56]

WHAT'S NEXT?

Recruiting is a critical first step in the staffing process. But once you've developed a recruiting strategy, the next challenge is selecting from among the interested applicants. In the next chapter, I'll describe the most common selection techniques and discuss their advantages and disadvantages.

FOR FURTHER READING

Bernstein, A. (2002, May 20). Too many workers? Not for long. *Business Week*, 127–130.
Matinez, M. N. (2001, August). The headhunter within. *HRMagazine*, 48–55.
Overman, S. (1999). Put overlooked labor pools on your recruiting list. *HRMagazine, 44*(2), 86–90.
Thomas, S. L. (2000, May/June). Recruiting and the web. *Business Horizons*, 43–52.

MANAGER'S KNOT 3.1

"I want to recruit a diverse workforce. How do I demonstrate a commitment to diversity during the recruiting process? And will an emphasis on racial and gender diversity turn off the White male applicants who make up the largest segment of my applicant pool?"

Avoid targeted searches that appear to exclude any groups— targeted searches can cause resentment among White men who fear they won't be considered for job openings, and may also be resisted by women and racial minority candidates who don't want to be perceived as affirmative action hires. Instead, create a recruiting process that emphasizes inclusion. Use specialized outlets (e.g., Internet sites and publications targeted to particular groups) to supplement your mainstream choices, not replace them. You'll also want to take a close look at your recruitment materials—the brochures, job announcements, and other materials you use during the recruiting process. Do the pictures in the brochure reflect the diversity you already have in your workforce? Does your organizational mission statement include a commitment to diversity? Research suggests that including statements about the organization's commitment to diversity in recruiting materials leads *all* applicants to rate the organization as more attractive—not just the female applicants, and not just the applicants who are members of racial minorities.[57]

MANAGER'S KNOT 3.2

"I rely heavily on our company's recruiters to find job applicants at college campuses and community job fairs. But recently I'm finding that the applicants these recruiters send to me are not good fits to the company culture or to the requirements of my jobs. What can I do to increase the effectiveness of these recruiting efforts?"

First, take a close look at the information you've provided to recruiters. Are recruiters familiar enough with the job content that they can knowledgeably address applicant questions? Recruiters often receive only a bare-bones sketch of the job requirements. That can discourage job applicants who try to probe for more details about the work environment. Second, check the message that you are sending to recruiters. Are you providing incentives for more applicants or for applicants who provide a better fit to the organization? Recruiters who are trying to fill quotas may be over-selling the job to potential applicants. By encouraging them to provide a realistic preview to job applicants, you communicate your commitment to finding qualified applicants, not just more applicants.

MANAGER'S KNOT 3.3

"I'm discouraged by my efforts to recruit employees for my small business. It seems like all the applicants want health insurance and other benefits I can't afford to provide. Is there any way that I can attract qualified applicants to my company?"

Small businesses often are unable to compete with large ones on financial terms. However, small businesses can offer job applicants more opportunities to gain hands-on experience and greater responsibilities than they might find at larger firms. Try emphasizing these nonfinancial benefits during your recruiting efforts. For example, students are frequently covered by their parents' health insurance plans, and might be less concerned about the lack of health benefits than applicants from other labor pools. But students would value flexible scheduling or training opportunities that allow them to gain work experience at the same time they are maintaining a full-time courseload.

MANAGER'S KNOT 3.4

"I finally convinced my boss that we should take the plunge into recruiting on the Internet. Any advice on doing this right?"

Take it slow! Start by using the Internet as a supplement to your traditional recruiting efforts, and systematically compare the yield ratios of Internet and non-Internet sources. You'll have more success in finding qualified applicants if you target specialized boards in your industry rather than using multi-purpose ones.

ENDNOTES

1. Joinson, C. (1998, September). Turn up the radio recruiting. *HRMagazine,* 64–70.
2. Overman, S. (1998, May). A creative net will snare the best. *HRMagazine,* 88–94.
3. Feldman, D., & Klaas, B. S. (2002). Internet job hunting: A field study of applicant experiences with on-line recruiting. *Human Resource Management, 41,* 175–192.
4. Work week. (1999, October 26). *Wall Street Journal,* p. A1.
5. Silverman, R. E. (2000, November 28). Software helps employers sift through work pool. *Wall Street Journal,* p. B14; Pollock, E. J. (1998, July 30). Inhuman resources. *Wall Street Journal,* p. A1.
6. Maher, K. (2002, January 29). Hitting the target. *Wall Street Journal,* p. B8.
7. Hogler, R. L., Henle, C., & Bemus, C. (1998). Internet recruiting and employment discrimination: A legal perspective. *Human Resource Management Review, 8*(2), 149–164.
8. Harrington, A. (2002, May 13). Can anyone build a better Monster? *Fortune,* 189–192.
9. Maher, K. (2003, January 14). Corporations cut middlemen and do their own recruiting. *Wall Street Journal Online.*
10. Moses, J. M. (1993, July 9). Employers face new liability: Truth in hiring. *Wall Street Journal,* pp. B1–B2; Work week. (1999, June 22). *Wall Street Journal,* p. A1; Lublin, J. S. (1999, December 21). Recent court case likely to push firms to be more candid with job applicants. *Wall Street Journal,* p. B17.
11. Silverman, R. E. (2000, February 22). The going rate. *Wall Street Journal,* p. B34.
12. Work week. (1997, October 23). *Wall Street Journal,* p. A1; Franco, M. D. (2002, November). Don't drop those incentives yet. *Catalog Age,* 29.
13. Silverman, R. E. (2000, January 25). Word of mouths. *Wall Street Journal,* p. B14.
14. Grensing-Pophal, L. (2001, August). *Credit Union Management,* 38.
15. It's all who you know, and who can last 90 days. (2000, November 1). *Wall Street Journal,* p. A1; Brown, E. (2000, October 30). Have friends, will hire. *Forbes,* 62.
16. Titunik, V. (2000, August 14). Get us an accountant, we give you the car. *Fortune,* 298.
17. Litvan, L. M. (1994, December). Casting a wider employment net. *Nation's Business,* 49–51.
18. Lambert, W. (1993, March 11). No bias seen in homogeneous work force. *Wall Street Journal,* p. B8.

19. Wysocki, B., Jr. (2000, March 30). Team effort. *Wall Street Journal,* p. A1.
20. Gilbertson, D. (1997, November 5). Frequent fliers turn headhunters. *Arizona Republic,* pp. A1, A15; Gilbertson, D., Sidener, J., & Davis, R. A. (1999, August 6). Southwest finds new way to use air-sickness bags. *Arizona Republic,* pp. E1–E2.
21. Work week. (1999, December 21). *Wall Street Journal,* p. A1; Vinzant, C. (2000, October 2). They want you back. *Fortune,* 271–272.
22. Williams, C. R., Labig, C. E., Jr., & Stone, T. H. (1993). Recruitment sources and posthire outcomes for job applicants and new hires: A test of two hypotheses. *Journal of Applied Psychology, 78,* 163–172.
23. Petzinger, T., Jr. (1996, September 20). They keep workers motivated to make annoying phone calls. *Wall Street Journal,* p. B1.
24. Useem, J. (1999, July 9). For sale online: You. *Fortune,* 67–78; Nakache, P. (1997, September 29). Cisco's recruiting edge. *Fortune,* 275–276.
25. Bernstein, A. (2002, May 20). Too many workers? Not for long. *Business Week,* 127–130.
26. Wysocki, B., Jr. (2001, July 10). When it is the job from hell, recruiting is tough. *Wall Street Journal,* pp. B1, B8.
27. Poe, A. C. (2001, April). Hiring in the hinterlands. *HRMagazine,* 81–88.
28. Hausman, T. (1998, October 20). Engineering perks. *Wall Street Journal,* p. B22.
29. Hausman, T. (1998, October 6). Handouts for the helpful. *Wall Street Journal,* p. B16.
30. Quintanilla, C. (1997, March 31). As jobs go begging, bosses toil nights—and improvise. *Wall Street Journal,* pp. B1, B8.
31. Richtel, M. (1999, November 19). Poaching in Silicon Valley. *International Herald Tribune,* business sect., p. 2.
32. Aeppel, T. (1999, October 5). A passage to India eases a worker scarcity in Ohio. *Wall Street Journal,* pp. B1, B18.
33. Harrington, A. (2000, May 15). Anybody here want a job? *Fortune,* 489–496; Grimsley, K. (1998, September 8). Employers go to prison to recruit new workers. *International Herald Tribune,* p. 9.
34. Harrington, A. (2000, May 15). Anybody here want a job? *Fortune,* 489–496.
35. Work week. (1999, April 27). *Wall Street Journal,* p. A1.
36. Work week. (1996, July 30). *Wall Street Journal,* p. A1.
37. Digh, P. (1999, October). Getting people in the pool; Diversity recruitment that works. *HRMagazine,* 94–98.
38. Johnson, J. L. (1997, April). The recruiting wars. *Discount Merchandiser,* p. 12.
39. Thaler, C. R. E. (2001, June). Diversify your recruitment advertising. *HRMagazine,* 92–100.
40. Anonymous (1996, December). In the moral minority. *Management Today,* pp. 4, 17.
41. Work week. (2000, June 6). *Wall Street Journal,* p. A1.
42. Nakache, P. (1997, September 29). Cisco's recruiting edge. *Fortune,* 275–276.
43. Useem, J. (1999, July 5). For sale online: You. *Fortune,* 67–78.
44. Sunoo, B. P. (1999, April). Temp firms turn up the heat on hiring. *Workforce,* 50–54.
45. Markels, A. (1998). Is anybody out there? *Working Woman, 23*(6), 40–46.
46. Munk, N., & Oliver, S. (1997, March 24). Think fast! *Forbes,* 146–151.
47. Useem, J. (1999, July 9). For sale online: You. *Fortune,* 67–78.
48. Boehle, S. (2000, May). Online recruiting gets sneaky. *Training,* 66–74; McConnell, B. (2002, April). Companies lure job seekers in new ways. *HR News,* pp. 1, 12.
49. Schodolski, V. J. (1995, November 6). Extension of benefits to gay partners on rise. *Chicago Tribune,* pp. 1–2.

50. Hammonds, K. H. (1991, November 4). Lotus opens a door for gay partners. *Business Week*, pp. 80, 85; Bulkeley, W. M. (1991, October 25). Lotus creates controversy by extending benefits to partners of gay employees. *Wall Street Journal*, pp. B1, B10.
51. Ray, S. P. (2001, May 7). Personal communication.
52. Rasmussen, E. (2000, May). Does your sales force need a new look? *Sales and Marketing Management*, 13.
53. Tight job market. (2001, January 31). *Arizona Republic*, p. E3.
54. Aley, J. (1995, October 16). The temp biz boom: Why it's good. *Fortune*, 53–55; Work week. (1999, September 21). *Wall Street Journal*, p. A1.
55. Quintanilla, C. (1997, March 31). As jobs go begging, bosses toil nights—and improvise. *Wall Street Journal*, pp. B1, B8.
56. Work week. (1997, October 23). *Wall Street Journal*, p. A1.
57. Williams, M. L., & Bauer, T. N. (1994). The effect of a managing diversity policy on organizational attractiveness. *Group and Organization Management, 19*, 295–308.

4

Hiring New Employees

If your recruiting efforts are successful, you will find yourself in the luxurious position of being able to select new hires from a pool of interested applicants. But how do you identify the applicants with the highest potential for success on the job? In this chapter, I'll describe some options that are available to assist in staffing decisions. I'll also highlight the advantages and disadvantages of the various options. You'll notice that one popular selection option, the selection interview, is conspicuously absent. That's because I've devoted the entire next chapter to discussing selection interviews in detail.

As with recruiting, it's important to first establish some criteria for evaluating selection procedures. In general, when we evaluate the relative effectiveness of selection methods, we need to consider both the cost of using the method and the accuracy of decisions resulting from the method. As a manager, you should be concerned about these criteria for both practical and legal reasons. On the practical side, we'd like to identify a selection method (or a combination of methods) that identifies the best candidates at the lowest cost. On the legal side, evidence regarding the accuracy of your hiring procedures is your first line of defense if your selection procedures are ever accused of being discriminatory.

The most accurate selection decisions result from using selection procedures that have high *validity*. Validity is a term used to describe whether the selection procedure (or test) accurately measures aspects of the applicant that are likely to be associated with job performance. There are three common forms of validity:

1. Criterion-related validity. *Criterion-related validity* is the extent to which a selection procedure predicts on-the-job success. Suppose you hired 100 employees last year. During the hiring process, applicants took a cognitive ability test. Six months after hiring, supervisors rated each employee's overall performance on the job. Now you have two pieces of information about each employee—their prehire score on the cognitive ability test, and their posthire job performance rating. The cognitive ability test has high criterion-related validity if scores on the cognitive ability test are strongly associated with the supervisors' ratings of performance. Usually, criterion-related validity is measured by a correlation coefficient—a statistical index of the strength of an association between two measures that can range from –1 to +1. Positive correlation coefficients indicate that scores on the two measures (in our example, the prehire test score and the posthire supervisory rating) covary in the same direction: The higher the employee scored on the cognitive ability test, the higher the supervisory rating (and, conversely, the lower the employee scored on the test, the lower the supervisor rating). However, it can also be desirable to have negative correlation coefficients. For example, higher cognitive ability test scores may be associated with lower turnover: The higher the employee scored on the cognitive ability test, the *less* likely he or she was to leave the organization in the first year (and, again, the lower the employee scored on the test, the *more* likely he or she was to leave the organization). The critical thing is the absolute value. In practice, correlation coefficients in the .5–.6 range indicate very high levels of criterion-related validity.

2. Content validity. *Content validity* is the extent to which a selection procedure directly samples the knowledge and skills needed to perform a job. For example, a selection procedure for a secretarial position would have high content validity if the applicants were screened using a test that measured typing and filing skills. There's no standard statistical test for content validity—instead, content validity is assessed by asking experts (people who are highly familiar with the job's content) to make an informed judgment as to whether the selection procedure accurately reflects on-the-job behavior.

3. Construct validity. In both of the previous types of validity (criterion-related and content validity), we were comparing the selection procedure to on-the-job behavior. But, in *construct validity*, we evaluate the selection procedure by comparing it to other procedures that are supposed to be measuring the same thing. We want to be sure that the selection procedure is measuring something that it's supposed to be

measuring, so we compare it to other procedures that are already accepted measures of that "something." For example, everyone would agree that being an accountant requires skill working with numbers. Let's say that I have developed a new selection procedure for hiring accountants that measures numerical ability. I would demonstrate that my test has construct validity by showing (using correlation coefficients) that applicants' scores on my new test were statistically associated with other indicators of numerical ability (e.g., college grades in mathematics classes, scores on the math component of the GRE).

In their Uniform Guidelines on Employee Selection Procedures,[1] the EEOC recognizes all three forms of validity as reasonable ways of evaluating the accuracy of a selection procedure. However, in practice, criterion-related validity is used more frequently than the other two types—in part because statistical measures of criterion-related validity make it possible to directly compare the predictive accuracy of different procedures. If you are interested in using a standardized test (i.e., a test that you purchase for use) in your selection procedure, the test's publisher should provide you with information about the test's criterion-related validity when it has been used to select employees in other organizations.[2] Later in this chapter, I'll provide some benchmarks to consider when you evaluate whether the criterion-related validity associated with a particular test is high enough to warrant adopting the test in your organization.

As a manager, you should also be concerned about content validity. Content validity, remember, describes the extent to which the selection procedure reflects skills and behaviors actually used on-the-job. Job applicants who take a test with high content validity are likely to see the test as a reasonable way of identifying the best candidates. However, as tests become more exotic (e.g., if the test asks obscure questions, or seems to invade the applicant's privacy), job applicants are more likely to see the test as inappropriate—even if the test has high criterion-related validity. Applicants who take tests that are not clearly job-related are likely to react negatively. They may develop an unfavorable impression of the organization, and decide they no longer want to be considered for the job.[3] In extreme cases, they may even challenge the legitimacy of the selection procedure in court.[4]

HIRING OPTIONS

In designing a selection procedure, there are a wide variety of options to choose among. I've organized the selection procedure options into two general categories: biographical information and standardized tests. During the recruiting process, you've probably accumulated a vast amount of biographical information about each job applicant—either through a resume that the applicant submitted when he or she indicated an interest in the job, or through an application form that the applicant submitted when he or she first inquired about the job. This biographical information represents one way that you can evaluate candidates and identify which ones have the highest potential for success on the job. In addition, you may choose to supplement this biographical information by asking applicants to take standardized tests as part of the hiring process. By asking all the applicants to take the same test, you can directly compare scores to assess their relative suitability for the position.

Biographical Information

Resumes and Application Blanks. Many managers fail to realize the wealth of information contained in resumes and application blanks. In fact, a recent survey found that 56% of managers admitted that they spent 5 minutes or less reviewing resumes.[5] Resumes and application blanks include information about dates of education, educational degrees earned, and the dates and type of prior employment. These data provide an objective way of comparing the qualifications of different candidates, and these biographical facts have been found to have good criterion-related validity across a wide range of occupations.[6]

In addition, the biographical data provide a written record that your organization can verify via outside checks. Background checks are becoming an important part of the hiring process for two reasons. First, there is increasing evidence that job applicants frequently provide false information on their applications. You might remember the media uproar that surrounded the resignation of a Notre Dame coach who had misrepresented his college football experience and postgraduate education on his resume.[7] Resume-padding and distortion is very common. Companies that screen prospective hires estimate that 33% of job applicants include some kind of falsehood on their resumes.[8] Managerial applicants, for example, may inflate their compensation by 10% to 20% (or more!) or misrepresent general business degrees as more specialized qualifications.[9]

Second, organizations are increasingly being held liable for *negligent hiring*.[10] Negligent hiring refers to situations in which an employer fails to use reasonable care in hiring an employee, who then commits a crime while in his or her position in the organization. For example, Avis Rent a Car hired a man without thoroughly checking his background. The employee later raped a female coworker. Avis was found guilty of negligent hiring and had to pay damages of $750,000. Had the company carefully checked the information provided in the man's job application, it would have discovered that he was serving a 3-year prison sentence during the time period he claimed he was attending high school and college.[11]

A background check can take many forms. Most employers at least try to verify an applicant's current position and salary with his or her current employer by telephone. Others get background reports from commercial credit rating companies in an effort to learn about an applicant's credit standing, indebtedness, and lifestyle.[12] Engaging an outside firm to conduct background checks can be relatively inexpensive ($5–$25 per check) for routine checks that verify the applicant's self-reported education and experience, but can be far more costly ($3,000–$10,000 per check) for detailed investigations.[13] Handled correctly, the background check can be an inexpensive and straightforward way to verify factual information about the applicant, such as current and previous job titles, current salary range, dates of employment, and educational background.[14]

Letters of Recommendation.   Many employers also ask the job applicant to provide letters of recommendation from people who know them—former supervisors, coworkers, or teachers. In general, managers report that these letters are not very helpful in their hiring decisions. In one study, 44% of human resource managers described reference letters as having "little" or "no" value in the hiring process.[15] Reference letters tend to be uniformly positive, making it hard to differentiate applicants.[16] Because applicants usually get to choose who writes the letter, they can identify only those writers who are likely to provide a glowing reference. In addition, some letter writers are reluctant to provide any negative information about a job applicant for fear that they might be sued for slander or defamation of character.[17]

Does this mean that letters of recommendation are useless? Not at all. Even when letters are uniformly positive, the content of letters may provide useful clues about the applicant's fit to the job that you can investigate further during an on-site interview. For example, if you are hiring a clerk who needs to maintain important records, the fact that 2 of the 3 letters of recommendation specifically mention the applicant's attention to detail might indicate that the applicant would be a good fit to the job. Intuit Corporation, the software company that produces Quicken, gets around the problem of overly positive letters of recommendation by requesting references in bulk—depending on the position, they might ask for as many as 12 letters of reference.[18] The first 2 or 3 letters submitted by the applicant invariably have nothing but positive things to say, but the other letters are likely to provide more candid information.

It's also important to note that courts in almost every state have held that employers, both former and prospective, have a *qualified privilege* to discuss an employee's past performance. These states have passed laws intended to protect the writers of reference letters and encourage them to provide accurate information to prospective employers.[19] The doctrine of qualified privilege protects employers who provide information about the job performance of former employees unless their behavior indicates a lack of good faith—that is, if the information provided by the employer is knowingly false or deliberately misleading, rendered with malicious intent, or violates any civil rights of the former employee.[20]

Selection Tests

Now, what about tests? Selection tests aren't necessarily limited to paper-and-pencil versions. Many selection tests are administered online, through the Internet or at kiosks located at retail outlets or malls.[21] Selection tests can offer a fast, cost-efficient way to screen prospective applicants.[22] Let's see what's out there.

Cognitive Ability Tests. You've probably taken several cognitive ability tests such as the SAT, the GRE, or the GMAT. These tests measure the applicant's general intelligence and his or her level of verbal and/or mathematical ability. In addition, there are more specialized tests that focus on assessing particular skills and abilities (e.g., computer programming knowledge, or accountancy skills).

Cognitive ability tests are among the most popular selection procedures, and with good reason—cognitive ability tests are inexpensive to administer and they have very high criterion-related validity. They are especially popular in the financial and consulting industries. Organizations in these industries have to screen large numbers of undergraduates and MBAs to fill vacant positions, and paper-and-pencil cognitive ability tests can be a cheap and effective way to make the first cut.[23]

Because cognitive ability tests measure general intelligence, the same test can predict performance in a wide variety of jobs that involve basic reading and writing skills, problem-solving skills, or logical reasoning skills. Bill Gates, when asked to describe Microsoft's hiring strategies, said that the company had a "bias" in hiring "toward intelligence or smartness over anything else, even, in many cases, experience." [24] It's probably not surprising that intelligence predicts job success among software designers or other professionals. But, in fact, intelligence predicts success on most, if not all, jobs. Consistently, research finds that scores on cognitive ability tests are associated with shorter training times, greater on-the-job productivity, and lower turnover rates.[25] If intelligence is what you're after, cognitive ability tests are the way to go. But keep in mind that there may be other attributes of employee performance (e.g., the employee's social skills, the employee's dependability) that are not addressed by cognitive ability tests.

Cognitive ability tests also have downsides. While cognitive ability tests have high criterion-related validity, they also are highly vulnerable to claims of adverse impact. In other words, organizations that use cognitive ability test scores as part of their hiring criteria may find that they are screening out disproportionate numbers of some racial or ethnic groups, or screening out disproportionate numbers of men or women. Why are cognitive ability tests so vulnerable to adverse impact? To answer this question, think back to the last time you took a standardized test in school (e.g., the SAT or the GRE). Remember all those reading comprehension problems, where you'd read a paragraph and then answer questions about the paragraph content? People of different backgrounds may be differentially familiar with the content in the paragraph, and those different levels of familiarity can affect their performance. Suppose that one cognitive ability test included reading comprehension paragraphs focusing on cooking and baking, and another cognitive ability test included paragraphs focusing on car mechanics. Would you expect members of both sexes to perform equally well on each test? Cognitive ability tests are also likely to be culturally biased—to reflect the culture of the test creators. Tests developed in the United States may overemphasize U.S. culture and knowledge, resulting in poorer scores for people who were raised in other cultures.[26] As a result of concerns about adverse impact, some organizations are reluctant to use cognitive ability tests. But that's throwing out the baby with the bathwater—cognitive ability tests can be a valuable part of a selection strategy. Some organizations guard against unintentional cultural bias by using paragraphs from their own shop manuals for testing.[27] These paragraphs provide information used directly on the job, so they are unlikely to be culturally biased.

A second problem with cognitive ability tests is that they measure general intelligence and reading/writing ability simultaneously. Paper-and-pencil cognitive ability tests necessarily require the test taker to have substantial reading and writing skills. However, many jobs in which performance is affected by jobholder intelligence may not require advanced reading and writing skills. For example, suppose you were hiring someone to maintain a storeroom and stock shelves with a diverse range of products. A more intelligent person might be a better performer, because he or she would be most likely to design a logical storage system and maintain accurate inventory records. But the actual level of reading and writing ability required in the job might be very low. Similarly, suppose you were hiring a carpenter to design and build office bookshelves. A more intelligent carpenter might make better use of supplies and take more accurate measurements—but, again, limited reading and writing abilities are required on a regular basis. A cognitive ability test, in which intelligence scores are highly affected by reading and writing skills, might screen out otherwise qualified candidates for these jobs.

Work Sample Tests. As a result of concerns about cognitive ability tests, some organizations have tried to develop selection procedures that move away from standard paper-and-pencil tests. In a work sample test, the organization designs a selection procedure that is a reasonable approximation of the actual behaviors required during on-the-job performance. As a result, scores on the work sample test should be affected only by those skills directly associated with job performance. If reading and writing skills are needed for the job, the work sample test should also require those skills. However, if reading and writing are not part of the job, scores on the work sample test should not be influenced by the applicant's reading and writing abilities. Work samples have always been widely used for managerial assessment, but they are beginning to catch on for other jobs as well. See Box 4.1 for some examples of how companies use work sample tests as part of their screening procedures.

Work sample tests offer benefits to both the hiring organization and to the job applicant. The organization learns how the applicant would per-

---

BOX 4.1
Work Sample Tests

Central Market HEB Houston, TX	Applicants work in small groups to build a product display. Assessors evaluate applicants' team skills.[28]
MicroTraining Plus Norwalk, CT	Applicants for computer training jobs deliver a speech on "anything but computers" (e.g., astronomy, a musical instrument, a foreign language). Assessors evaluate how well applicants can communicate complex subjects to a novice audience.[29]
Toyota Georgetown, KY	Applicants participate in a "Day of Work" in which they spend 4 full hours on the assembly line—moving heavy equipment, checking for defects, and generally enduring the monotony and repetition associated with an assembly line job.[30]
Rosenbluth International Philadelphia, PA	Potential executive hires at this travel management company are sometimes flown to the company's North Dakota ranch to help repair fences or drive cattle. How well they perform doesn't really matter—the company is measuring how pleasant and nice the candidates can be under difficult circumstances.[31]

form under conditions very similar to the actual job, and the applicant learns more about the job during the selection procedure. In a way, work sample tests offer a *realistic job preview*—remember our discussion of realistic job previews from the last chapter? Toyota's "Day of Work" is tough (see Box 4.1), but it is no worse than the conditions applicants would deal with on the job if they were hired. Still, some applicants find the experience unbearable; one applicant asked for a restroom break and disappeared for good, leaving her nametag on the restroom sink.[32]

What's the downside of work sample tests? They are expensive to design and administer. Unlike cognitive ability tests, where the same standardized test can be used for a wide variety of jobs, a unique work sample test has to be designed for every job in the organization. Then a scoring key has to be developed, and raters need to be trained to assess performance on the work sample. That can be time consuming and costly. Also, despite their high content validity, work sample tests tend to have lower criterion-related validity than cognitive ability tests. The lower validity associated with work sample tests is probably a function of rater error. Cognitive ability tests have a clear right or wrong answer and can be computer scored with no error. In contrast, the grading of a work sample often requires a more subjective assessment and is more prone to rater error.

Personality Tests. Personality tests are becoming a popular part of selection procedures. There are many different kinds of personality tests, but the most common tests measure the "Big Five" dimensions of personality:

- Extraversion (the extent to which a person is talkative and sociable)
- Agreeableness (the extent to which a person is tolerant of other people and cooperative)
- Conscientiousness (the extent to which a person is dependable and organized)
- Emotional stability (the extent to which a person is secure and calm)
- Openness to experience (the extent to which a person is curious and insightful)

Standardized tests are available that reliably measure these aspects of personality. The question is, are these tests *valid*? Do personality tests predict on-the-job performance?

Research suggests that personality does have a small but important association with on-the-job performance. In particular, conscientiousness is associated with performance across jobs. Many low-skilled jobs (including cashiers, janitors, and gardeners) require logical thinking, good control, and judgment—none of which are trainable.[33] Conscientiousness can predict how likely an employee is to arrive on time for work, whether the employee will check his or her work carefully, and more generally, whether the employee will be a dependable worker.[34] These may be important aspects of job performance, but because these behaviors are not associated with employee ability, they are not likely to be predicted by the employee's performance on cognitive ability or work sample tests. Extraversion also has been found to be related to performance in jobs with a large social component, such as sales and management positions.[35]

There is a catch, however. Applicants often react negatively when they are asked to take personality tests as part of the hiring process. In one survey, 26% of jobseekers said that they would be reluctant to take employer-mandated personality tests, and 12% of jobseekers said they would withdraw from the selection process to avoid taking the test.[36] Depending on the size and quality of your applicant pool, you may not be willing to risk losing 12% of your applicants. Job applicants' negative reactions are partly a response to several widely publicized cases in which organizations were using personality tests inappropriately. For example, Dayton Hudson (the parent company of Target stores) received a lot of negative publicity when the public learned that they were using a psychological test including questions like "I believe in the second coming of Christ," "I prefer baths to showers," and "I hardly ever feel pain in the back of my neck" to hire security guards. These questions were part of an instrument called the Minnesota Multiphasic Personality Inventory, which was initially developed to identify severe psychiatric disorders such as schizophrenia and paranoia.[37] In practice, the personality tests used in personnel decisions are more likely to assess the Big Five dimensions I described earlier, and ask the job applicant to indicate their preference for alternative situations. For example, questions asking job applicants to indicate their preference for different activities (meeting new people at a party or reading a good book) might be used to assess extraversion.[38]

In response to applicant privacy concerns, few organizations use personality tests on a widescale basis, and many organizations tend to limit their use during tight labor markets.[39] Still, a 2002 survey of human resource managers found that 22% of the respondents reported using personality tests as part of the hiring process.[40] Personality testing is becoming especially common when organizations are filling upper level positions. For example, Supply Pro (a San Diego startup) used true-or-false questions like "To me, crossing the ocean in a sailboat would be a wonderful adventure" to see if their management applicants were likely to be risk takers. And when Hewlett Packard was choosing a CEO, the company assessed the emotional volatility of candidates by asking whether statements like "When I bump into a piece of furniture, I don't usually get angry" were true or false.[41]

Occasionally you hear about companies trying to assess applicants' personalities through more indirect means—handwriting analysis, for example. Sigmund Warburg, the founder of a British merchant bank, specified in his will that all job applicants to the bank have to submit a handwriting sample, which is then sent off for analysis to a London company called Graphology Services.[42] Handwriting analysis is popular in some European countries, where job applicants are routinely asked to provide handwriting samples as part of their job application.[43] It's harder to get a firm fix on how many U.S. firms use handwriting analysis in their selection procedures—most companies don't like to go on record as using it, and handwriting analysts protect the privacy of their clients.[44] However, there is evidence that a growing number of U.S. firms, including United Parcel Service and J.C. Penney, are asking job applicants to submit handwriting samples.[45]

How does handwriting analysis work? Usually, the job seeker is asked to spontaneously write on a blank page, and the handwriting sample is then sent to a handwriting analyst, who prepares a personality profile. The analyst uses characteristics of the handwriting to draw inferences about the writer's personality. For example, if the writer's handwriting is particularly clear and easy to read, the analyst might infer that the writer is generally neat. Evidence that the writer presses hard on paper might suggest that the writer is tense. People whose handwriting is large and round are likely to be described as nurturing.[46] Writers who eliminate extra strokes and don't dot their *i*s are predicted to be efficient.[47]

Is it a good idea to use handwriting analysis as a basis for hiring decisions? In a word, No! There's no basis for claims that people's handwriting predicts on-the-job performance. One well-designed study asked 115 real estate agents and brokers to provide two handwriting samples to a group of 20 handwriting analysts. The analysts used the handwriting samples to predict the agents' personality and sales performance. The analysts were fairly consistent in the personality traits they attributed to the writers, but they were *not* successful in using their analysis to predict job performance.[48] In other words, the analysts could tell the researchers something about the writers' personalities, but they couldn't predict whether the writers' personality was going to influence on-the-job performance. If you want to consider an applicant's personality as part of your hiring decision, then use a Big Five personality test. There's no reason to include a handwriting analysis in your selection procedures, especially since job applicants are likely to react as negatively to a handwriting analysis as they would if you asked them to take a polygraph test during the hiring process.[49]

Integrity Tests (or Honesty Tests). Employee theft costs U.S. organizations between $35 and $50 billion a year and employers suffer a greater financial loss from employee theft than from shoplifters.[50] Until the late 1980s, organizations who wanted to screen job applicants for their potential to steal from the organization asked job applicants to take a polygraph test. However, due to recent legislation, it is illegal for most companies to use the polygraph for hiring purposes. As a result, organizations are increasingly likely to substitute paper-and-pencil tests that measure a person's integrity or honesty. These tests include questions like:

- Would you consider buying something from somebody if you knew the item had been stolen?
- If you found $100 that was lost by a bank truck, would you turn the money over to the bank even though there was no reward?
- Do you think it is all right for one employee to give another employee a discount even though the company does not allow it?
- Have you ever overcharged someone for your personal gain?

Research suggests that applicants' responses to these types of questions predict theft behavior as well as other counterproductive behaviors such as violence on the job, tardiness, and absenteeism.[51] In one study, convenience store employees who were terminated for theft had scored significantly lower on a prehire honesty test than employees who were not terminated.[52]

Looking at that list of sample integrity test questions, you'll notice that the questions are generally very direct and "transparent." It might seem easy for a dishonest person to "cheat" on an integrity test and present himself or herself as an honest, forthright citizen. However, about 6% of the U.S. population readily admits to engaging in criminal activity on these types of tests. People who fall into this 6% believe that "everyone does it" and don't hesitate to disclose dishonest behavior.[53] In fact, research suggests that integrity tests predict behavior even when test takers are trying to present a positive impression to employers. In one study, researchers hired students to take a battery of selection tests and instructed them to take the tests as if they really wanted the job. Afterward, researchers intentionally overpaid the students, and scores on an integrity test included in the battery predicted who returned the overpayment.[54]

By the way, some organizations (including Best Buy and Pic'n Pay shoe stores) administer integrity tests by phone so that they can track the response time associated with different questions. If it takes applicants too long to answer questions like "Should an employee be fired for stealing $1?" or "To get a job, would you lie?," their hesitancy may count against them.[55]

Designing a Selection Procedure

By now you've seen that each selection option has its own advantages and disadvantages. Table 4.1 summarizes the costs and criterion-related validity associated with each of the tests we've discussed. The Validity column in the table reports a correlation between test scores and on-the-job performance (measured either by supervisory ratings or actual productivity indicators). This is the average correlation researchers have observed across tests, across organizations, and across jobs[56]—this information is provided as a general benchmark. Of course, the specific criterion-related validity you might find in your organization depends on the particular test you are using, and the organizational context.

The table suggests that either cognitive ability tests or work sample tests can provide high criterion-related validity—these two selection options regularly result in criterion-related validities in the .53 (cognitive ability tests) and .44 (work samples) range. When you design a selection procedure, you'll probably want to include either a cognitive ability test or a work sample.

TABLE 4.1
Costs and Criterion-Related Validities Associated With Selection Tests

	Cost/Applicant	Validity
Cognitive ability tests	$5–$100	.53
Work samples	$50–$500	.44
Big Five personality tests	$1–$100 and up	.02–.15
Integrity tests	$9–$100	.18

Manager's Checkpoint

Use the following questions to decide whether cognitive ability tests or work samples would be best for your hiring needs:

- How many applicants do I expect to screen? (If you will be screening a large number of job applicants, you need a measure that is easy to administer and inexpensive. That suggests using a cognitive ability test rather than a work sample.)

- How many different jobs am I trying to fill? (If you are filling one job, or a few jobs, you can consider designing work sample tests. But because a work sample has to be designed for each job, they probably are not a viable option if you are trying to fill many unique positions.)
- To what extent does on-the-job performance depend on reading and writing abilities? (If reading and writing are not part of the jobs you are trying to fill, a work sample test may be more appropriate than a paper-and-pencil cognitive ability test.)

As shown in Table 4.1, the criterion-related validities associated with the next two selection options (personality tests and honesty tests) are quite a bit less. The criterion-related validity associated with personality tests is only .02–.15, with tests measuring conscientiousness and extraversion at the high end of this range. That's substantially lower than the criterion-related validity associated with either cognitive ability tests or work sample tests. But it's important to remember that personality tests may be tapping different elements of performance than either cognitive ability tests or work sample tests. A good measure of employee conscientiousness may help you to identify those employees who are unlikely to be reliable or dependable in their job performance.

Similarly, the criterion-related validity of integrity tests (.18) may seem low in comparison with cognitive ability tests or work samples. Table 4.1 presents the average validity of integrity tests in predicting supervisory performance ratings. However, the *primary* purpose of integrity tests is to predict employee theft and other counterproductive behaviors. The average validity of integrity tests in predicting these outcomes is considerably higher (theft = .36; general counterproductivity = .32).[57] I can't think of a situation in which I would advise using personality tests or integrity tests *instead* of a good cognitive ability test or a work sample. But either personality tests or integrity tests may be useful *supplements* to a cognitive ability test or a work sample.[58] These tests predict aspects of an employee's behavior (reliability, dependability, integrity) that contribute to success on the job—aspects that are not likely to be measured by cognitive ability tests or work samples.

Manager's Checkpoint

The following questions might help you to decide whether you want to integrate personality tests or integrity tests into your selection procedures:

- Am I experiencing problems associated with employee reliability—e.g., high absenteeism rates, high error rates? (If yes, then a
  measure of conscientiousness might be worth including in your
  selection procedures.)
- Am I experiencing problems associated with employee theft? (If
  yes, then a paper-and-pencil integrity test could be included in
  your selection procedures.)
- Am I currently having a hard time attracting qualified applicants?
  (If your applicant pool is very small, you may not want to risk the
  perception that your selection procedure is intrusive by including
  personality tests or integrity tests.)

WHAT'S NEXT?

Ready to move on to our discussion of the selection interview? Interviews
are commonly used (and misused!) in organizational selection procedures, so we'll devote the entire next chapter to discussing their advantages and disadvantages.

FOR FURTHER READING

Behling, O. (1998). Employee selection: Will intelligence and conscientiousness
    do the job? *Academy of Management Executive, 12*(1), 77–85.
Lachnit, C. (2002, February). Protecting people and profits with background
    checks. *Workforce*, 50–54.
Sackett, P. R. (1994). Integrity testing for personnel selection. *Current Directions in
    Psychological Science, 3*, 73–76.
Tyler, K. (2000, January). Put applicants' skills to the test. *HRMagazine*, 74–80.

MANAGER'S KNOT 4.1

*"I know how important it is to check references before hiring a job ap-
plicant, but I never feel like I'm getting good information from applicants' former employers. I always get off the phone with a list of bland
strengths and weaknesses that tell me very little about the applicant's fit to the job."*

Try changing the questions you ask applicants' former employers. Rather than
asking for general information about the applicant's responsibilities at the organization, or the applicant's strengths and weaknesses, try giving the reference more background about your job and your organization. For example,

describe your company (Is it formal or laid-back? Is it fast-paced or relaxed?) and ask the reference whether that environment is likely to be a good fit for the job applicant. Or describe some of the challenges the applicant is likely to face on the job (Is it demanding customers? Relentless work loads?) and ask whether the reference has observed the applicant manage these or similar demands. Sometimes providing more detailed background information can help the reference to provide a more useful assessment of the applicant.

MANAGER'S KNOT 4.2

"The job I'm trying to fill is a critical one in my organization—the employee will work in a very sensitive position, and we want someone who has an impeccable background. However, I've gotten a huge quantity of applications, and paying for a thorough background check on each one will break the bank. What can I do?"

Good question—and a common problem for organizations who frequently receive a large number of applications in response to job openings. You don't need to send every job applicant for a background check. Instead, you can design a *multihurdle* selection procedure. In a multihurdle selection procedure, the organization sequences the various selection tests. You can design a sequence in which the cheaper tests, or those that are easiest to administer, are given first. After applicants pass the initial hurdles, the organization may administer additional, more expensive procedures. For example, you might first use a standardized cognitive ability test to identify the best candidates for your position. The highest scoring applicants then are invited to a face-to-face interview. The background check can be used as a final hurdle for the most promising candidate.

MANAGER'S KNOT 4.3

"My organization uses a huge battery of tests to screen job applicants. In fact, we've acquired a reputation in the community as a company that 'over-tests.' I'd like to reduce the number of different tests we use—how I can identify which ones should be eliminated?"

Administering too many tests is trying for both the organization and the applicants. There are two issues to consider here. First, check the criterion-related validity of each of your selection procedures. Some tests in the battery may not be strongly related to performance on the job. The tests with the lowest criterion-related validity should be the first ones you eliminate. Second, check for redundancy in the kinds of information that each test provides. Are you using two standardized tests that both measure general intelligence? Are you using two different methods (e.g., a paper-and-pencil test and a handwriting analysis) to measure personality? You may be able to eliminate one without a reduction in the overall quality of information you acquire about each applicant.

ENDNOTES

1. Equal Employment Opportunity Commission. (1978). Uniform guidelines on employee selection procedures. *Federal Register, 43*, pp. 38290–38315.
2. Flynn, G. (2002, June). A legal examination of testing. *Workforce*, 92–94.
3. Rynes, S. L., & Connerley, M. L. (1993). Applicant reactions to alternative selection procedures. *Journal of Business and Psychology, 7*(3), 261–277; Steiner, D. D., & Gilliland, S. W. (1996). Fairness reactions to personnel selection techniques. *Journal of Applied Psychology, 81*, 134–141; Smither, J. W., Reilly, R. R., Millsap, R. E., Pearlman, K., & Stoffey, R. W. (1993). Applicant reactions to selection procedures. *Personnel Psychology, 46*, 40–76; Gilliland, S. W. (1995). Fairness from the applicant's perspective: Reactions to employee selection procedures. *International Journal of Selection and Assessment, 3*, 11–19.
4. Gilliland, S. W. (1993). The perceived fairness of selection system: An organizational justice perspective. *Academy of Management Review, 18*, 694–734.
5. Resumes get only a glance. (2001, March 8). *USA Today*, p. B1; Accountemps (2001). Snap decision. Retrieved April 29, 2002, from http://www.accountemps.com/PressRoom?LOBName=AT&releaseid=169
6. Childs, A., & Klimoski, R. J. (1986). Successfully predicting career success: An application of the biographical inventory. *Journal of Applied Psychology, 71*, 3–8; Harvey-Cook, J. E., & Taffler, R. J. (2000). Biodata in professional entry-level selection: Statistical scoring of common format applications. *Journal of Occupational and Organizational Psychology, 73*, 103–118. Rothstein, H. R., Schmidt, F. L., Erwin, F. W., Owens, W. A., & Sparks, C. P. (1990). Biographical data in employment selection: Can validities be made generalizable? *Journal of Applied Psychology, 75*, 175–184.
7. The George O'Leary incident. (2001). *Sports Illustrated, 95*(25), 32.
8. Jarman, M. (2001, September 15). Employee screeners see surge in business. *Arizona Republic*, p. D1.
9. Schellhardt, T. D. (1994, February 23). While the recruiter checks your resume, investigate the firm's. *Wall Street Journal*, p. B1.
10. Segal, J. A. (1994, June). When Charles Manson comes to the workplace. *HRMagazine*, 33–40; Kondrasuk, J. N., Moore, H. L., & Wang, H. (2001, Summer). Negligent hiring: The emerging contributor to workplace violence in the public sector. *Public Personnel Management*, 185–195.
11. Kaufer, S. (2001). Corporate liability: Sharing the blame for workplace violence. Retrieved April 29, 2002, from http://www.noworkviolence.com/articles/corporate_liability.htm
12. Greengard, S. (1995, December). Are you well armed to screen applicants? *Personnel Journal*, 84–95.
13. Jarman, M. (2001, September 15). Employee screeners see surge in business. *Arizona Republic*, p. D1; Dunham, K. J. (2001, August 1). Checking out. *Wall Street Journal*, p. B13; Grainger, D. (2001). You just hired him. *Fortune, 144*(8), 205–206;

Lachnit, C. (2002, February). Protecting people and profits with background checks. *Workforce*, 50–54.

14. Adler, S. (1993). Verifying a job candidate's background: The state of practice in a vital human resources activity. *Review of Business, 15*(2), 3–8.

15. Von der Embse, T. J., & Wyse, R. E. (1985, January). Those reference letters: How useful are they? *Personnel*, 42–46.

16. Muchinsky, P. M. (1979). The use of reference reports in personnel selection: A review and evaluation. *Journal of Occupational Psychology, 52*, 287–297.

17. Greenburg, J. C. (1995, November 30). Reference ill will spurs worker suits. *Chicago Tribune*, sect. 3, pp. 1–2; Barada, P. W. (1996, November). Reference checking is more important than ever. *HRMagazine*, 49–51.

18. Greengard, S. (1995, December). Are you well armed to screen applicants? *Personnel Journal*, 84–95.

19. McMorris, F. A. (1996, July 8). Ex-bosses face less peril giving honest job references. *Wall Street Journal*, pp. B1, B6.

20. Kroeker, K. M., & Arnold, D. W. (1996, October). Initiatives to protect employers from defamation charges. *Security Management*, 79.

21. Overholt, A. (2002, February). True or false: You're hiring the right people. *Fast Company*, 110–114; Gale, S. F. (2002, April). Three companies cut turnover with tests. *Workforce*, 66–69.

22. Tyler, K. (2000, January). Put applicants' skills to the test. *HRMagazine*, 74–80.

23. Silverman, R. E. (2000, December 5). Sharpen your pencil. *Wall Street Journal*, p. B16.

24. Stross, R. E. (1996, November 25). Microsoft's big advantage—hiring only the supersmart. *Fortune*, 159–162.

25. Seligman, D. (1997, January 13). Brains in the office. *Fortune*, 38.

26. Roberson, L., & Block, C. J. (2001). Racioethnicity and job performance: A review and critique of theoretical perspectives on the causes of group differences. *Research in Organizational Behavior, 23*, 247–325; Flynn, G. (2002, June). A legal examination of testing. *Workforce*, 92–94.

27. Flint, J. (1995, October 9). Can you tell applesauce from pickles? *Forbes*, 106–108.

28. Turner, M. (2001). Creative hiring replaces yesterday's staid interview. *Houston Business Journal*. Retrieved March 12, 2001 from http://houston.bcentral.com/houston/stories/2001/03/12/focus1.html

29. Work week. (1995, December 28). *Wall Street Journal*, p. A1; Behling, O. (1998). Employee selection: Will intelligence and conscientiousness do the job? *Academy of Management Executive, 12*(1), 77–85.

30. Maynard, M. (1997, August 11). Toyota devises grueling workout for job seekers. *USA Today*, p. 3B.

31. Martin, J. (1998, January 12). So, you want to work for the best .... *Fortune*, 77–78.

32. Maynard, M. (1997, August 11). Toyota devises grueling workout for job seekers. *USA Today*, p. 3B.

33. Work week. (1994, February 22). *Wall Street Journal*, p. A1.

34. Barrick, M. R., & Mount, M. K. (1991). The big five personality dimensions and job performance: A meta-analysis. *Personnel Psychology, 44*, 1–26; Hough, L. M., Eaton, N. K., Dunnette, M. D., Kamp, J. D., & McCloy, R. A. (1990). Criterion-related validities of personality constructs and the effect of response distortion on those validities. *Journal of Applied Psychology, 75*, 581–595.

35. Barrick, M. R., & Mount, M. K. (1991). The big five personality dimensions and job performance: A meta-analysis. *Personnel Psychology, 44*, 1–26.

36. Some job seekers are squeamish about personality tests. (2000). CareerBuilder Inc. Retrieved September 18, 2000, from http://corp.careerbuilder.com/cfm/newsview.cfm?type=release&ID=77

37. Hays, C. L. (1997, November 28). Trying to get a job? Check yes or no. *New York Times*, p. D1; O'Meara, D. O. (1994, January). Personality tests raise questions of legality and effectiveness. *HRMagazine*, 97–100.

38. Hays, C. L. (1997, November 28). Trying to get a job? Check yes or no. *New York Times*, p. D1.

39. Some firms drop tests of workers. (2000, August 13). *USA Today*, p. D1.

40. Terry, S. (2002, March 11). Hiring firms give weight to "style." *Christian Science Monitor*, p. 19.

41. Do you have a personality for success? (2000). *Business Week Online*. Retrieved October 16, 2000, from http://www.businessweek.com/careers/content/oct2000/ca20001013_818.htm

42. The power of the written word. (1990). *The Economist, 315*(7659), 97–98.

43. Driver, R. W., Buckley, M. R., & Frink, D. D. (1996). Should we write off graphology? *International Journal of Selection and Assessment, 4*(2), 78–86.

44. Leonard, B. (1999, April). Reading employees. *HRMagazine*, 67–73.

45. Armour, S. (1998, July 21). Fine print: Hiring through handwriting analysis. *USA Today*, p. 1B; Bianchi, A. (1996, February). The character-revealing handwriting analysis. *Inc.*, 77–79; Fowler, A. (1991). An even-handed approach to graphology. *Personnel Management, 23*(3), 40–43; Uhland, V. (2000). Employers using more tests. *Denver Rocky Mountain News*, p. 1J.

46. Lewis, D. E. (1997, January 26). Prospective employers looking for the write stuff. *Boston Globe*, p. F1.

47. Bianchi, A. (1996, February). The character-revealing handwriting analysis. *Inc.*, 77–79

48. Rafaeli, A., & Klimoski, R. (1983). Predicting sales success through handwriting analysis: An evaluation of the effects of training and handwriting sample content. *Journal of Applied Psychology, 68*, 212–217.

49. Kravitz, D., Stinson, S., & Chavez, T. (1995). Evaluation of tests used for making selection and promotion decisions. *International Journal of Selection and Assessment, 4*(1), 24–34.

50. Lipman, M., & McGraw, W. R. (1988). Employee theft: A $40 billion industry. *Annals of American Academy of Political and Social Sciences, 498*, 51–59; Budman, M. (1993, November/December). The honesty business. *Across the Board*, 34–37; Geller, A. (2002, March 25). Theft by U.S. employees rises. *The Arizona Republic*, pp. D1, D4.

51. Ones, D. S., Viswesvaran, C., & Schmidt, F. L. (1993). Comprehensive meta-analysis of integrity test validities: Findings and implications for personnel selection and theories of job performance. *Journal of Applied Psychology, 78*, 679–703.

52. Bernardin, H. J., & Cooke, D. K. (1993). Validity of an honesty test in predicting theft among convenience store employees. *Academy of Management Journal, 36*, 1097–1108.

53. Murphy, K. R. (1993). *Honesty in the workplace.* Belmont, CA: Brooks/Cole.

54. Cunningham, M. R., Wong, D. T., & Barbee, A. P. (1994). Self-presentation dynamics on overt integrity tests: Experimental studies of the Reid Report. *Journal of Applied Psychology, 79*, 643–658.

55. Work week. (2000, June 27). *Wall Street Journal*, p. A1; Work week. (1994, March 22). *Wall Street Journal*, p. A1.

56. Hunter, J. E., & Hunter, R. F. (1984). Validity and utility of alternative predictors of job performance. *Psychological Bulletin, 96*, 72–98; Barrick, M. R., & Mount, M. K. (1991). The big five personality dimensions and job performance: A meta-analysis. *Personnel Psychology, 44*, 1–26; Ones, D. S., Viswesvaran, C., & Schmidt, F. L. (1993). Comprehensive meta-analysis of integrity test validities: Findings and implications for personnel selection and theories of job performance. *Journal of Applied Psychology, 78*, 679–703.

57. Ones, D. S., Viswesvaran, C., & Schmidt, F. L. (1993). Comprehensive meta-analysis of integrity test validities: Findings and implications for personnel selection and theories of job performance. *Journal of Applied Psychology, 78*, 679–703.

58. Schmidt, F. L., & Hunter, J. E. (1998). The validity and utility of selection methods in personnel psychology: Practical and theoretical implications of 85 years of research findings. *Psychological Bulletin, 124*, 262–274.

5

Interviewing Job Applicants

In the previous chapter, I presented a variety of strategies managers can use to find the best candidates in an applicant pool. In that chapter, I didn't discuss one of the most important selection techniques: selection interviews. Selection interviews are one of the most popular methods of selecting job candidates—estimates of organizations using interviews for selection range from 70% to 99%.[1]

Let's think about the traditional interview first. What I mean by a "traditional" interview is one in which the manager conducts the interview in an unstructured way. The manager might start with an open-ended question ("tell me about yourself") and the interview then proceeds in a haphazard fashion depending on the applicant's answer to that first question. Interviewees for the same job may or may not be asked the same questions. The manager follows his or her "gut" in pursuing one line of questioning or another. Now, remember our discussion of criterion-related validity in chapter 4? Criterion-related validity is a statistical measure of the extent to which scores on a selection device are associated with on-the-job performance. As a benchmark, the criterion-related validity of cognitive ability tests tends to hover around .53, and the criterion-related validity of work sample tests is .44. In contrast, a 1984 review of research on the traditional interview found it to have a criterion-related validity of about .14![2]

That's not a typo—one of the most popular selection devices has lousy criterion-related validity. How is that possible? Well, research finds that the traditional selection interview tends to have certain problems—and we'll get to those in a minute. But don't worry about the interview—we've learned a great deal since 1984 about how to conduct selection interviews that *do* predict job performance. As you'll see later in this chapter, by using some simple techniques to structure the interview process, the criterion-related validity of a selection interview can compete with the best selection devices. So I'm giving you the punchline first: the more structured the interview, the greater the criterion-related validity.

WHAT'S WRONG WITH INTERVIEWS?

First, interviewers tend to overweight negative information. Before a job applicant shows up for a formal job interview, he or she has already survived some initial prescreening. All the applicants that are interviewed by the decision maker meet the job's minimum criteria in terms of educational requirements and prior job experience. As a result, the interviewer is evaluating a series of qualified candidates—any one of whom is probably capable of doing the job. This can lead the interviewer to frame the selection process as one of elimination and to go on a search for negative information.[3]

Second, research finds that interviewers tend to base their hiring decisions on very limited data. If interviewers review test scores or application blanks before conducting the interview, this information can influence the questions interviewers ask and their evaluation of the applicant's answers.[4] As a result, the interview doesn't contribute much new information into the selection decision. Also, interviewers make up their minds about an applicant's suitability very quickly. In one often-cited study, a researcher concluded that interviewers made their decisions within the first 3 to 4 minutes of the job interview![5] That 3- to 4-minute estimate is probably extreme, but recent research finds that interviewers express confidence that they have made a final decision 15 to 16 minutes into the interview.[6] Interviews usually take 30, 45, even 60 minutes—what is the interviewer doing the rest of the time? Once an initial decision is made, interviewers spend the rest of the interview confirming the decision. In other words, they go on a hunt for information that will justify their initial impression. You may have experienced this when you were on the receiving end of a job interview. Ever have an interview where things went wrong very early? Let's say the interviewer learns something negative, but minor, about you at the beginning of the interview (like, you got a *D* during your freshman year in a college calculus course—and then went on to get straight *A*s in all your other courses). The interviewer is likely to return to that *D* again and again during the interview, and ask questions designed to elicit other negative information ("Tell me

about another time that you had trouble getting started in something new."
"Tell me about other examples where you had difficulty working with numbers."). At the end of this search-and-destroy mission, the interviewer has
accumulated a consistent body of negative information, justifying his or
her initial negative impression of the job candidate.

Third, interviews are very vulnerable to contrast and order effects.[7] The
impression an interviewer forms of an average candidate is very much influenced by the candidate who he or she interviewed *before* the average candidate. A superstar who makes a positive impression on the interviewer can
make subsequent candidates look worse by comparison, and a lackluster interview can make subsequent candidates look pretty good! This can be a
problem in on-campus interviewing where recruiters meet with a long list of
college students interested in the job. It's very difficult to keep impressions of
the early candidates from influencing impressions of the later ones.

A final criticism of the interview is that it is labor intensive and expensive.
Unlike cognitive ability tests that can be administered to a large group and
computer-scored, interviews take up a lot of a manager's time. A total of 6
to 8 person hours per candidate is not uncommon, and this investment
can be much higher for managerial or professional positions.[8]

That's a long laundry list of problems! Despite these problems, it's unlikely that organizations will be abandoning interviews entirely. So it's important to avoid the problems with selection interviews and try to get them
done right. In this chapter, you'll learn some ways to ensure that you're getting your money's worth from selection interviews. But first let's consider
the strengths of interviews: What do they do well?

WHAT INTERVIEWS DO WELL

Interviews are really good at measuring three distinct areas of applicant
competency. First, interviews can be a way of learning about applicants'
abilities in certain technical areas. Some technical skills may be so unique
or specialized that no standardized tests are available—these are areas that
can be discussed and probed in the job interview.

Second, interviews can be a way of assessing applicants' problem-
solving skills. Paper-and-pencil ability tests can identify whether an applicant gets the right answer—but they don't identify whether the applicant
got there by guessing or through systematic reasoning. Some organizations (especially Silicon Valley companies) like to ask "puzzlers"—interview questions that require "reasoning out" to get an answer. Try this one:
"How many gallons of white house paint are sold in the U.S. every year?"[9]
Unless you work for Home Depot or some other store that sells house
paint, chances are you have no idea what the right answer might be. But
the interviewer asking this question is less interested in the accuracy of

your answer than in observing the process by which you arrive at an answer and seeing how you work through the problem. How did you use information you already had (e.g., a ballpark figure of the U.S. population) to extrapolate to information you *didn't* have (e.g., an estimate of the number of houses in the United States)? To what extent did you think "outside the box" (e.g., Did you remember that house paint is used to cover both internal and external walls)?

Finally, interviews give the organization an opportunity to assess the applicant's verbal and presentation skills. As a manager, you want the opportunity to assess how the applicant interacts with other people—information that can't be obtained through arms-length assessment tools. When Bellagio built a huge new resort in Las Vegas, they had 24 weeks to screen 84,000 people for customer service positions.[10] Clearly, they couldn't conduct an extended sit-down interview with each job applicant. Instead, job applicants completed applications at computer terminals. Applicants then proceeded to a checkout desk. Not just a formality, the clerks at the checkout desk were screening each applicant for communication skills and overall demeanor—and thereby weeded out about 20% of the applicants.

Beyond what the interview measures, interviews also provide the organization with two valuable opportunities. First, this is an opportunity for the organization to explore "fit" issues with the applicant. Remember our discussion of *realistic job previews* in chapter 3? Organizations use realistic job previews to convey information to an applicant about the positive and negative aspects of a job—information that can help the applicant to make an informed decision about whether to accept the job if it's offered. In a face-to-face interview, organizational representatives can give an applicant accurate, realistic information about life on the job. Egon Zehnder, the founder of executive search firm Egon Zehnder International (EZI), explained in a *Harvard Business Review* article how he used selection interviews as opportunities to highlight the company's unique compensation system. EZI emphasizes organizational seniority in its pay system rather than pay for performance. The company believes that this system promotes a collaborative organization culture, and encourages individuals to be more concerned about the group's success rather than their personal outcomes. However, this system is very different from the compensation system at many professional firms, so it can come as a surprise to job candidates. To better prepare them, Egon Zehnder would say in the interview: "Do you know that even if you have the highest billings in the firm and are responsible for 60% of the profits of your office, you won't get an extra penny for it? Picture yourself in that situation. Are you comfortable with it? If you aren't don't join us. You'll be very unhappy."[11]

Second, many organizations view interviews as a public relations opportunity. People value the chance to meet one-on-one with company representatives and have a chance to "show their stuff." Applicants frequently view the job interview as one of the fairest ways to make hiring decisions—even if they have been turned down for the job.[12] That kind of positive reaction can pay dividends. You may not be interested in hiring this applicant now, but you might be interested in them (or their family or friends) later. As you can see, despite their problems, job interviews play an important role in the selection process. So let's turn now to ways that the interview process can be improved.

IMPROVING THE INTERVIEW

Interviewers frequently gripe about job seekers who are poorly prepared for job interviews—who show up for interviews with food stuck to their clothes, who bad-mouth their former employers, or who interrupt the interview to take personal calls on their cell phones.[13] Have you heard the one about the job applicant who asked if she could use the interviewer's phone so she could call in sick to her current employer?[14] After dialing, she proceeded to fake a coughing fit. Or how about the job applicant who, when asked where she wanted to be in 5 years, responded "I don't plan that far ahead .... I could be hit by a bus tomorrow"?[15]

But, at the same time, job seekers have plenty of complaints about the quality of the interviewers they encounter.[16] In a recent survey conducted by Bernard Haldane Associates, a career management organization based in New York, 20% of job seekers said that they have been "insulted" by interviewers' questions.[17] Why are interviews handled so poorly? Part of the problem is that interviewers frequently haven't received training in how to conduct an effective interview. Fewer than one half of large corporations require interviewers to receive training before conducting interviews on college campuses.[18] Organizations often send recent graduates back to their alma maters to interview prospective applicants. These graduates may have only limited experience with the job and the organization—and even less experience interviewing prospective candidates. But even professional interviewers may not be well prepared for the interview. In a survey conducted by Hanigan Consulting, 200 professional interviewers and recruiters were given a list of 12 inappropriate questions—70% of the respondents thought that at least 5 of the questions were acceptable lines of inquiry.[19]

But here's some good news: it's not that hard to improve the quality of job interviews. There are two primary steps you can take to ensure that your interviews are both legally defensible and likely to predict on-the-job performance. First, you need to structure them—ask the same job-related questions of every applicant. Second, you need to use situational or behavioral questions (I'll explain what those are a little later). Let's take a closer look at those two steps.

Step One: Structuring the Job Interview

The first step in preparing for a high-quality interview process is developing an interview protocol—a standard list of interview topics that you will discuss with every applicant. This protocol should be developed before you meet with *any* applicants face-to-face. Start by reviewing the job's requirements, and generating a set of questions that relate directly to each requirement. That list of questions will establish the general structure of every interview you conduct. After the interview process is completed, you'll have compiled a common set of information about the applicants, and their relative quality and suitability can be assessed directly.

A structured interview protocol will help you to avoid one of the most common pitfalls in employment interviews. Interviewers often "shoot from the hip" and ask questions spontaneously. Some of those unscripted questions may be triggered by a candidate's demographics or appearance—and make an applicant feel "singled out." Are you only asking the Hispanic applicants about their language fluency? Are you only asking about age when the applicant appears to be older than the typical jobholder? Are you only asking health-related questions when the applicant has a visible disability? If you are, these questions might raise concerns of disparate treatment—because only certain types of applicants are being evaluated on these dimensions.

Job applicants sometimes believe that there is a magic list of "illegal" questions that interviewers are forbidden from asking—but that's not an accurate belief. You'll recall from chapter 2 that in the United States, EEO laws prohibit discrimination based on race, sex, national origin, disability, age, and other demographic dimensions. As a manager, you are not forbidden from *asking* about those dimensions, but you are prohibited from *using* those dimensions in your hiring decision. Interview questions become problematic when the content of these questions can be used to infer discrimination against certain job applicants. Here's a sampling of problematic questions:

- What is your ancestry? (could indicate national origin discrimination)
- How old are you? (could indicate discrimination against older job applicants)
- What religious holidays do you observe? (could indicate discrimination against members of certain religious groups)
- How is your health? (could indicate disability discrimination)

Now, why would interviewers ask questions like that? Sometimes, perfectly reasonable hiring criteria are hidden behind these problematic questions. But the true purpose is obscured because the interviewer has made an inference about the relation between the job's requirements and the applicant's personal characteristics. Here are similar questions, rewritten to eliminate the disparate treatment inference:

- Many of our customers are more comfortable speaking and writing in languages other than English. Do you speak, read, or write fluently in any languages other than English?
- This job involves serving alcohol to restaurant customers. The law says that you must be 21 to serve alcohol. Do you meet that job requirement?
- This job involves frequent travel to other parts of the country. Since training sessions start very early on Monday morning, we usually travel on Sundays. Would that be a problem for you?
- This job involves working with chemicals that can have a negative impact on the health of people who have a suppressed immune system. Does your physical condition enable you to work with these chemicals?

As you can see, the law doesn't stop you from gathering information that is job-relevant. As long as you can explicitly and directly link your question to a job requirement, the question is appropriate. That's why the initial interview protocol (based on the job requirements) is so important—it helps you to identify, before being confronted with any individual applicant, what you need to know in order to make an informed hiring decision.

Some managers are reluctant to develop structured interview protocols. They fear that the structure will limit their ability to gather information and ask revealing questions. But using a protocol doesn't mean you have to become an interview robot! One of the big advantages of interviews is their flexibility, and you should take advantage of that flexibility. The protocol is just a framework that helps to structure the overall interview. Once you've ensured that each applicant is being given the opportunity to provide information relevant to the underlying job requirements, you can feel free to follow up on interesting answers and probe for additional details.

Step Two: Using Situational or Behavioral Questions

As a result of developing your interview protocol, you should be clear on *what* you want to know about each applicant. But how should you frame questions to elicit the information you really want? Let's say, for example, your review of the job requirements indicates that successful applicants will need to juggle multiple competing tasks. If you just go in and ask every applicant, "How are you at multitasking?" 95% of them will say "Great!" and you won't have learned a thing. We need to make sure that applicants' answers to interview questions will be predictive of actual on-the-job performance. We'll talk about two kinds of predictive questions: *situational interview questions* and *behavioral description interview* questions.

Situational Interview Questions. Situational interviews ask the applicant to respond to a series of hypothetical situations—the applicant explains, in considerable detail, how he or she would handle each situation.[20] The questions are open-ended, but the interviewer has a scoring key that enables him or her to quantitatively evaluate the quality of the applicant's answer.

Remember my earlier example about the Bellagio resort? The Bellagio needed to fill a large number of customer service positions, including working the front desk. Here's an example of a situational interview question they used: "You are working at the front desk, and a guest arrives very late. You can't find the guest's reservation—what would you do?"[21] Before using a question like this in a job interview, the manager needs to sit down and think about the applicants' possible answers, and develop a scoring key to evaluate them. If your organization is in a customer service industry (like Bellagio) you may be most concerned about hiring individuals who will take initiative to solve customers' problems. Therefore, answers that reflect a high regard for customer service, and an ability to satisfy the customer above all else, would receive a high score ("I'd make sure that the guest was settled into a room tonight, and ask a manager to help solve the reservation problem in the morning"). Answers that showed less initiative but still tried to address the customer service problem might receive fewer points ("I'd see if I could call one of the managers at home, and ask what to do"). Answers that reflected a low regard for the customer receive 0 points ("I'd tell the customer that I couldn't do anything without a valid reservation, and suggest that he try another hotel down the street"). You'll find more examples of situational interviews used by employers in the top half of Box 5.1.

Behavioral Interview Questions. In a behavioral interview, the interviewer asks the job applicant to reflect on his or her *past* experience.[22] The idea is to find links between this job's requirements and the applicant's history in dealing with similar issues in the past. For example, suppose that you are hiring a trainer to teach people how to use a complicated graphics package. The applicants you are interviewing have a great deal of technical experience with the software, but limited experience in teaching or training. How can you identify the ones with the highest potential for success? One strategy might be to ask the applicants to describe an experience they had explaining difficult material to someone else—even if it occurred outside of a formal teaching context. This would allow an applicant, for example, to describe how he helped his elderly aunt to complete her income taxes last year.

BOX 5.1
Sample Situational and Behavioral Questions

Company	Situational Interview Questions
Colgate-Palmolive New York, NY	Applicants are asked how they would get employees to wear hard hats in a dangerous factory area. "Cop" answers (docking the pay of people who didn't wear their hats) are less valued than "coach" answers (having management set a good example by always wearing their hats).[23]
Hyperion Solutions Stamford, CT	"You've been asked a question by a client on a product that you don't support, and it's after-hours on Friday. Where do you find the answer?"[24]
Boston Consulting Group Boston, MA	"A client makes two types of refrigerators: the traditional kind, with the freezer on top, and the larger variety, with the freezer on the side. In the 1990s, the company was making money on both lines. But a few years back, the top-mounted division started to falter. Now things are so bad that the black from the side-mounts is barely keeping pace with the red from the top-mounts. Given this, what would you advise the client?"[25]
Company	**Behavioral Interview Questions**
Southwest Airlines Dallas, TX	"Tell me about a time that you experienced a stressful situation and were able to solve the problem with humor."[26]
Capital One Financial Corp. Richmond, VA	"Describe a project where you had to collaborate with others. How do you work in developing people?"[27]
BellSouth Mobility Atlanta, GA	"Tell us about a person you supervised who had performance issues. What was the problem? How did you diagnose it? What steps did you take to fix it?"[28]

The bottom half of Box 5.1 presents some sample behavioral questions used by employers. These questions reflect important requirements of the job being filled. Capital One, for example, wants to ensure that the people they hire are able to work in a team environment. Southwest Airlines knows that one of the most difficult situations for an airline employee is announcing a flight cancellation—and Southwest Airlines wants employees who can handle that situation with humor.

Choosing Between Situational and Behavioral Interview Questions. If you use situational or behavioral questions in the interview, the criterion-related validity skyrockets to around .50[29]—about the same as the criterion-related validity of cognitive ability tests. That's pretty impressive. But should you use situational (hypothetical) *or* behavioral (past experience) questions? Both of these options improve the criterion-related validity of the interview, but research suggests that behavioral interviews have higher validity than situational interviews.[30] Behavioral interviews (focusing on past experience) can be especially useful in situations where the applicants have little direct experience with your job or industry. For example, many of Southwest Airline's applicants come from customer service positions outside the airline industry; they may never have had to announce a cancelled flight, but they can still describe their ability to use humor under pressure (see Box 5.1). Similarly, if you manage a call center, you'll want to know how applicants will handle irate customers who call about billing errors. Job applicants may not know enough about your organization's policies or billing procedures to provide very specific answers in response to a situational question. However, they can respond to a question focusing on their past experience: "Tell me about a time when you had to deal with someone who was angry about something that wasn't your fault. How did you resolve the situation?" The applicant's answer may reflect experience he or she gained in another industry, in his or her personal life, or at school.

Manager's Checkpoint

Use the following questions to help you improve your job interviews:

- Do I have a clear sense of the skills required to do the job well? (Being very specific about the job requirements will help you to design questions that get directly at those requirements, rather than relying on vague impressions of the job applicant. Developing a complete list of job requirements may require consultation with other people in the organization.)
- Have I developed a standard list of topics and starter questions that can be asked of every candidate? (Remember that you

should address the same issues and topics with every candidate, in order to avoid impressions of disparate treatment.)

- Am I asking predictive questions? (Predictive questions, whether
they focus on an applicant's past experience or ask the applicant
to respond to hypothetical scenarios, should be developed for
each of the skill areas you are trying to assess.)

- Am I primarily hiring people with experience in my particular industry, who are likely to be familiar with the job content? (If you
hire from within the industry, applicants will understand the hypothetical situations and be able to respond to them effectively. If
you are hiring from outside the industry, or hiring applicants with
limited job experience, questions about past experience may
give applicants the opportunity to show that they have the skills
required to perform.)

INTERVIEW TWISTS

So far, we've discussed interviews that use a traditional format in which a
job applicant is scheduled for a one-on-one face-to-face meeting with a
single interviewer. However, some organizations are experimenting with
other methods of interviewing, with positive results. We'll discuss two other
options—one that involves more evaluators in the interview process, and
one that substitutes a computer-mediated interview for at least part of the
traditional interview.

Panel Interviews and Video Interviews

Some organizations, including Federal Express and Holt, Rinehart and
Winston, involve more than one person in the interview process. In these
organizations, job applicants meet with a panel of two to six interviewers
who take turns asking questions. Interviewers on the panel may be selected
exclusively from management ranks, or may include peers who would be
working alongside the candidate on the job.[31] Early evidence suggests that
panel interviews result in greater acceptance of the final decision on both
sides.[32] On the organizational side, interviewers have more confidence in
their hiring decisions if multiple people have had an opportunity to interact
with the job applicant. And on the job applicant's side, panel interviews can
avoid the sense of not having gotten on well with a primary/single interviewer. Multiple people can evaluate the applicant's potential, and the applicant doesn't have to rehash the same material over and over again in a
sequence of one-on-one meetings.

Probably the biggest problem with a panel interview is the scheduling nightmare it can cause. It can be difficult to have all the relevant parties available at the same place, at the same time, to meet with a job applicant. An alternative is to use video interviews. Video interviews are becoming popular as an option for organizations that want to involve multiple people in the interviewing process, but want to save costs at the same time. In a video interview, applicants are sent to interview centers where they are videotaped as they respond to a standard set of questions.[33] Video interviews have several advantages: First, they save travel costs associated with interviewing.[34] Second, they standardize the interview across applicants—all applicants are asked the same standard set of questions, which allows direct comparisons to be made across the applicants.[35] Finally, the video can easily be passed around the organization (or viewed on the Internet) so that all interested parties have a chance to evaluate the applicant.[36]

Even if you don't convene a formal panel, you may want to involve other people in the interview process and get their perspective on the job applicant. The Container Store, for example, allows any current employee (even part-timers) to accept applications and prescreen job applicants. Company representatives say that the policy serves a positive public relations function by communicating the company's culture to the job applicant.[37] However, it's important to remember that when non-managerial employees get involved in the interviewing process, they also need to know and follow EEOC guidelines. Employees should receive guidelines on how to ask questions that are related to the job requirements and do not venture into areas protected by EEO law.[38]

Computerized Interviews

As interviews become more and more structured, you might wonder why you even need a human interviewer! Couldn't the organization administer a job interview via a computer, and ask the applicants to type in their answers to a standard set of questions? You might even get better, more candid information—research suggests that people are more likely to disclose information that might reflect negatively on them to a computer than to a person.[39] For example, one study found that job applicants reported their grade point averages and scholastic aptitude scores more accurately (with less inflation) in computerized interviews than in face-to-face interviews.[40] Also, with computerized interviews you never have to worry about the interviewer asking inappropriate questions or skipping over important questions. Several years ago, Neiman Marcus learned that one way to identify which job applicants were likely to stay with the retailer once hired was simply to ask them: "How long do you plan to stay with us if a job is offered?"

However, managers frequently failed to collect this information because they felt uncomfortable asking applicants face-to-face about their intentions. Now Neiman Marcus includes the question as part of a pre-interview computerized screening. "I am amazed at how many people come right out and tell us they only plan to work a few months," says a human resource manager for the company.[41]

Some job hunters see computerized interviews as more depersonalized than the traditional interview,[42] especially when used to hire into high-status organizational positions.[43] Computers are unlikely to replace human interviewers completely, largely because of the public relations function served by the interview. However, many organizations, including Nike, Target stores, Publix supermarkets, and Blockbuster Video, are using computers in the interview process for prescreening.[44] In a typical computerized interview, the questions are presented in a multiple choice format, one at a time, and the applicant responds to the questions by pressing a key corresponding to his or her desired response. Computer-aided interviews are generally used to reject totally unacceptable candidates, and to select those who will move on to a face-to-face interview. One organization that has invested in computerized interviews in a big way is Home Depot.[45] Home Depot established a company-wide customized computer system called the Job Preference Program (JPP) as part of their response to complaints from women who claimed that they were being steered into low-paying cashier positions. Job seekers apply at computer kiosks, and the computer adjusts its questions depending on the amount of applicant experience. When managers are ready to fill an opening, the computer gives them the names of prescreened candidates as well as suggesting interview questions to ask. Managers can only interview people who have expressed an interest in the job via the JPP system. Since JPP was introduced, the number of female managers at Home Depot has increased by 30% and the number of minority managers by 28%. But the system has other added benefits. Managers, for example, are thrilled that they no longer have to waste time interviewing people who are clearly a poor fit to the job—the computerized prescreening weeds out unqualified candidates before a live interview takes place.

Manager's Checkpoint

The following questions might help you to decide whether you want to add these twists into your interviewing process:

- Do I need to screen a large number of job applicants? (As the number of applicants increases, it may be worth considering the use of computerized prescreening.)
- Am I uncomfortable asking some of the questions that would help me to identify qualified applicants? (If your answer is yes, you might consider delegating these "sensitive" questions to a computer.)
- Has my organization had problems in the past with interviewers asking inappropriate or irrelevant questions in the job interview? (If your answer is yes, computerized or videotaped interviews can minimize these problems.)
- Am I unfamiliar with some of the job requirements? Will the job applicant need to work closely with other people after hiring? (If your answer to either question is yes, you might want to consider involving other people in the interview process. For example, you could conduct panel interviews or show a videotaped interview to other interested parties.)

WHAT'S NEXT?

At this point in the employment process, you've effectively recruited and screened applicants and hired the ones who were best-qualified. But now that your newly hired employees are on the job, how are you going to measure their performance? In the next chapter, we'll examine the performance appraisal process.

FOR FURTHER READING

Gladwell, M. (2000, May 29). The new-boy network: What do job interviews really tell us? *The New Yorker*, 68–86.

Graves, L., & Karren, R. (1996). The employee selection interview: A fresh look at an old problem. *Human Resource Management, 35*(2), 163–180.

Mornell, P. (1998, March). Zero defect hiring. *Inc.*, 74–83.

Segal, J. A. (2002, June). Hiring days are (almost) here again! *HRMagazine*, 125–134.

MANAGER'S KNOT 5.1

"I'm trying to fill a position that requires long hours and extensive travel. I don't see how anyone with small children or other family responsibilities could do the work. I want to address these concerns in my interviews with job candidates—how can I bring up these issues without being perceived as discriminating?"

First, make sure you clearly and unambiguously describe the job requirements during the interview—this will give job candidates who cannot meet the demands of the work the opportunity to opt out. Second, provide this information to *all* job candidates—not just the women, and not just the candidates who tell you they have small children at home. Don't assume who can do the work and who can't.

MANAGER'S KNOT 5.2

"We've had a lot of trouble with employee theft at my company. Our employees are responsible for stocking expensive computer equipment, and our stores have experienced an increasing amount of inventory 'shrinkage' that we attribute to employee theft. However, we'd like to avoid using standardized integrity tests. Is there a way to get at integrity issues using an interview?"

You can design an interview to gather predictive information about almost any on-the-job behavior. If you wanted to conduct a situational interview, you could develop behavioral dilemmas that reflect on-the-job situations ("Suppose you learned that a coworker was taking computer equipment off site during her lunch break. What would you do?"). Or you could ask applicants how they handled similar situations in the past ("Tell me about a time when you learned that someone you knew was doing something unethical or illegal. How did you handle that situation?")

MANAGER'S KNOT 5.3

"I interview prospective applicants at job fairs. I try to break up the interviews and allow a little recovery time between them, but often my schedule is packed solid. What can I do to make sure that my assessments of the candidates are accurate and not influenced by order effects?"

You've already taken the first step—just recognizing that order effects can occur will put you on your guard and make you less susceptible to them. Another precaution is to avoid making a final decision during the interview itself. Instead, take notes about an applicants' strengths and weaknesses, using concrete examples that will help to jog your memory later. Then, at the end of the day, review your notes and make decisions in the context of the entire applicant pool.

MANAGER'S KNOT 5.4

"I supervise a team of people with highly technical skills. But I'm not a techie myself, and so I feel uncomfortable interviewing people for open positions. How can I effectively interview people whose technical skills far exceed my own?"

Your problem is not unusual. Managers frequently have to hire individuals with specialized skills. Here are a few suggestions: First, do these technical skills have to be assessed in the interview? Perhaps there is a standardized test or a work sample that could be used to evaluate technical expertise, freeing your interview time to address other issues. Second, this might be a good opportunity to involve other people in the interviewing process. You don't have skills in the applicant's technical area, but are there members of your team who do? You could invite these individuals to participate in a panel interview. They can ask the technical questions, and you can ask the non-technical questions, but you can observe the applicants' ability to handle both types of questions. If you don't want to conduct a panel interview, you can still involve the other members of your team by asking them to suggest relevant questions to ask (and getting their feedback on the quality of applicant answers). Finally, don't hesitate to acknowledge your lack of technical expertise in the interview. Remember, the person you hire has to be able to communicate effectively with you—and that includes being able to communicate technical information in a straightforward way without unnecessary jargon. By letting the applicant know up front that you are unfamiliar with the specifics of the technical area, you give the applicant an opportunity to demonstrate his or her communication skills.

ENDNOTES

1. Dipboye, R. L. (1992). *Selection interviews: Process perspectives*. Cincinnati, OH: South-western Publishing; McDaniel, M. A., Whetzel, D. L., Schmidt, F. L., & Maurer, S. D. (1994). The validity of employment interviews: A comprehensive review and meta-analysis. *Journal of Applied Psychology, 79*, 599–616.
2. Hunter, J. E., & Hunter, R. F. (1984). Validity and utility of alternative predictors of job performance. *Psychological Bulletin, 96*, 72–98.
3. Springbett, B. M. (1958). Factors affecting the final decision in the employment interview. *Canadian Journal of Psychology, 12*, 13–22; Dipboye, R. L., Stramler, C., & Fontenelle, G. A. (1984). The effects of the application on recall of information from the interview. *Academy of Management Journal, 27*, 561–575.

4. Tucker, D. H., & Rowe, P. M. (1979). Relationship between expectancy, causal attributions, and final hiring decisions in the employment interview. *Journal of Applied Psychology, 64,* 27–34; Dougherty, T. W., Turban, D. B., & Callender, J. C. (1994). Confirming first impressions in the employment interview: A field study of interviewer behavior. *Journal of Applied Psychology, 79,* 659–665; Macan, T. M., & Dipboye, R. L. (1988). The effects of interviewers' initial impressions on information-gathering. *Organizational Behavior and Human Decision Processes, 42,* 364–387.

5. Springbett, B. M. (1958). Factors affecting the final decision in the employment interview. *Canadian Journal of Psychology, 12,* 13–22.

6. Buckley, M. R., & Eder, R. W. (1988). B. M. Springbett and the notion of the "snap decision" in the interview. *Journal of Management, 14,* 59–67; Tucker, D. H., & Rowe, P. M. (1977). Consulting the application form prior to the interview: An essential step in the selection process. *Journal of Applied Psychology, 62,* 283–288; Initial minutes of job interview are critical. (2000). *USA Today Magazine, 128*(2656). Retrieved April 15, 2001, from http://www.britannica.com/magazine/article?query=Saving+Silverman&id=5&smode=1

7. Wexley, K. N., Yukl, G. A., Kovacs, S. Z., & Sanders, R. E. (1972). Importance of contrast effects in employment interviews. *Journal of Applied Psychology, 56,* 45–48.

8. Rosse, J., & Levin, R. (1997). *High impact hiring: A comprehensive guide to performance-based hiring.* San Francisco: Jossey-Bass.

9. Frase-Blunt, M. (2001, January). Games interviewers play. *HRMagazine,* 106–114.

10. Breen, B. (2001, January). Full house. *Fast Company,* 110–122.

11. Zehnder, E. (2001, April). A simpler way to pay. *Harvard Business Review,* 53-61.

12. Gilliland, S. W. (1995). Fairness from the applicant's perspective: Reactions to employee selection procedures. *International Journal of Selection and Assessment, 3,* 11–19; Steiner, D. D., & Gilliland, S. W. (1996). Fairness reactions to personnel selection techniques in France and the United States. *Journal of Applied Psychology, 81,* 134–141.

13. Maher, K. (2002). How best to land that job? Step One: Brush your teeth. *Wall Street Journal Online.* Retrieved November 19, 2002 from online.wsj.com

14. Buxman, K., & Sweeney, T. (2002, February). Interview blunders. *Credit Union Management,* 6.

15. Buxman, K., & Sweeney, T. (2002, February). Interview blunders. *Credit Union Management,* 6.

16. In bad taste. (2001, May 8). *Wall Street Journal,* p. B12.

17. Work week. (1999, September 28). *Wall Street Journal,* p. A1.

18. Rynes, S. L., & Boudreau, J. W. (1986). College recruiting in large organizations: Practice, evaluation, and research implications. *Personnel Psychology, 39,* 729–757.

19. Woo, J. (1992, March 11). Job interviews pose rising risk to employers. *Wall Street Journal,* pp. B1, B5.

20. Latham, G. P., & Saari, L. M. (1984). Do people do what they say? More studies of the situational interview. *Journal of Applied Psychology, 69,* 569–573; Latham, G. P., Saari, L. M., Pursell, M. A., & Campion, M. A. (1980). The situational interview. *Journal of Applied Psychology, 65,* 422–427.

21. Breen, B. (2001, January). Full house. *Fast Company,* 110–122.

22. Janz, T. (1982). Initial comparisons of patterned behavior description interviews versus unstructured interviews. *Journal of Applied Psychology, 67,* 577–580.

23. Saltzman, A. (1991, May 13). To get ahead, you may have to put on an act. *U.S. News and World Report,* 90.

24. Taking questions to a hire level. (2001, March 23). *National Post,* p. C02.

25. Kay, J. (2000, May 1). Walk me through your head. *National Post,* p. 66.

26. Turner, M. (2001). Creative hiring replaces yesterday's staid interview. *Houston Business Journal*. Retrieved March 9, 2001, from http://Houston.bcentral.com/Houston stories/2001/03/12/focus1.html

27. Trotsky, J. (2001, January 8). Oh, will you behave? *Computerworld*, 42–43.

28. Brackley, H. J. (1998, October 5). Canned answers won't cut it at new-style job interviews. *Miami Herald*, p. 9.

29. Campion, M. A., Campion, J. E., & Hudson, J. P., Jr. (1994). Structured interviewing: A note on incremental validity and alternative question types. *Journal of Applied Psychology, 79*, 998–1002.

30. Campion, M. A., Campion, J. E., & Hudson J. P., Jr. (1994). Structured interviewing: A note on incremental validity and alternative question types. *Journal of Applied Psychology, 79*, 998–1002; Pulakos, E. D., & Schmitt, N. (1995). Experience-based and situational interview questions: Studies of validity. *Personnel Psychology, 48*, 289–308.

31. Frase-Blunt, M. (2001, December). Peering into an interview: Peer interviewing can reveal the perfect candidate for your team—if it's done right. *HRMagazine*, 71–76; Martin, J. (1998, January 12). So, you want to work for the best .... *Fortune*, 77–78; Warmke, D. L., & Weston, D. J. (1992). Success dispels myths about panel interviewing. *Personnel Journal, 71*(4), 120–126.

32. Frase-Blunt, M. (2001, December). Peering into an interview: Peer interviewing an reveal the perfect candidate for your team—if it's done right. *HRMagazine*, 71–76; Warmke, D. L., & Weston, D. J. (1992). Success dispels myths about panel interviewing. *Personnel Journal, 71*(4), 120–126.

33. Frazee, V. (1996). Solve the long-distance hiring dilemma. *Personnel Journal*, recruitment staffing sourcebook suppl., 18–20; Gunsch, D. (1991, August). Smile, you're on a hiring camera. *Personnel Journal, 16*; Frost, M. (2001, August). Video interviewing: Not yet ready for prime time. *HRMagazine*, 93–98.

34. Lublin, J. S. (1999, April 27). Hunting CEOs on a 32-inch screen. *Wall Street Journal*, pp. B1, B4; Frazee, V. (1996). Solve the long-distance hiring dilemma. *Personnel Journal*, recruitment staffing sourcebook suppl., 18–20; Work week. (1995, November 21). *Wall Street Journal*, p. A1; Frost, M. (2001, August). Video interviewing: Not yet ready for prime time. *HRMagazine*, 93–98.

35. Cronin, M. (1994, September). Try taping those interviews. *Inc.*, 120; Johnson, M. A. (1991, April). Lights, camera, interview. *HRMagazine*, 66–68.

36. Johnson, M. A. (1991, April). Lights, camera, interview. *HRMagazine*, 66–68; Dawson, C. (1986, May). Using video as an aid to selection. *Personnel Management*, 67; Frost, M. (2001, August). Video interviewing: Not yet ready for prime time. *HRMagazine*, 93–98.

37. Turner, M. (2001). Creative hiring replaces yesterday's staid interview. *Houston Business Journal*. Retrieved March 9, 2001, from http://Houston.bcentral.com/Houston/stories/2001/03/12/focus1.html

38. Segal, J. A. (2002, June). Hiring days are (almost) here again! *HRMagazine*, 125–134; Frase-Blunt, M. (2001, December). Peering into an interview. *HRMagazine*, 71–77.

39. Evan, W. M., & Miller, J. R., III. (1969). Differential effects on response bias of computer vs. conventional administration of a social science questionnaire: An exploratory methodological experiment. *Behavioral Science, 14*, 216–227.

40. Martin, C. L., & Nagao, D. H. (1989). Some effects of computerized interviewing on job applicant responses. *Journal of Applied Psychology, 74*, 72–80.

41. Stamps, D. (1995, April). Cyberinterviews combat turnover. *Training*, 43–47.

42. Bulkeley, W. M. (1994, August 22). Replaced by technology: Job interviews. *Wall Street Journal*, pp. B1, B4.

43. Martin, C. L., & Nagao, D. H. (1989). Some effects of computerized interviewing on job applicant responses. *Journal of Applied Psychology, 74,* 72–80.
44. Thornburg, L. (1998, February). Computer-assisted interviewing shortens hiring cycle. *HRMagazine,* 73–79; Overholt, A. (2002, February). True or false: You're hiring the right people. *Fast Company,* 110–114; Richtel, M. (2000, February 6). Online revolution's latest twist: Job interviews with a computer. *New York Times,* p. 1.
45. Daniels, C. (2000, April 3). To hire a lumber expert, click here. *Fortune,* 267–270; Gilbertson, D. (1999, September 19). Computers replacing job-application paper. *Arizona Republic,* pp. D1, D6; Bulkeley, W. M. (1994, August 22). Replaced by technology: Job interviews. *Wall Street Journal,* pp. B1, B4; Henkoff, R. (1994, October 3). Finding, training, and keeping the best service workers. *Fortune,* 110–122.

III

Measuring and Evaluating
Employee Performance

#

Conducting
Performance Appraisals

Sweaty palms, upset stomach, pounding heart—these are symptoms frequently associated with performance appraisals in organizations. If you've ever waited to find out whether your test scores were high enough to admit you to your preferred college, or sat by the phone hoping for a job interview callback, you know how stressful life can be when you're on the receiving end of performance feedback. But you might be surprised to know that managers report that *giving* performance feedback is one of the most difficult parts of their jobs. The performance rating you give to your subordinate can affect the employee's pay raise and promotion opportunities—not to mention his or her self-esteem and motivation. That kind of pressure is bound to cause a few sleepless nights.

Think of the performance appraisal process as having two distinct stages. In the first stage, the manager uses a standard form provided by the organization to rate each of the employees he or she supervises. We'll call that part the performance appraisal *rating*. In the second stage, the manager shares the rating with each employee during a performance appraisal *meeting*. Later in this chapter, I'll discuss each of these stages. But let's get one thing straight right at the beginning. There is no perfect performance appraisal method! In organizations, performance appraisals are conducted for a variety of administrative (e.g., salary recommendations, promotion and layoff decisions) and developmental (e.g., training recommendations) purposes. The goals associated with administrative and developmental appraisals can conflict with one another, and even when the goals are reasonably compatible, one performance appraisal method is unlikely to be the best match for every purpose. As you'll see in this chapter's material, every performance appraisal method offers trade-offs. Your responsibilities in the performance appraisal process include managing these trade-offs, limiting as many appraisal errors as you can, and delivering performance feedback effectively to your employees. With those goals in mind, let's talk more about who the rater is in the performance appraisal process.

RATER CHOICES

In most organizations, the primary person evaluating employee performance is the immediate supervisor. But more and more organizations are involving other people in the evaluation process. In many jobs, the immediate supervisor may not have access to all of the relevant information about employee performance. Imagine, for example, a police officer who spends most of his time patrolling local neighborhoods with his partner or a salesperson who spends most of her time meeting with clients. The supervisor may have information about the bottom line (e.g., the number of arrests made, the amount of sales), but no information about the process contributing to those outcomes. In these cases, coworkers and customers may be able to fill in the gaps. At some organizations, employees are encouraged to identify a couple of coworkers with whom they work closely; at review time, the manager asks these "accountability partners" to evaluate the employee's contributions.[1] Other organizations gather feedback from internal or external customers to evaluate sales and services employees.[2] Some organizations are also involving employees' subordinates in the performance evaluation process. Subordinates can provide useful feedback to the employee about his or her management skills.[3] These upward appraisals are especially beneficial for higher-level executives, who are often excluded from traditional top-down appraisal systems.[4]

Performance appraisal systems that involve multiple raters in the evaluation process are called *360 degree* systems. By inviting supervisors, subordinates, peers, and customers to participate in the evaluation process, the employee can receive performance feedback from every possible vantage point—from above, below, and on all sides. Studies show that about 12% of American organizations are using full 360 degree systems (taking advantage of supervisor, subordinate, *and* peer ratings), 25% are using upward appraisals in which subordinates evaluate their supervisors, and 18% are using peer appraisals.[5] 360 degree feedback can involve a handful of raters, or many. Larger organizations (e.g., Boeing) conduct 360 performance evaluations through the Internet, and involve 20 or more raters per employee.[6] 360 degree feedback can be very useful in the performance appraisal process, especially in its ability to provide the employee with developmental feedback.[7] People may be completely unaware of their strengths and weaknesses in interpersonal relationships unless the people they work with provide candid feedback about their behavior. The key word here is *candid*—coworkers must feel comfortable in providing both positive and negative information to the employee.[8] For that reason, the 360 feedback collected by an organization is usually aggregated and summarized before being presented to the employee. This preserves the confidentiality of the individual raters and gives the employee a "big picture" view rather than pages and pages of detail.[9]

RATER ERRORS

No matter how experienced, raters are susceptible to a number of *rater errors* (see Table 6.1). Some raters are "easy graders" and give all employees, regardless of their actual performance, scores at the high end of the performance rating scale—this is known as the *leniency error*. Other raters tend to be "hard graders" and give all employees scores at the low end of the performance rating scale (*severity error*). Still others tend to give scores that cluster at the scale midpoint (*central tendency error*). These errors are problematic because they misrepresent the actual range and distribution of employee performance.

A very common rater error is called *halo error*. Halo error occurs when the rater assigns ratings on the basis of a global impression of the employee as either a good or poor performer. Suppose a manager has observed an employee make excellent presentations to clients. As a result of this observation, the manager now thinks of this employee as an excellent performer. The manager commits a halo error when she assumes that the employee also meets deadlines, has technical expertise, and gets along well with his team members—without having actually observed these performance dimensions. Managers can also commit the halo error in a negative direction when they assume, for example, that an employee who is chronically late for work is a poor performer in other respects. When raters commit the halo error, the performance evaluation process loses accuracy—we don't know the specific ways that an employee's performance is good or bad, and therefore we don't know what kinds of training or other developmental opportunities might be used to improve performance.

Extended time gaps between appraisals can give rise to a rater error called *recency error*. In most U.S. organizations, managers are asked to evaluate employee performance on an annual basis.[10] Let's say, for exam-

TABLE 6.1

Common Rater Errors

Leniency error	A rater consistently rates employees at the high end of the scale
Severity error	A rater consistently rates all employees at the low end of the scale
Central tendency error	A rater consistently rates employees at the scale midpoint
Halo error	A rater's evaluation of an employee on one performance dimension creates an overall positive or negative impression that drives ratings on other dimensions
Recency error	A rater's evaluation is heavily influenced by the employee's most recent performance
Contrast error	A rater's evaluation of an average employee is boosted after rating a poor employee, or lowered after rating an excellent employee
Similar-to-me error	A rater's evaluation of an employee is inflated because of a personal connection

ple, that your organization asks managers to submit performance evaluations at the end of the calendar year. On December 15, you sit down at your desk and diligently evaluate each employee who reports to you. After completing your ratings, employee evaluations may not cross your mind again until the following November, when your organization sends you a reminder memo that evaluations are coming due. When you get ready to evaluate your employees this time, will you remember what they were doing in January and February? More likely, your performance rating will be heavily influenced by your employees' recent performance—information that is very accessible in your memory banks. Recency errors reduce the accuracy of performance ratings, particularly if some employees have had highly variable performance over the year.

Most managers conduct performance appraisals of all of their employees at one time. If raters evaluate a series of employees, their performance standards can be anchored by the first few employees they review, giving rise to *contrast errors*. Suppose you supervise three employees: Alicia, Bobby, and Cora. Alicia is a dream employee—her work is outstanding. Cora is a problem employee—she is constantly on the verge of being fired. Bobby's performance is somewhere in between. If you evaluate Alicia first, you may find that your performance expectations are pulled up—and subsequently evaluate Bobby a little more harshly than he deserves. But if you evaluate Cora first, you may find that Bobby's performance looks good by comparison and give him a higher rating.

There's one more rater error to consider—the *similar-to-me* error. Raters tend to evaluate employees more positively when the rater and the employee have something in common. Maybe the rater and the employee went to the same college, share a love of sports, or have similar values. These similarities can boost performance ratings.

Thinking about all these potential rater errors can be discouraging, but there are ways to guard against them. As we review the various performance methods, you'll see that some methods are especially effective in reducing leniency, severity, and central tendency errors. You can conduct an informal check on these errors yourself by incorporating comparative judgments into the appraisal process. After evaluating all your employees, go back and create a loose ranking of your employees by asking yourself: "Is this employee's overall performance generally stronger than, the same as, or weaker than the performance of other employees I supervise?"[11] The resulting distribution created by your answers to this question should roughly correspond to your evaluations of individual employees—deviations may indicate rater errors. For example, if you have no difficulty identifying one employee as performing more poorly than his or her coworkers, but you still gave that employee high scores on all the performance dimensions, you may be exhibiting the leniency error.

As for the other errors, you can structure your decision-making process to minimize their influence. To reduce recency error, you can schedule regular evaluation checkpoints at which you jot down a few notes to yourself about how each employee is currently performing.[12] These notes can be useful for jogging your memory when the official performance evaluation deadline rolls around. To guard against contrast error, try evaluating employees on one day, shuffling the order, and reevaluating them on another day in a different sequence.

RATING METHODS

Performance appraisal methods can be organized into four basic types. Rating methods ask the rater to assess (1) the employee's personal characteristics or *traits*; (2) the employee's work *behaviors*; (3) the employee's work *results*; or (4) the employee's overall value, or worth *in comparison to* other employees. Within each of these types, there are many variations. We'll discuss the advantages and disadvantages of each type, and I'll give you an example or two to illustrate each one.

Trait Methods

In trait rating methods, raters evaluate performers on underlying charac-teristics (or *traits*) such as dependability, ability to work with others, and leadership. Trait methods include graphic rating scales and the essay method (or narrative method).

Graphic Rating Scales.   Several examples of graphic rating scales are shown in Fig. 6.1. Graphic rating scales ask the rater to evaluate the em-ployee on a series of scales. The rater chooses a number, a descriptive category, or a point on the scale that best describes the employee. The or-ganization might provide the rater with a brief definition of the trait being evaluated—beyond that, the rater usually receives little guidance from the organization about how the trait might operate in the work context or how to evaluate employee performance in terms of the trait. In other words, it's the rater's responsibility to consider how "leadership" would be displayed on the employee's job, and to decide whether the employee has demonstrated enough leadership to warrant a high score on the graphic rating scale.

Essay Method.   Another option in the trait methods category involves asking raters to write an essay or a narrative describing the performance of each employee. Usually, raters are instructed to address the em-ployee's strengths and weaknesses in terms of a handful of dimensions (dependability, ability to work with others, and leadership are typical di-mensions) and make recommendations for the employee's further devel-opment (e.g., training opportunities that the employee should pursue).

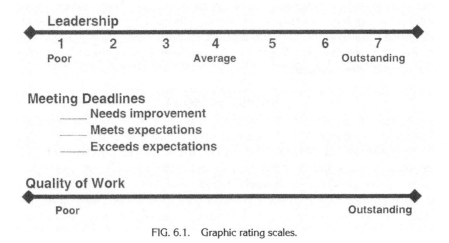

FIG. 6.1.   Graphic rating scales.

Some raters find it difficult to create employee narratives from scratch—it can be intimidating to stare at a blank computer screen and try to generate employee narratives—but computer software has been marketed to provide some structure to the process. Several programs (such as Performance Now! by Knowledge-Point and Review Writer by Avantos Performance Systems) ask raters to evaluate employees on graphic rating scales first—then the software generates a narrative that the rater can customize with specific examples.[13] These software packages can make it easier to generate narrative reviews, but be careful! If you are too quick to accept the software's canned text, your reviews of different employees may sound too much alike, and may miss some of the strengths and weaknesses unique to each employee.

Advantages and Disadvantages of Trait Methods. Trait methods, especially graphic rating scales, are probably the most commonly used performance evaluation method used in organizations today. A quick glance at the examples in Fig. 6.1 explains why trait methods are popular—they can be used in almost any job, in virtually every organization. Graphic rating scales are intentionally general. The same graphic rating scale can be used to evaluate the performance of a janitor, a secretary, a computer programmer, or a top-level manager. For example, at Home Depot, *all* of the salaried associates, from the CEO on down, are rated on identical criteria such as "gets results," "drives change," and "displays character."[14] The fact that one single performance appraisal form can be used throughout the entire organization means that the organization can create a performance appraisal system that is flexible and inexpensive. Similarly, essay methods can be used in any job. Raters can create essays that focus on the same underlying dimensions regardless of the particular job being performed.

But the flexibility of trait methods is a double-edged sword. The flexibility of trait methods means that there is a lot of opportunity for rater error to enter into the process. Because raters are free to define for themselves what expectations they have for "meeting deadlines," one manager may evaluate employees very harshly for missing a deadline by 24 hours, while a manager in the next department may think that missing a deadline by 24 hours is standard operating procedure and meets expectations. It can be very frustrating to be on the receiving end of trait method performance evaluations. A graphic rating scale provides no direct information to an employee about what he or she needs to do to raise a "5" score on the "leadership" scale to a "6" or "7." This places a heavy burden on the manager's shoulders to fill in the gaps and provide the necessary developmental feedback during the performance evaluation interview or in an accompanying essay.

Behavioral Methods

In contrast to the trait methods (which focus on employees' personal characteristics), behavioral methods focus on the specific behaviors displayed by employees. Instead of using general terms like "dependability" or "leadership," behavioral methods ask raters to consider the extent to which employees perform certain behaviors. There are two main variations of behavioral methods—Behaviorally Anchored Rating Scales and Behavioral Observation Scales.

Behaviorally Anchored Rating Scales.   Behaviorally Anchored Rating Scales (BARS) are well-named, because these scales give the rater a behavioral anchor for each point on the scale. Figure 6.2 provides an example of a BARS for a customer service representative job. Rather than letting the rater make his or her own judgment about what constitutes a "5" on a graphic rating scale, the BARS defines a "5" for the rater: A customer service representative who deserves a rating of "5" is someone who uses positive phrases to describe a product when interacting with customers. Where do these behavioral anchors come from? In designing a BARS performance appraisal system, an organization will ask supervisors and other organizational experts to reach a shared understanding of what constitutes good, average, and poor performance on a particular job. In our example, the organization might have involved supervisors of customer service representatives in sharing examples of what they consider good or poor behaviors exhibited by the employees they supervise.

Behavioral Observation Scales.   There's a variation of BARS performance evaluation systems. In Fig. 6.2, you'll notice that each number in

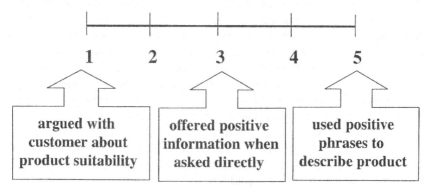

FIG. 6.2.   Behaviorally anchored rating scales.

the BARS is associated with a specific behavior. In a Behavioral Observation Scale (BOS), each number is associated with a behavioral frequency. For example, we could convert the BARS scale in Figure 6.2 to a BOS scale by asking the rater to assess *how often* the customer service representative uses positive phrases to the describe the product to customers. In this case, a 5 might be anchored with "every time he or she speaks with a customer," a 3 might be anchored with "about half of the time the rep speaks with a customer," and a 1 might be anchored with "never."

Advantages and Disadvantages of Behavioral Methods.   BARS and BOS evaluation systems have several advantages. These behavioral methods avoid many of the rater errors described earlier. Because the scales are developed by getting supervisors to reach a consensus on what constitutes poor, average, and good performance, BARS and BOS tend to reduce the errors that occur when each supervisor defines the scale for himself or herself (i.e., leniency, severity, and central tendency errors). In addition, because these scales are based on employee behaviors, employees receive built-in developmental feedback when they learn their scores on a BARS or BOS scale. An employee who wants to raise her score from a "3" to a "5" on a BOS knows that she needs to be using positive phrases to describe the product to customers all of the time, not just 50% of the time. That's good, right? But you might be surprised to learn that BARS and BOS performance evaluation systems are not commonly used in organizations. Many organizations are unwilling to invest the time and resources required to develop a unique BARS or BOS system for every job in the organization, even though these methods are superior (in a measurement sense) to trait methods.

Results-Oriented Methods

The behavioral methods we were just discussing focus on what the employee actually does—the behaviors the employee exhibits on the job. In contrast, results-oriented performance appraisal methods focus on what the employee achieves. These methods use external, objective measures as indicators of employee performance. The exact measures depend on the job, but they might include things like the amount of sales, the number of new clients, or the quality or quantity of production an employee achieved during the appraisal period. For example, Philip Morris' Kraft General Foods unit and other companies use computerized sales information from checkout counters as a quantitative indicator of marketing employee performance. The better a promotional campaign's results, the bigger the bonus awarded to its creators.[15]

The most common, comprehensive result-oriented performance evaluation methods use some version of Management-by-Objectives (MBO). In an MBO system, the supervisor and the subordinate sit down together and develop a series of performance objectives. At the same time, they agree on a way of measuring progress toward the objectives, and set goals for the upcoming performance evaluation period. Figure 6.3 shows an MBO system for an employee in the human resources function. The employee and his or her supervisor have identified three objectives to focus on during the upcoming evaluation period: reducing the time needed to fill open positions, increasing the use of web-based recruiting, and making advertising more cost-effective. But these objectives are too broadly defined and open-ended. The next step is to quantify them into measurable goals. So, as shown in Fig. 6.3, the goal of reducing time to fill open positions has been translated into a specific goal of getting the time to fill open positions down to 14 days. The employee begins the 2003 evaluation period with this as a specific goal, and his or her performance at the end of the period is evaluated against the goal.

Advantages and Disadvantages of Results-Oriented Methods. Organizations that use results-oriented methods like MBO frequently report that they are very effective, highly motivating performance evaluation systems. MBO systems communicate to employees exactly what is expected of them, and provide clear behavioral benchmarks for performance. Developmental feedback is inherent in the entire MBO process, because the employee's skills and abilities are taken into account at the front end when goals are initially set and along the way as progress toward the goals is measured. MBO systems can be very useful if you supervise employees with different performance and skill levels. For example, you wouldn't expect a new trainee to perform at the same level as a seasoned veteran. Giving the trainee a low evaluation on a graphic rating scale or a BARS scale may accurately reflect his or her performance—but it may be very discouraging and demotivating for the employee. In an MBO system, goals are highly personalized and reflect the employee's experience and training.

Objective	Method of Measurement	2003 Goal	2003 Result
Reduce time to fill open positions	Average time to fill open positions	14 days	21 days
Increase use of web-based recruiting	Percentage of new hires that make initial contact via Internet	50%	60%
Make advertising more cost effective	Advertising costs per hire	$10,000	$9,500

FIG. 6.3.   Management by objectives.

But there are always trade-offs. Because MBO systems design each employee's goals to be appropriate for his or her skill and ability level, it can be difficult to make performance comparisons across employees. Let's say you supervise two employees, Joe and Catherine. Joe has achieved 100% of his goals, and Catherine has achieved 50% of hers. You can't assume that Joe is the better performer, because Catherine's goals may have been much more difficult than Joe's. Catherine may have taken on a new, challenging assignment that was disrupted by outside factors. If you supervise only a handful of employees, you'll be aware of these factors and take them into consideration as you review the MBO results, but that adjustment gets more difficult as your supervisory responsibilities increase.

Notice, too, that there are other challenges associated with MBO systems. Managers find MBO systems to be extremely labor-intensive and time-consuming to do well. The performance appraisal is not constrained to a single meeting—instead, MBO systems demand regular, ongoing meetings between the subordinate and supervisor. For some jobs, you may find it difficult to identify specific, quantitative ways of measuring objectives. For example, you may have an employee whose responsibilities include improving morale within the department—how would you measure "morale," and how much improvement is appropriate? In addition, the goals that employees are working toward may not always be under their own control. Many goals can be thwarted by supplier problems, economic variations, inclement weather, and other external factors.

Comparative Methods

In the performance evaluation methods we've discussed to this point, it's possible for *all* employees to be rated "excellent." When a rater evaluates employees using trait, behavioral, or results-oriented systems, the rater compares the performance displayed by a particular employee against a performance scale (or to a performance goal), not against other employees. In many situations, that's appropriate. If you've done a careful job of hiring and training employees, you may be in the luxurious position of supervising a group of outstanding employees. Unfortunately, many organizational decisions require employee-to-employee comparisons. For example, your department has been allocated a limited pool of bonus money—how can you make sure that the bonuses are going only to the very best performers? Or, in contrast, you've been told to downsize your workforce by 10%—how can you identify the poorest performers? These decisions are not well-served by any of the methods we've discussed so far. Instead, comparative methods are needed. Examples of comparative methods include ranking systems and forced distributions.

Ranking Systems.   One simple comparative system involves directly ranking employees within a given workgroup or department. Raters are asked to identify the best employee, followed by the second-best employee, and so forth. For example, employees at Microsoft who do the same job in the same unit receive a "stack ranking" that tells them their position in an array ranging from most valuable to least valuable.[16] Sometimes variations are used, such as when raters identify the best employee and the worst employee, followed by the second-best employee and the second-worst employee, and so on.

Forced Distributions.   More commonly, raters are asked to group the employees they supervise into a forced distribution. You may be familiar with forced distributions from your schooldays, when a teacher would say that the top 10% of the class would get *A*s. Forced distributions in business organizations look a lot like the schoolday versions; raters are told to group their employees so that a certain percentage get *A*s, a certain percentage get *B*s, and a third percentage get *C*s. Employees who receive *C*s are unlikely to receive raises or bonuses, and employees who receive *C*s over multiple evaluation periods may eventually be asked to leave.

General Electric (GE) has used a forced distribution system for years. In the GE system, managers can categorize only 20% of their employees as outstanding and 70% as high performers; the remaining 10% must be rated as "in need of improvement." The bottom 10% are not likely to stay unless their performance improves. Jack Welch, former CEO of GE, argued that this system improves the organization's ability to build an "all-star team," because the process of differentiation raises the bar higher each year and increases the overall caliber of the organization.[17]

Advantages and Disadvantages of Comparative Methods.   Comparative performance evaluation methods are becoming more popular as organizations are asked to make difficult downsizing and promotion decisions. Would this tough love system work in your organization? Maybe. Low performers can be a drain on the organizational system—many organizations find that instituting a forced distribution performance evaluation system raises productivity by eliminating "deadwood." The problem occurs when managers are asked to find the lowest 10% year after year. Eventually, managers may feel that they are cutting into the real heart of their workforce. If managers supervise a particularly talented or productive unit, even the lowest 10% may still be effective employees. At GE, managers played every game in the book to avoid identifying the lowest 10%—even listing employees who had died![18] But that insistence on *every* manager identifying the lowest 10% is the strength of comparative systems—these systems virtually eliminate the leniency, severity, and central tendency errors that result when different managers define performance standards differently.

Although comparative systems can be useful for administrative purposes, they fall short in terms of providing developmental feedback to employees. Learning that your supervisor ranked you 20th out of 50 employees (in a ranking system) or receiving a *B* grade (in a forced distribution) provides little information about how to improve performance. Just as with graphic rating scales, the burden of supplementing comparative methods with developmental feedback falls to the supervisor. These comparative systems work best when they are linked to clear objective criteria that are known to employees. Otherwise, a supervisor's decisions about who is ranked first, or who gets an *A*, can be perceived as politically motivated or capricious.[19]

No two employees ever do the exact same job with absolutely identical responsibilities (even among employees in the same job classification), so comparative systems rely on the rater's evaluation of overall performance. These apple-to-orange comparisons can sometimes be perceived as overly subjective and raise complaints of bias—see Box 6.1 for recent examples of some very public controversies. Employees also perceive (often correctly) that these systems are setting the groundwork for future layoff decisions, leading them to be derisively described as "rank and yank" systems.[20] The advantages of having comparative information available for

---

BOX 6.1
Controversies Surrounding Comparative Performance Appraisal Methods

Ford Motor Company Detroit, MI	Graded employees as A, B, or C. Company rules required that 10% of employees be given a C. The system was discontinued after employee lawsuits claimed that the system favored younger and non-White employees.[21]
Goodyear Akron, OH	Used an A-B-C grading system in which about 10% were given As, 80% Bs, and 10% Cs. Workers receiving Cs weren't eligible for merit raises and were warned that further Cs could lead to demotions or firing. The company is altering the system but faces a lawsuit charging that the system discriminated against older workers.[22]
Conoco Houston, TX	Ranked employees 1 to 4. Lawsuit alleging bias against U.S. citizens in favor of British, Norwegian, and Canadian professionals was eventually settled out of court.[23]
Procter & Gamble Co. Cincinnati, OH	Requires that 20% of employees be ranked 1, 65% be ranked 2, and 15% ranked 3, with 3 indicating that performance issues must be addressed. A lawsuit charged that the system discriminated against older workers.[24]

administrative decisions needs to be balanced against the potential for backlash from organizational members.

Choosing Among the Different Methods

You've seen that every performance evaluation method has advantages and disadvantages. I've summarized these advantages and disadvantages in Table 6.2. So, how do you know what performance evaluation system is best for your organization? It depends on the primary purpose for which you are designing the evaluation system. To see what I mean, try this thought experiment. Imagine yourself occupying each of three organizational roles. First, imagine that you are the CEO, and you have a plan to downsize your workforce dramatically over the next few years. Which performance evaluation system would help you to identify the employees who should be let go? Second, place yourself in the shoes of a frontline supervisor. In this role, your primary concern is justifying employee raises and motivating future performance. Which performance evaluation system would help you to communicate to employees the reasons behind a small merit increase and give employees clear behavioral feedback about improving performance in the upcoming year? Finally, imagine that you are a newly

TABLE 6.2

Advantages and Disadvantages Associated with Different Performance Appraisal Methods

	Advantages	*Disadvantages*
Trait methods • Graphic rating scales • Essay method	Inexpensive; the same rating form can be used for all jobs in the organization	Prone to rater error; subjective
Behavioral methods • BARS • BOS	Reduce rater error; provide behavioral feedback to employees	Expensive; unique rating forms must be developed for every job in the organization
Results-oriented methods (MBO)	Tailored to individual employee's needs and abilities; excellent for providing developmental feedback	Not easily used for many administrative decisions, because employees are not evaluated on a common scale
Comparative methods • Ranking • Forced distributions	Good for administrative decisions	Eliminates some rater errors, but may be perceived as subjective; not very effective in providing developmental feedback

hired entry-level employee. At this career stage your primary concern is developing new skills and receiving detailed feedback. Which performance evaluation system would you prefer? My guess is that you selected different performance evaluation systems in each case. As a CEO making downsizing decisions, you need a comparative system. As the frontline supervisor, you want systems that include behavioral feedback—a BARS or BOS system would work well here. But as the entry-level employee your primary concerns are developmental, and best met by a results-oriented system like MBO. It's unreasonable to expect that the same performance evaluation could meet each person's needs equally well.

Manager's Checkpoint

Use the following questions to decide which performance evaluation system is right for your needs:

- Will the performance evaluation system primarily be used for administrative decisions? (If you are using the performance evaluation system to distribute a limited bonus pool or training dollars, you need a comparative system that will identify the most deserving employees. Similarly, if you are using the performance evaluation system to identify employees who are most expendable, you need a comparative system.)
- Is my primary concern employee development? (If your primary concern is developing employee potential, an MBO system can help you to identify each employee's strengths and areas in need of further development.)
- Do my employees perform similar kinds of work or do they each perform unique idiosyncratic jobs? (If you supervise employees who do similar work, you can develop a behavioral system (BARS or BOS) that can be used across employees. If the employees you supervise are engaged in very dissimilar work, you might want to use an MBO system to provide personalized feedback.)

PERFORMANCE APPRAISAL MEETINGS

Let's move on to the second stage of the performance appraisal process. You've followed your organization's performance appraisal system and made an evaluative judgment about each employee. Now you need to schedule a face-to-face meeting with each employee to share your evaluative rating. What are your goals for that session? At a minimum, you probably have two goals. First, you want to make sure that your employee understands the reasons for the rating and feels fairly evaluated. And second, you want to motivate the employee to strive for better performance in the future.

Managers often complain that these two goals inherent in performance evaluation interviews require them to occupy two roles simultaneously—roles that make contradictory demands.[25] To achieve the first goal, the manager needs to act as a judge. In this role, the manager is the boss and maintains control of the communication. The manager focuses on the employee's past performance and explains what it was about the employee's past performance that contributed to the current performance rating. A good judge is factual, focusing on the objective performance evidence. But, in order to achieve the second goal, the manager needs to consciously switch gears and act as a coach. In this role, the manager is supposed to motivate the employee to keep improving performance. A good coach is encouraging and supportive, focusing on the emotional and behavioral obstacles to future performance. And a good coach actively involves the employee in identifying these obstacles and generating ways to overcome them. That's a tall order for one manager to achieve in one brief meeting!

Most managers find it impossible to meet both of these goals in the same performance meeting. In fact, research finds that performance evaluation interviews fall into three distinct types.[26] In the first type, called the *tell-and-sell* interview, the manager concentrates on the judge role. In a tell-and-sell interview, the manager tells the employee the reasons for his or her performance rating and tries to sell a prepackaged improvement plan. The second type is called the *tell-and-listen* interview. In this type, the manager starts out as a judge. But, partway through the interview, the manager turns the interview reins over to the employee, encouraging the employee to share his or her plans for improvement. The final type of performance evaluation, called a *problem-solving* interview, keeps the manager in the coach role throughout the entire interview. Although a tell-and-sell or a tell-and-listen interview can be very effective in communicating the performance rating to the employee, only the problem-solving interview actively engages the employee in his or her own evaluation and motivates future behavioral change.

Increasingly, organizations like American Express, Avon Products, and Harley-Davidson are encouraging managers to separate the performance evaluation meeting into two distinct components.[27] The manager presents the performance rating in the first meeting, along with any implications the rating might have for the employee's pay raises or promotion potential. Then, in a second meeting, both the manager and the employee turn their sights to the future and focus on employee development. If you do choose to separate these two performance appraisal meetings, you should make sure that they are distinctly separate in time to prevent the two roles from spilling over—3 months might be about right.[28] However, some recent research suggests that separating the roles into two meetings may be unnecessary and may even interfere with the effectiveness of the performance appraisal.[29] Pay is an important outcome, and avoiding the pay implications of developmental feedback may feel forced and artificial. Whether you choose to conduct two meetings or one, the important thing to remember is that your goals of communicating performance feedback and conducting a developmental discussion require you to occupy two distinct roles (judge and coach), and these two roles require very different behaviors. So let's take them one at a time.

The Manager's Role as Judge

In your role as judge, you need to clearly communicate the reasons for the performance rating. Let's eavesdrop on a performance appraisal interview for a moment.

> Lisa, thanks for coming in today to talk about your performance. Let's see, your performance has really improved since your last review. But there are a few problems. You've been absent six times this month. Your reports are consistently overdue. Oh, and you aren't bringing in enough new accounts. But I'm confident you can overcome these problems and I'm glad to have you on our team!

How do you think Lisa is going to react to that opening? This example illustrates several common mistakes that managers make when they convey performance feedback. First, notice that the positive feedback provided by the manager is very broad and general. The manager says that Lisa's performance "has really improved" but doesn't provide any details, leaving Lisa wondering "*In what way? Along which dimensions?*" If Lisa is unaware of what she is doing right, she may decide that those behaviors are not very important and eventually stop doing them.

Second, notice that Lisa's manager presented her with a laundry list of problems. Because most performance reviews are scheduled annually, managers sometimes feel like they have just this one chance to put all their concerns on the table. Unfortunately, Lisa's interpretation of the meeting may be "*I'm not doing anything right—why even bother trying?*" It's better to focus on the one or two areas most in need of improvement. If more than a couple of performance issues need to be addressed, schedule a series of meetings to handle them instead of trying to tackle them all in one meeting.[30]

Finally, notice the sequence of the feedback Lisa received. Lisa's manager gave her a "feedback sandwich" by putting a thick slab of negative feedback between two slices of positive feedback. Managers use feedback sandwiches to make themselves more comfortable in a stressful situation. By opening the meeting with some "good news," managers can postpone talking about the more difficult negative material. And once they get the "bad news" out of the way, managers try to close the meeting on an upbeat note. But feedback sandwiches don't work for the recipient.[31] Over time, feedback sandwiches train Lisa to be suspicious of any positive openings—because they signal the negatives to come. And the closing positive feedback falls on deaf ears—because Lisa is still reeling from the negative blows.

So, what could Lisa's manager have said instead? There's no single best way to present feedback—every manager has to find his or her own personal style. But here's one example of how Lisa's manager could have presented the same message:

> *Lisa, thanks for coming in today to talk about your performance. I want to use our time here to give you a clear picture of your performance—both your strengths and weaknesses. In your last review, we focused specifically on your teamwork skills and your client relationships. Both of these areas have shown a great deal of improvement. For example, your coworkers told me how you stayed late last week to finish up that big presentation. And several clients have said that they enjoy working with you because you respond so quickly to their requests. Those are real strengths. Now, there is one specific area of improvement I'd like us to address in the next couple of months—your reports are consistently overdue. In the last six months, only one of your reports was turned in on time, and the others were turned in anywhere from two days to weeks late. Late reports are a problem because they delay our ability to get feedback to the client. What's the problem with the reports? How can we address it?*

Notice that in this alternative script, the manager gave Lisa several specific examples of good performance. The manager also focused on one specific area that needed improvement and explained why this area needed attention. And, finally, the manager turned the floor over to Lisa—making a smooth transition from judge to coach.

The Manager's Role as Coach

In the manager's role as coach, the goal is to encourage the employee's active participation and commitment to change. This may be easy to accomplish or difficult. Some employees may be eager to participate, and have engaged in a good deal of self-reflection prior to the performance appraisal meeting. However, other employees may be surprised to learn that they have performance areas in need of improvement, and be reluctant to participate in a forthright discussion of their strengths and weaknesses. How can a manager encourage employee participation? Some organizations have established procedures that clearly communicate to employees their interest in having employees participate actively in the evaluation process. For example, Parkview Medical Center in Pueblo, Colorado, requires that managers and their employees complete an APOP (that stands for "Annual Piece of Paper").[32] Unlike traditional performance appraisal forms, APOP works bottom-up—asking employees to tell their managers what obstacles they are facing on the job, and describing what the manager could be doing to make their jobs easier. But, even if your organization doesn't have these kinds of mechanisms in place, there are several things you can do informally to encourage participation.

Ask the employee to do a self-appraisal before the performance evaluation meeting. It may be difficult for an employee to participate "cold." But doing a thorough self-assessment before the performance evaluation meeting can get the employee reflecting on his or her performance ahead of time.[33] Some managers worry that their subordinates will be too lenient in evaluating their own performance, and the resulting discrepancy between their self-ratings and the managerial ratings will have a negative impact on the quality of the discussion. But an interesting finding has been observed with respect to self-appraisals: When employees evaluate themselves privately, their ratings often are unrealistically favorable.[34] However, these leniency effects are diminished when subordinates know that their self-appraisals will be revealed to their supervisors[35] or verified against other data sources.[36] When a subordinate knows that he or she will have to justify and explain the self-appraisal in the performance appraisal meeting, the self-appraisal is more likely to be critical and thorough.

Ask the employee to identify the problem. As the manager, you may have several areas that you think need improvement. But having the employee identify a particular area on which to focus encourages the employee to "own" the problem. Employees are more likely to be committed to solving a problem that they personally have identified as a problem. For example, Lisa's late reports may be causing her conflict with her coworkers—leading her to recognize this as a problem area and motivate change.

Ask the employee to generate a solution. Once the area in need of improvement has been identified, the problem needs to be diagnosed and a plan of attack developed. The problem with Lisa's late reports could be addressed in several ways: Lisa could set longer, more realistic deadlines. Lisa could establish milestones that keep her work on target over the deadline period. Lisa could make better use of departmental resources and coworkers to delegate parts of the work that would free her to move the project along. Lisa's manager may have a preference for one of these strategies, but ultimately the best strategy is the one that Lisa is able to use.

Manager's Checkpoint

The following questions might help you to prepare to discuss performance issues with your employees:

- Am I ready to perform as a judge? Have I compiled behavioral examples that illustrate both the positive and negative aspects of the employee's performance?
- Have I identified the one or two areas of the employee's performance that I want to focus our discussion on?
- Have I prepared the employee to be an active participant in the discussion (e.g., by asking the employee to conduct a self-appraisal before the meeting)?

WHAT'S NEXT?

Performance evaluation is often used as a basis for allocating organizational rewards, including merit increases and performance bonuses. In the next chapter, I'll describe the most common incentive systems used in organizations and discuss their advantages and disadvantages.

FOR FURTHER READING

Fandray, D. (2001, May). The new thinking in performance appraisals. *Workforce*, 36–40.

Grote, D. (2002, November/December). Forced ranking: Behind the scenes. *Across the Board*, 40–45.

Joinson, C. (2001, March). Making sure employees measure up. *HRMagazine*, 36–41.

Waldman, D. A., Atwater, L. E., & Antonioni, D. (1998). Has 360 degree feedback gone amok? *Academy of Management Executive, 12*(2), 86–94.

MANAGER'S KNOT 6.1

"My organization uses graphic rating scales in its performance appraisal process. When an employee asks me to explain why he or she got a '4'on the 'dependability' scale instead of a '5,' I never know what to say."

This is a common problem for managers, because most organizations continue to use graphic rating scales. You can convert graphic rating scales to BARS or BOS-type scales for your own use. Ask yourself what kinds of behaviors would be good, clear indicators of excellent performance—and which behaviors would be good, clear indicators of poor performance. Developing these behavioral anchors before you evaluate any individual employees can ensure that you are consistent in applying the scale across employees. Having behavioral anchors ready can also be helpful later in the performance evaluation interview. When an employee asks why he or she received a "4" on the scale (and what it would take to get a "5"), you'll have some specific behavioral feedback ready at your fingertips.

MANAGER'S KNOT 6.2

"I know I'm supposed to provide specific positive feedback. But in my job as manager, my attention is focused on the problems. How can I make sure that I remember specific examples of positive performance?"

One strategy is to keep a performance journal for each employee—scheduling specific times (perhaps weekly) to reflect on each employee's performance and to jot down specific examples of positive behavior. Some managers ask employees to keep a "hero file." Each employee can keep track of their own contributions and the things they did right—and pass the information on to you on a regular basis.

MANAGER'S KNOT 6.3

"Our organization uses a standard performance appraisal form for all jobs. One question asks about the employee's ability 'to work with others.' One of the employees I supervise works at night as a security guard—he doesn't interact with anyone except potential intruders. Should I just leave that question blank?"

This problem results from organizations having a "one size fits all" performance appraisal form. The critical issue here is to find out the consequences of skipping an item. If the performance appraisal is primarily used to provide developmental feedback on each performance dimension, skipping one dimension is not a problem. But if personnel decisions (e.g., pay raises, promotion potential) are based on an overall score (computed by adding or averaging across items), the employee may be penalized if you fail to answer a question. If that's the case, be careful to correct the employee's total score so that it accurately reflects only those items that pertain to the employee's job requirements.

MANAGER'S KNOT 6.4

"My organization evaluates employees on a series of 7-point scales. This past year I gave ratings to my employees that I thought accurately reflected their performance. I gave a couple of employees an average score of 7.0, but I rated most of my employees as performing at a 5 or 6 level. Now the HR department says there's only enough bonus money to reward employees who got a perfect 7.0! How can I keep my employees from being screwed in the reward process?"

This problem occurs when the same performance appraisal system is used for both administrative and developmental purposes. In the long run, your organization's performance appraisal system will lose its feedback potential, as more and more managers inflate their employees' ratings to justify bonuses. One possibility is to use your organization's performance appraisal system as an administrative tool—remembering that the appropriate anchor on "7" is "deserves bonus." Then you can create a "shadow" performance appraisal form that further differentiates those "7's" into subgroups—based on specific behavioral criteria that you can use to structure the feedback you provide in the performance appraisal interview.

ENDNOTES

1. Lancaster, H. (1998, December 1). Performance reviews: Some bosses try a fresh approach. *Wall Street Journal*, p. B1.
2. Budman, M., & Berkeley, R. (1994, February). The rating game. *Across the Board*, 34–38.
3. McEvoy, G. M. (1987). Using subordinate appraisals of managers to predict performance and promotions: One agency's experience. *Journal of Police Science and Administration, 15*(2), 118–124; Hegarty, H. H. (1974). Using subordinates' ratings to elicit behavioral changes in supervisors. *Journal of Applied Psychology, 59*, 764–766.
4. Longnecker, C. O., & Gioia, D. A. (1988). Neglected at the top: Executives talk about executives' appraisal. *Sloan Management Review, 29*(2), 41–47.
5. Antonioni, D. (1996, Autumn). Designing an effective 360 degree appraisal feedback process. *Organizational Dynamics*, 24–38.
6. Edwards, M. R., & Ewen, A. J. (1996, March). Automating 360 degree feedback. *HRFocus*, 3; Toquam-Hatten, J., & DeMay, C. C. (2001, April). *360-degree assessment at the Boeing Company: DRC's dual-process (web/paper) approach.* Paper presented at annual meetings of the Society for Industrial-Organizational Psychology, San Diego; Huet-Cox, G. D., Nielsen, T. M., & Sundstom, E. (1999, May). Get the most from 36-degree feedback: Put it on the Internet. *HRMagazine*, 92–103.
7. DeNisi, A. S., & Kluger, A. N. (2000). Feedback effectiveness: Can 360-degree appraisals be improved? *Academy of Management Executive, 14*(1), 129–139; Peiperl, M. A. (2001, January). Getting 360 degree feedback right. *Harvard Business Review*, 142–147.
8. Church, A. H. (1995, August). First-rate multirater feedback. *Training and Development*, 42–43.
9. Antonioni, D. (1996, Autumn). Designing an effective 360 degree appraisal feedback process. *Organizational Dynamics*, 24–38.
10. Lee, C. (1996, May). Performance appraisal: Can we manage away the curse? *Training*, 44–59.
11. Segal, J. A. (2000, October). 86 your appraisal process? *HRMagazine*, 199–206.
12. Painter, C. N. (1999, June). Ten steps for improved appraisals. *Supervision*, 11–13.
13. Sprout, A. L. (1995, April 17). Surprise! Software to help you manage. *Fortune*, 197–204; Fryer, B. (1994, August). An easier way to write performance reviews. *PC World*, 109; Baig, E. C. (1994, August 22). So you hate rating your workers? *Business Week*, 14; Lewis, P. H. (1993, December 19). The executive computer. *New York Times*, sect. 3, p. 10.
14. Sellers, P. (2002, June 24). Something to prove. *Fortune*, 86–98.
15. Gibson, R. (1991, August 1). How product check out helps determine pay. *Wall Street Journal*, p. B1.
16. Abelson, R. (2001, March 20). Rating workers with grades earns companies an "A" in litigation. *International Herald Tribune*, p. 18.
17. Welch, J. (2001, September 17). Jack and the people factory. *Fortune*, 75–86.
18. Welch, J. (2001, September 17). Jack and the people factory. *Fortune*, 75–86.
19. Fisher, A. (2002, September 2). Do I fire the bottom 10% just because Jack did? *Fortune*, 210.
20. Hymowitz, C. (2001, May 15). Ranking systems gain popularity but have many staffers riled. *Wall Street Journal*, p. B1.

21. Ford nears settlement of some bias suits. (2001, November 17). *Arizona Republic*, p. D2; Shirouzu, N., & White, J. B. (2001, July 9). Ford assesses job ratings amid bias suit. *Wall Street Journal*, pp. A3, A14; Shirouzu, N. (2001, July 11). Ford stops using letter rankings to rate workers. *Wall Street Journal*, pp. B1, B4; Eldridge, E. (2001, December 19). Ford settles two lawsuits by white male workers. *USA Today*, p. 3B.

22. Dawson, B. (2002, September 16). Failing grade: Goodyear faces lawsuit over evaluation system it will alter. *Rubber and Plastics News*, 1.

23. Jones, D. (2001, May 30). More firms cut workers ranked at bottom to make way for talent. *USA Today*, p. 1B; Horn, C. (2001). *The dangers of forced ranking*. *Personneltoday.com*. Retrieved July 31, 2001, from http://www.zigonperf.com/resources/pmnews/danger_forced_ranking.html

24. Nelson, E. (2001, August 2). P&G executive, in federal suit, claims firm discriminates against older workers. *Wall Street Journal*, p. B5.

25. Meyer, H. H., Kay, E., & French, J. R. P. (1965, March). Split roles in performance appraisal. *Harvard Business Review, 43*, 123–129.

26. Maier, N. R. F. (1958). *The appraisal interview: Objectives, methods and skills*. New York: Wiley.

27. Lopez, J. A. (1993, May 10). Companies split reviews on performance and pay. *Wall Street Journal*, p. B1.

28. Lee, C. (1996, May). Performance appraisal: Can we manage away the curse? *Training*, 44–59.

29. Prince, J. B., & Lawler, E. E. (1986). Does salary discussion hurt the developmental performance appraisal? *Organizational Behavior and Human Decision Processes, 37*, 357–375.

30. Peters, P. (2000, May). 7 tips for delivering performance feedback. *Supervision*, 12–14.

31. Tyler, K. (1997, April). Careful criticism brings better performance. *HRMagazine*, 57–62.

32. Imperato, G. (1998, September). How to give good feedback. *Fast Company*, pp. 144–156; Lee, C. (1996, May). Performance appraisal: Can we manage away the curse? *Training*, 44–59.

33. Lawrie, J. W. (1989, January). Your performance: Appraise it yourself! *Personnel*, 2–33; Grote, D. (1998, October). Painless performance appraisals focus on results, behaviors. *HRMagazine*, 52–58; Farh, J., Werbel, J. D., & Bedeian, A. G. (1988). An empirical investigation of self-appraisal-based performance evaluation. *Personnel Psychology, 41*, 141–156.

34. Meyer, H. H. (1980). Self-appraisal of job performance. *Personnel Psychology, 33*, 291–295.

35. Parker, J. W., Taylor, E. D., Barrett, R. S., & Martens, L. (1959). Rating scale content: Relationship between supervisor- and self-ratings. *Personnel Psychology, 12*, 49–63; Bassett, G. A., & Meyer, H. H. (1968). Performance appraisal based on self-review. *Personnel Psychology, 21*, 421–430.

36. Farh, J., Werbel, J. D., & Bedeian, A. G. (1988). An empirical investigation of self-appraisal-based performance evaluation. *Personnel Psychology, 41*, 141–156; Fox, S., Caspy, T., & Reisler, A. (1994). Variables affecting leniency, halo and validity of self-appraisal. *Journal of Occupational and Organizational Psychology, 67*, 45–56.

7

Designing Reward Systems

W hat determines your salary? This isn't a naïve question—organizations, especially large ones, frequently develop complex, Byzantine compensation systems that make it difficult for an individual to understand which parts of his or her paycheck are associated directly with the job, and which parts covary with his or her performance.

In general, organizational compensation systems should accomplish three goals. Compensation packages should be designed to *attract* quality job applicants, *motivate* employees to be high performers, and encourage long-term employee *retention*. To accomplish these goals, we have several elements of the compensation package we can work with: base salary, short-term incentive systems (incentives that operate over 1 year or less), long-term incentive systems (multiyear incentives), and benefits. These compensation elements are differentially effective in achieving organizational goals (see Table 7.1). High base salaries and generous benefit packages do a good job of attracting and retaining employees. But because salary and benefits are generally based on organizational membership and not job performance, they play a limited role in employee motivation. Short-term incentive systems (e.g., performance bonuses) do a good job of attracting and motivating quality performers, but generally have only moderate ability to retain employees over the long run—the exact opposite of long-term incentive systems (e.g., stock ownership).

TABLE 7.1

Compensation System Goals

	Attracting	Motivating	Retaining
Base salary	High	Low	High
Short-term incentives	High	High	Moderate
Long-term incentives	Moderate	Moderate	High
Benefits	High	Low	High

As a result, it's difficult (if not downright impossible) to design a compensation package that is effective at achieving all three goals. That's why organizations are always tinkering with their compensation packages—they are trying to design a compensation package that addresses their current problems. In this chapter, we'll consider each of these compensation components: salary, short-term incentives, long-term incentives, and benefits.

BASE SALARY

How do organizations decide on an appropriate base salary for a job? Imagine that you are hiring your first employee—a secretary. You are drafting a want ad to place in the local newspaper, and you want to provide a salary range. How do you decide the appropriate salary? A very simple, straightforward answer to this question is "I'd look at the market." Exactly—you'd try to find out what other companies in your area are paying secretaries these days, and to set your base salary somewhere in that vicinity. Many Internet Web sites (e.g., salary.com, jobstar.org, wageweb.com) provide detailed salary information organized by job type and by geographic location. These sites can provide useful comparison data as you establish base salaries for jobs in your organization.

The market rate is a useful basis for salary setting when organizations are filling jobs from the outside—jobs that have counterparts in other organizations. These jobs include secretaries, entry-level accountants, nurses, and many others. These are *firm-general* jobs, meaning that the skills and responsibilities associated with these jobs are common across organizations. However, we can't rely on the market for salary setting in all situations.

First, there may be jobs within your organization that do not have an adequate market comparison. For example, suppose you operate a law firm in a tiny Midwest community and you are hiring a lawyer specializing in patent law. The closest patent lawyer is 300 miles away in a large metropolitan area. Is that person's salary a good comparison for your job? Probably not—the two jobs are associated with different geographic areas, with different costs of living, and so on.

Second, the longer people stay in your organization, the more likely they are to acquire *firm-specific* skills. That secretary you hired is learning about your organization's clients, filing system, and accounting practices. This information is valuable inside your organization, but it may not be transferable to another company. So, the longer people remain with the organization, the more difficult it becomes to use the external market to estimate the value of their contributions. Organizations try to overcome this problem by establishing *job ladders*—sequences of jobs. They hire people into the lowest rungs on these ladders. As employees acquire more firm-specific skills, they progress up the job ladder and move into progressively higher salary ranges. For example, your organization may have a series of accountancy positions (Accountant Level I, Accountant Level II, Accountant Level III) or secretarial positions (Secretary Level I, Secretary Level II, Secretary Level III). Once employers are past the bottom rungs of these ladders, an external market comparison is usually inadequate for determining base salaries. Instead, organizations rely on internal comparisons as a basis for salary decisions.

Job Evaluation

Let me start with an analogy. Suppose I gave you an apple and an orange, and asked you to decide which one was "better." Your first reaction might be, "No way! You're asking me to compare apples with oranges—it can't be done!" But upon reflection, you'd think about what, in general, makes a fruit good. You'd generate some general dimensions (e.g., vitamin content, fiber content, ripeness) that could be applied to both apples and oranges. You'd evaluate the apple and the orange on these dimensions, and the fruit with the highest score would be judged the "better" of the two.

Job evaluation follows a similar process. In *job evaluation*, we are trying to determine the relative value of dissimilar jobs—jobs in which people have different skills and perform different tasks. The only way to compare these diverse jobs is by generating a set of dimensions common to all these jobs. In job evaluation, these dimensions are called *compensable factors*. The factors organizations use to evaluate jobs include the educational requirements, experience requirements, level of responsibility, physical demands, and working conditions.

Once an organization has identified a set of compensable factors, it has to decide how much weight to place on each of those factors. Let's assume that we're working with a 1,000-point system. An organization that equally valued education, experience, responsibility, physical demands, and the quality of the working conditions might allocate 200 points to *each* of those dimensions. But consider a university. A university has very few jobs that have really onerous working conditions—no matter which job they perform, employees are unlikely to be exposed to hazardous chemicals or fumes on the job. As a result, there's unlikely to be much variation in the working conditions people experience in their university jobs, and the little variation that does exist doesn't necessarily reflect the relative value of the jobs to the university. On the other hand, variations in educational require-ments directly reflect the extent to which a job contributes to the univer-sity's mission—education. So a university might shift the weight allocation to place somewhat greater weight on educational requirements and less weight on working conditions. In general, the relative weight placed on dif-ferent dimensions should reflect what's most important to the organiza-tion's overall goals.

Table 7.2 shows a sample compensable weighting system for an organi-zation. This organization places a heavy weight on educational and experi-ence requirements, with less weight on responsibility, and even less weight on physical demands and working conditions. The next step is to develop a scoring system for each factor. For example, this organization has allo-cated 300 points to the education factor, which means that an individual job can "earn" up to 300 points for its educational requirements. Table 7.3 shows a scoring system associated with the education factor. In our sample organization, jobs that only require an eighth-grade education are worth 20 points, jobs that require a high school diploma are worth 90 points, and so on. Jobs that require a postgraduate degree are worth the highest number of points—the 300 maximum.

Once the organization has developed a scoring key for each compen-sable factor, every job in the organization can be evaluated. For each job, we would use the scoring keys to award the job points associated with its educational demands, its experience requirements, and the

TABLE 7.2
Job Evaluation: Compensable Factors

Education	300
Experience	300
Responsibility	200
Physical demands	100
Working conditions	100
Total points	1,000

TABLE 7.3
Job Evaluation: Education Factor

Eighth-grade education	20 points
High school diploma	90 points
Two-year college degree	160 points
Four-year college degree	230 points
Postgraduate degree	300 points

other factors. At the end of this process, we will have a "score" for every job in the organization. Jobs with a similar value are grouped together, and these groups are ranked according to their relative value to the organization.

At this point, we still haven't assigned salaries to the jobs, though. All we know is that jobs at the top of this rank ordering (i.e., jobs that are more valuable to the organization) should be paid more than jobs at the bottom of this rank ordering (i.e., jobs that are less valuable). To assign wages to this rank ordering, the organization looks for jobs within this range that are firm-general. For these jobs, a market rate is available. These jobs serve as benchmarks in the overall compensation system; wages of the benchmark jobs are tied to the market, and wages of the jobs near the benchmark in the salary array are tied to the benchmark.

The wage-setting system I just described is standard in many organizations, and it explains some common problems with salaries in organizations. For example, employees frequently complain about *wage compression*. Wage compression occurs when salaries paid to people in jobs of a lower rank start bumping up against the salary range of jobs of higher rank. This happens because wages in entry-level positions are based on the external market—and so wages in these jobs tend to rise faster than wages of the firm-specific jobs. When faced with the choice of raising the base pay for entry-level jobs or failing to fill those positions, organizations generally increase the base salary at the point of hire and worry about internal inequities later.[1] Once the salaries associated with the entry-level positions jump up, they tend to stay up, narrowing the gap between entry-level positions and the higher positions on the job ladder. (But never say never—some organizations are taking a close look at these entry-level jobs and cutting back salaries. For example, several law firms recently rolled back starting salaries for their first-year associates, suggesting that salaries had gotten ahead of the market.)[2]

Another issue here is *pay dispersion*—the salary spread across organizational levels. For lower level firm-general jobs, the external market is efficient—organizations tend to offer similar wages to employees performing these jobs. But for higher level firm-specific jobs, there are weaker market constraints. Some organizations have a very wide pay dispersion, so that upper level executives make a great deal more than the lower level employees. But other organizations try to maintain a more egalitarian pay spread. Whole Foods, for example, has a policy precluding any employee from earning more than 10 times the company's average annual salary.[3] For many years, Ben and Jerry's Homemade held the CEO's pay to 7 times the salary of the lowest paid employee.[4] In contrast, the highest paid employees at a Fortune 500 company might make more than 100 times the salary of a low-level employee.

Manager's Checkpoint

Use the following questions to help you understand how base salaries should be set for jobs in your organization:

- Are most of the jobs in my organization firm-general or firm-specific? (The more firm-general jobs, the more you can rely on the market as an indicator of the appropriate wage. However, firm-specific jobs require more of an internal assessment. Firm-specific jobs are more likely to be found in high-technology or knowledge-intensive industries, but even companies operating in traditional industries such as construction or manufacturing are likely to have some firm-specific jobs.)
- How widely do I recruit to fill firm-general jobs in my organization? Do we attract job applicants only from the local metropolitan area, or do we draw applicants from other areas of the state, or the nation? (Answering these questions will help you identify the relevant market comparison.)
- What are some common factors—such as education, responsibility, or physical demands—that reflect the relative value of jobs in my organization? (Identifying these compensable factors will help you to position firm-specific jobs in relation to firm-general jobs that are tied to the market rate.)

Merit Pay

I mentioned earlier that base salary tends not to be motivating—but what about merit pay? *Merit pay* is an increase in base pay that a person receives based on individual performance. Merit pay is usually expressed as a percentage. For example, your manager might tell you that based on your annual performance appraisal, you will be receiving a 5% increase in your base pay. This is traditionally how organizations have tried to build in a motivating component into the base pay. Unfortunately, most of the evidence suggests that merit pay doesn't motivate good performance. There are several reasons for this:

First, merit pay increases tend to be small. Last year, the Conference Board reported that the median pay raise was about 4%. However, research suggests that there is a critical threshold at about 6% to 7% of base pay. When merit raises are below this threshold, people's reactions range from neutral to negative.[5] Further, only a tiny portion of the pay raise shows up in the employee's weekly paycheck. For someone who makes $40,000 a year, a 4% pay raise means that he or she will be making $30 more each week.

Second, merit pay generally does not make strong distinctions between average and outstanding performers. An average performer gets a 4% raise, and an outstanding performer gets 4.5%. The average $40,000/year employee's weekly paycheck will increase by $30, while the outstanding employee's paycheck increases by $35. Is the potential of earning an extra $5 per week going to inspire the average employee to boost performance to an outstanding level?

Third, merit pay is weakly linked to past performance. Many employees have a hard time distinguishing the merit part of their raise from other increases (e.g., cost of living) that are folded into their overall paycheck. And by the time the pay raise appears in their paycheck, they may have forgotten the performance activities on which it's based. Think about it: A manager evaluates the employee's performance in December, taking into account the employee's activities over the entire calendar year. After the performance evaluation, it might take weeks or months for payroll to issue the raise. There's an initial lag between employee performance and the performance appraisal, and then there's another lag between the appraisal and the actual reward.

Finally, merit pay is even more weakly linked to future performance. Because the merit pay is now part of the employee's base salary, the employee continues to get the higher amount even if performance declines during the following year.

INCENTIVES

Short-Term Incentives

As a result of the shortcomings associated with merit pay, many organizations have been deemphasizing merit pay and implementing bonuses and other incentives that have to be re-earned every year. Today, more than 75% of salaried and hourly workers have a compensation system that includes some form of variable pay, up from fewer than half that number 10 years ago.[6] Take a look at Box 7.1 to see some examples of how organizations are rewarding individual employees for their performance—without affecting the base salary. The examples in Box 7.1 show the wide variety of incentive systems organizations are using to motivate employees and direct their activities.

Bonuses.   One popular form of short-term incentives is an individual-level bonus. A *bonus* is an incentive payment beyond base pay. Most bonuses are planned and based on achieving a set goal. For example, an or-

---

BOX 7.1
Rewarding Individual Performance

⚬ At First Third Bank, sales employees earn as much as 125% over their base salary as a result of incentive pay. But even nonsales employees, including security guards, pick up extra cash: $15–$25 for persuading someone to apply for a credit card, $25 for a mortgage application, and $25 for a consumer loan that is approved.[7]

⚬ Forget that old "employee of the month" plaque. At Lanier Worldwide Inc., an Atlanta-based office-machine supplier, regional executives who surpass targets have the opportunity to meet one-on-one with top corporate brass— in Europe.[8]

⚬ Technology Professionals Corporation (TPC) believes that the best employee rewards are customized to the employee's needs and inter-ests—like a getaway golf weekend for the employee who loves the game. TPC's vice president of corporate culture has even arranged for a staff member to fly on an F17 bomber.[9]

⚬ Nortel Networks and other organizations are increasingly offering on-line incentive systems. These systems reward employee performance with award points that can be "cashed in" for tangible awards. The awards offered in the online catalog include housewares, toys, elec-tronics, and exotic travel opportunities, including African safaris and barge trips through Burgundy.[10]

⚬ At Wolverton Inn, a small upscale hotel near Stockton, NJ, every housekeeper is given a 40-item checklist for each room. Rooms are checked at random, and employees who meet 95% of the criteria over a 6-month period are given an extra week's salary.[11]

---

ganization might promise employees a bonus if they bring in several new accounts, or if they produce 10% more widgets than they produced last year. From the organization's perspective, bonus systems are less risky than traditional merit pay systems. The organization only pays the bonus if employees achieve the goal. And having achieved the goal, there are no guarantees for the next pay period. New goals will be set, and the bonus has to be re-earned. In addition, many organizations guarantee a bonus based on individual performance, but the actual size of the bonus depends on the organization's profitability. In 2001, for example, companies paid the low-est bonuses since 1995 due to a downturn in the economy.[12]

Organizations that rely heavily on bonuses have been very enthusiastic about the results. Here's a quote from James M. Colbin, Vice President of Human Resources at Nucor, a steel company: "If you give a bonus to somebody of 15%, of course they like it …. But if you give them a bonus of 100%, you get their attention big-time, and when they start seeing 150%

bonus or 160% bonus, they are focused on that bonus. And when they know it's not going to be changed, like ... putting a ceiling on it ... they catch fire."[13] Wow! A 150% bonus sound pretty good in comparison to that 4% merit increase, doesn't it? But before you get too excited, you should know that Nucor sets its base pay at about half of the competition's. A highly motivated, high-achieving employee at Nucor can make a great deal more than he or she would make working at another steel company, but a less productive employee makes considerably less. By emphasizing a bonus system, Nucor has shifted the risk onto the employee's shoulders.

If you're going to rely heavily on incentive-based systems, you really need a performance appraisal system that is up to snuff. Technology is now available that monitors employee performance in some jobs on an ongoing basis—and ties that performance to the incentive system. A variety of organizations, including Hewlett-Packard, General Electric, Sun Microsystems, and British Airways are using software that directly tracks the behavior of customer service representatives. The software can track employee work time, sales, and customer complaints—and base incentives on the digital records. These systems can also be used to provide direct, ongoing feedback to the employees. At Hewlett-Packard, for example, an incentive calculator allows sales and marketing executives to see just how much they'll earn if they double their performance goals.[14]

Bonuses can be a terrific way to focus employees' attention on a goal. But keep in mind that goal-directed behavior has its own costs. Employees may be so focused on goal achievement that they neglect other parts of their work—or they may become fixed on reaching the goal at all costs. Green Giant, for example, offered employees a bonus for removing insect parts from the vegetables they were packaging—only to learn that some enterprising employees were bringing insects from their backyards and "finding" them in the veggies at work to get their bonuses.[15]

Spot Bonuses.   A *spot bonus* is an unplanned bonus that is unrelated to any established performance measure. That's what differentiates spot bonuses from traditional bonuses. Spot bonuses are unexpected; they are used when a manager "catches an employee doing something right." The employee is publicly recognized for doing a good job. One example of a company who uses spot bonuses effectively is Valassis, a firm that makes advertising inserts. When employees do something right, managers have the opportunity to give that employee $5, $50, or even $500, depending on the value of the employee's contribution. Managers stand the honored employee on a chair, ring bells, and celebrate the achievement publicly. And at Lands' End, spot bonuses can be even more generous—as high as $2,000 for a job well done.[16]

Some companies empower nonmanagerial employees to award spot bonuses. Take the case of Scitor, a systems engineering consulting firm in California. Scitor employees have the opportunity to award one another "be my guest" bonuses that usually range between $100 and $300.[17] These bonuses are used to recognize employees who work late to help a coworker, met impossible deadlines, or pitch in to finish up a project. Employees can use the gift certificates to have a nice dinner with the family or treat themselves to a spa day, or they can save up the gift certificates to buy a VCR or a refrigerator.

Team Bonuses.   Bonuses and spot bonuses can be used to reward groups as well as individuals. Group level bonuses are used to encourage collaboration. By offering an incentive based on team performance, the organization creates a situation in which team members are mutually dependent on one another. One of the most interesting examples of team incentives was applied by Phillips-Van Heusen. Chairman Larry Phillips promised the executives who headed up 11 different divisions that each of them would receive a $1 million bonus—*if* the company's earnings per share grew at a 35% compound annual rate over a 4-year period.[18] In response, each division found new ways to make its core business more profitable—for example, by establishing a new mix of suppliers. But, more importantly, the anticipated bonus encouraged the divisions to cooperate in new ways. For example, salespeople in the shirt and sweater divisions teamed up to make sales calls and boosted sales for both divisions by selling color-coordinated combinations. The company's earnings jumped, and Phillips-Van Heusen enjoyed record profits. Unfortunately, the executives didn't quite make the goal—and didn't get the $1 million bonus. But you don't have to feel sorry for the 11 executives because the bonus plan had built-in milestones associated with lower bonuses, and the executives still managed to earn about $100,000 each in bonus awards.[19]

When applying group bonuses, one thing to consider is the size of the group. In the Phillips-Van Heusen example, the group size was only 11—and every executive had a personal relationship with each of his or her teammates. As group size increases, it may be harder for team members to appreciate the impact that their personal effort has on the group's performance. Don't get me wrong—you can still use team bonuses to motivate large groups. You just need to be extra careful to ensure that team members understand the role they play in influencing the team's outcome. In 1995, Continental Airlines initiated a "team" bonus system that involved the entire nonmanagerial workforce—that's 35,000 employees! Under this system, each employee would get a $65 cash bonus in any month that Continental ranked among the top five airlines for on-time departures.[20] By focusing on on-time departures, Continental selected a performance criterion that could be accurately and objectively measured. But, more importantly, it was a measure that staff and crew knew was directly affected by their actions. It worked—Continental went from being one of the worst-performing airlines to one of the best. To maximize the motivational impact of the program, Continental made an important administrative decision about how the bonuses would be distributed. Each month, supervisors handed a separate bonus check directly to each worker—in the full amount of $65. The bonus was taxable income, but Continental listed the taxes associated with the bonus on the employee's regular paycheck.

Gainsharing Plans. *Gainsharing plans* are incentive programs in which financial gains resulting from improved productivity are shared with employees. The idea behind gainsharing plans is this: Employees have a great deal of know-how about their jobs. They are the best source of information about how their jobs can be performed more effectively, at a lower cost. Gainsharing plans encourage employees to make suggestions to improve productivity. When employee suggestions are implemented and save the company money, a portion of those cost savings is returned to the employees. Gainsharing plans are especially popular in manufacturing settings. The plans focus on things that are under employees' direct control—the amount of waste in the manufacturing process, the length of time machines are shut down, the number of rejected parts. For example, Westinghouse measures improvements in quality, cost, and productivity compared to established baselines and then gives each plant employee an equal lump sum payment.[21] One critical component of gainsharing plans is that they involve a good deal of employee participation. There's usually a committee established to review suggestions from employees about how to improve the system and save money. Premium Standard Brands used a gainsharing plan to improve productivity at their meat processing plant. A single employee-initiated change resulted in savings of $13,000/month, and total monthly savings can run as high as $300,000. When a portion of those savings were passed back to employees, annual payouts for 2000 exceeded $1000/employee.[22]

Long-Term Incentives

The incentives we've discussed so far were all short-term incentive systems in which employees receive payouts at frequent intervals (monthly or annually). However, incentives can also have a more long-term focus. In these incentive programs, employees may not receive a payout for several years.

Profit-Sharing Plans. In a *profit-sharing plan*, employees are promised a payment beyond base pay that is based on company profits. That might sound a little like gainsharing, but profit-sharing plans differ from gainsharing plans in several ways. First, in a profit-sharing plan, the target employees are shooting for organizational profit—not productivity. There are a lot of things that get in the way between an employee's effort and organizational profit—advertising effectiveness, the general state of the economy, and so on. Second, there usually is less focus on participation in a profit-sharing plan than in a gainsharing plan. Third, while gainsharing plans generally have frequent (monthly) payoffs, profit-sharing plans are usually treated as deferred income. For all these reasons, profit-sharing plans (and other long-term incentive systems) tend to have less of a motivating function than gainsharing. Like other long-term incentive systems, the focus of profit sharing plans is long-term retention.[23]

Stock Options.   *Stock options* are opportunities for employees to purchase a specified number of shares of company stock in the future at a guaranteed price. For example, suppose that your company's stock is currently selling at $10/share. Your company gives you options to purchase stock at $10/share. Five years later, the stock is selling at $30/share—but you exercise your options, purchase the stock at $10/share, resell it for $30/share, and pocket the profit. (Of course, there's no guarantee that the stock price will go up. An alternative scenario is that 5 years later the stock is selling at $5/share and your options are "underwater.") Employees can only exercise stock options during a specified period. At the front end, employees cannot exercise options until the options have "vested" (generally a period of 3–5 years).[24] Unvested options generally must be surrendered to the company if the employee leaves before the vesting period is over. And once the options have vested, employees have a limited period (usually 10 years) in which to exercise them.[25] It's that time delay that makes stock options a long-term incentive. During the 3 to 5 years that the employee is waiting to exercise his or her options, the company hopes that the options will inspire a feeling of ownership, motivating employees to improve their productivity and in turn improve the company's stock price.

Stock options used to be exclusively reserved for rewarding managers and executives. The idea was that these individuals were primarily involved in the decision-making policy-setting activities that would have the most impact on the stock price. Now stock options are viewed as a retention tool, and may be made available to employees at every level of the organizational hierarchy. More than 40% of companies now offer stock options to employees, up from just 8% in 1991.[26] Texas Instruments, for example, gave managers the authority to grant stock options to their best performers, and turnover among engineers went from 15% to 7% in a 6-year period.[27]

Employee Stock Ownership Plans.   In an employee stock ownership plan, the company contributes shares of its stock to a trust. The trust holds the stock in individual employee accounts—employees earn stock based on pay and seniority. The trust then distributes stock to the employees (or their families) when employees leave the company—as a result of retirement, death, or termination. In other words, the company is contributing stock into employee accounts. Employees can then sell back the stock when they leave the company—and use that money for their retirement.

More than 11,000 ESOPs exist in the United States, and there are a number of rousing success stories.[28] However, recent evidence suggests that company enthusiasm for ESOPs has stalled.[29] In some cases, individual employee-owners retired sooner than expected, draining their accounts and putting companies in perilous financial position.[30] More commonly, however, morale suffers when company profits decline and employee financial security is threatened.[31] One problem is that ESOPs lock employee retirement money into the stock of the company for which they work. So, as the company's stock declines, so do employee nest eggs.[32]

BENEFITS

Private and not-for-profit employers in the United States are required by federal and state law to offer three benefits to their employees: employer contributions to Social Security, unemployment insurance, and workers' compensation insurance. In addition, since the passage of the Family and Medical Leave Act of 1993, many employers are required to provide up to 12 weeks' unpaid leave to permit employees to care for newly born or newly adopted children, to care for sick family members, or to take care of their own health problems. These legally mandated benefits comprise only a small portion of the benefits offered by organizations, with the remainder (almost 80%) of employee benefits provided voluntarily by employers. Discretionary benefits may include health care benefits, vacation time, sick leave, life insurance, tuition reimbursement programs, and pension plans.

However, the terms "voluntary" and "discretionary" may be misleading. Some voluntary benefits are so commonly offered that they have become institutionalized, and employees have come to expect these benefits to be a standard part of compensation packages. For example, a large national survey conducted by the Society for Human Resource Management found that 99% of respondents' organizations offered some kind of health insurance coverage.[33] A large employer that did not offer health insurance coverage would be regarded as highly unusual in today's marketplace, and would be likely to have difficulty attracting and retaining a quality workforce.

Large organizations are also likely to voluntarily offer employees family-friendly benefits such as paid family leaves, child care referrals or on-site child care, and lactation programs for nursing mothers.[34] An emerging benefit in this family-friendly category is elder care. As the U.S. population ages, employees increasingly find themselves caring for elderly parents, often at the same time that they are raising young children. More than 14 million U.S. workers are the primary caregivers for older family members,[35] and more than 10% of caregivers say that they have given up promotions or jobs to meet family obligations.[36] Therefore, accommodating the needs of these caregivers can boost employee retention. Elder care benefits come in a variety of shapes and sizes. The most basic programs provide a toll-free telephone number or Web site that employees can access for information about federal and state elder care programs, and more comprehensive elder care programs provide flexible hours for caregivers and direct access to experienced professional geriatric specialists.[37] Ford Motor Company now offers employees free house calls by geriatric-care managers to assess the health of elderly relatives and develop plans for their care, and Fannie Mae employs a full-time elder care case manager to help employees coordinate care for family members.[38]

Over time, it has become increasingly expensive for companies to provide competitive benefits to employees. In the mid-1990s, benefit expenses represented less than 20% of employers' payroll costs. By 2000, benefits represented about 40% of payroll, and by 2007 the projected benefit bite is expected to be greater than 50%.[39] To manage these costs, employers are increasingly asking employees to share the costs of certain benefits (e.g., through copayments or higher deductibles), especially medical coverage.[40]

Unfortunately, organizations often do not get much bang for their benefit buck. A majority of employees are unable to accurately name the benefits they receive from their employers and "more than 75 percent of employees perceive the value of their benefits at less than half the actual cost to their employers."[41] To get a good return on the investment companies are making in employment benefits, it's important to provide benefits that employees value and appreciate. Decisions about which benefits to offer are too often based on benchmarking what the competition is doing, rather than on the actual needs and preferences of the workforce.[42] In one survey, less than one third of high-tech companies reported that they had conducted a benefits-related attitude survey in the last 2 years.[43] Without accurate information about employee needs, organizations can offer expensive benefits for years and have no positive impact on employee attraction or retention.

In addition, employees need to have a clear understanding of the benefits that are offered, and their role in the total compensation package. Organizations are making increased efforts to communicate the value of benefits in straightforward, easy to understand language.[44] For example, some companies distribute a benefit summary to each employee that lists each benefit the employee receives, and the dollar amount that each benefit costs the company. These summary statements might cost a company $10 to $20 per employee, but they show employees exactly what they are getting in the benefit package.[45]

To accommodate the individual needs of employees, there is a trend toward offering *flexible benefits* plans, also known as *cafeteria plans*.[46] These plans enable individual employees to choose the benefits that are best suited to their particular needs, and prevent benefits from being wasted on employees who have no need for them. Typically, employees are offered a basic or core benefits package of life and health insurance, sick leave, and vacation. Requiring a core set of benefits ensures that employees have a minimum level of coverage to protect against unforeseen financial hardships. Employees are then given a specified number of credits they may use to "buy" additional benefits they would like.[47]

These personalized benefit systems are more complex to administer, so many organizations are also instituting computer-based interactive employee benefit systems.[48] Interactive employee benefit systems are now mainstream at many employers, such as Booz, Allen and Hamilton, Silicon Graphics Inc., and LG&E Energy.[49] Organizations use the Web to facilitate annual benefit enrollments, personal data changes, 401(k) changes, and family status changes.[50] The Internet can give employees immediate access to benefit information, allowing both greater control and ownership of the benefits offered them.

DESIGNING COMPENSATION SYSTEMS

Now put it all together. How can a compensation system be assembled from the various components discussed? Try this thought experiment. Imagine that you are a brilliant entrepreneur starting up a software company. What kind of compensation system would you need at the following junctures?

- Your first problem is hiring people with the right mix of technical skills. You need to persuade them to join your organization instead of the competition. What parts of the compensation package will you emphasize?
- Now you've got your technical staff on board—but you find that they leave your company a year later. How can the compensation package be changed to boost retention?
- You're coming close to the software package launch date. You need employees to give it one big push to get the product out the

door. How can you motivate employees to give their all to meet the deadline?

Each of these stages calls for attention to a different part of the compensation package. At the early stage, where your primary concern is employee attraction, you'll want to devote a large proportion of the compensation budget to base salary and benefits. When retention is a problem, you want to emphasize long-term incentives like stock options or profit-sharing plans. Short-term motivational needs call for short-term individual or team bonuses.

Manager's Checkpoint

Use the following questions to consider what kind of compensation package is right for your needs:

- Is my primary concern employee attraction, motivation, or retention? (All three goals are important, but with limited resources you need to make some tough choices about whether your compensation package should maximize attraction and retention by devoting more dollars to salary and benefits, or maximize motivation by developing a system that permits more variable pay based on performance.)

- Do I have objective, accurate ways to measure employee performance? (Remember that measurement and rewards go hand-in-hand. If you can't accurately measure performance at the individual level, you won't be able to establish clear individual-level goals or to reward employees for their achievements.)

- Can performance be objectively measured at the team or organizational level? Do employees have a clear sense of how their individual behavior influences these team- or organization-level outcomes? (If your answer to both questions is yes, you might want to consider incentive systems that rely on measures of team or organizational performance, such as gainsharing or profit-sharing.)

- Is my workforce fairly homogeneous, or is it diverse in terms of employee age and other demographics? (If your workforce is homogeneous, you may be able to identify a limited set of benefits that would appeal to employees. The more diversity in your workforce, the more you might want to consider flexible benefit plans instead.)

PAY SECRECY

Here's one more thing to consider: Should your compensation system be "open" or "closed"? Managers often argue that employees are more satisfied when pay is kept secret, that is, when employees know their own pay and no one else's.[51] In 1996, more than 50% of all employers banned workplace discussions of pay.[52] However, that percentage has been steadily dropping, partly in response to recent cases in which employees effectively argued that workplace bans on salary discussions violate their rights to discuss the terms and conditions of their employment.[53] In general, it's a very risky move to try and control the content of employee conversations by prohibiting salary discussions. But employers still have a great deal of latitude about how much information they choose to provide about organizational salary systems. There's been a general trend toward making salary systems more transparent—providing more information about wage-setting procedures and organizational wage distributions. "Open" pay systems can promote a sense of fairness in the organization, while keeping salaries secret can lead employees to think that the organization has something to hide.[54]

"Open" organizations usually disclose only salary ranges. For example, American Express now makes available to employees the market pay ranges for most positions.[55] But at Whole Foods Inc. a notebook listing every employee's annual compensation, including gross wages and bonuses, is available for all workers to peruse.[56] This can scare some people off—in fact, some employees have decided not to join Whole Foods because they were so horrified by the open system. But Whole Foods management says that publishing salary information is one way to show team members that the company is serious about eliminating inequity in the pay system. When inequities are brought to light, they can be swiftly corrected. As organizations move toward more open pay systems, it's important that employees understand how wages are set; for example, organizations need to inform workers how factors such as education, prior experience, and years of service influence their pay.[57] Right now, most employees *don't* understand the wage-setting process. In one survey, less than one half of the respondents said they understood how increases in their base pay were determined. But the same survey found that in companies that had made an effort to explain pay processes, employees were more satisfied with their compensation, more likely to stay with the company, and more committed to the organization.[58]

WHAT'S NEXT?

In the last two chapters, we've focused on how to measure and reward employee performance. Now it's time to think about employee development over the life span. In the next chapter, we'll consider employee career development.

FOR FURTHER READING

Duncan, W. J. (2001, Summer). Stock ownership and work motivation. *Organizational Dynamics*, 1–11.

Frase-Blunt, M. (2001, August). What goes up may come down. *HRMagazine*, 85–90.

Hutchins, J. (2002, March). How to make the right voluntary benefit choices. *Workforce*, 42–48.

Wiscombe, J. (2001, August). Can pay for performance really work? *Workforce*, 28–34.

MANAGER'S KNOT 7.1

"One of my best employees told me that he is considering another opportunity that offers a substantial increase over his current salary. He's already at the top of his pay grade. What can I do?"

This is the basic problem underlying job-based salary systems. At some point, employees "top out" and the only way to offer higher salaries without changing the underlying system is to promote employees into higher paying jobs. Are there open positions at higher levels in your employee's job ladder? If no promotion opportunities exist, or if the employee is ideally suited to his current position, look carefully at the nonsalary elements of the compensation package. Can you increase the value of the employee's overall compensation package by offering short-term bonuses or long-term stock options? In the long run, however, it might be wise to review the market data associated with the employee's pay grade. It may be that your problem isn't limited to this employee. If jobs in your organization are undervalued relative to benchmark jobs (and the external market), it may be time to adjust the salary ranges associated with the job ladder.

MANAGER'S KNOT 7.2

"My company uses an individual incentive system in which nonmanagerial employees can earn substantial bonuses for meeting production goals or sales goals. When I checked the payroll records recently, I realized that several of my employees will be making more this year than I do."

Many managers who supervise production or sales employees make similar observations. An incentive system that rewards employees for reaching specific goals can result in compensation exceeding that earned by the employees who supervise them. That's actually good news. By not imposing artificial caps on the bonus amounts employees can earn, your organization has demonstrated that it is trustworthy, and will live up to the promises it makes. There's another benefit to this system: Because the organization makes it possible for employees to substantially supplement their income, employees are less likely to be concerned about promotions into higher paying jobs (including yours). But if you are concerned about possible inequities in the incentive system, you might want to make a proposal to take the bonus system organization-wide and apply it to managerial personnel as well. What kinds of measurable outcomes do you affect in your job? These outcomes might form the basis of goals that can be tied to short- or long-term incentives for you and other managerial employees.

MANAGER'S KNOT 7.3

"My organization frequently needs marketing and production to collaborate on new products, but members of these two divisions don't get along. We tried department-level performance bonuses, but that just seemed to increase the feuding and backbiting. How can I reduce the bickering and encourage cross-functional collaboration?"

Offering department-level bonuses may have increased the sense of competition between marketing and production employees. Instead, try offering bonuses to employees based on collaborative goals. Start by identifying some clear, measurable goals that are affected by the activities of both departments, then reward members of both departments when the goals are met (e.g., when a product is developed on time and under budget).

MANAGER'S KNOT 7.4

"I was stunned when several members of my department left recently to work for a competitor. The other company offered higher salaries—but I know our benefits contribute to a better compensation package overall. How can I keep more people from leaving?"

There are two issues to consider here. First, do your employees know the value of their benefits? You might need to educate your employees about their benefit choices, and the value of the various benefits you offer. This can be done through seminars or through informational booklets. Second, make sure that the benefits you're offering are a good fit to your workforce. When was the last time you conducted a benefit survey? It may be that the needs of your workforce have changed and your company's benefit package has not.

ENDNOTES

1. Wanderer, M. (2000, Fourth Quarter). Dot-comp: A "traditional" pay plan with a cutting edge. *World at Work Journal*, 15–24.
2. Dunham, K. J. (2002, January 22). Cutting back. *Wall Street Journal*, p. B6.
3. Markels, A. (1998, April 9). Blank check. *Wall Street Journal*, p. R11.
4. Johnson, B. (1997, December 15). Frozen assets behind heart-warming hype. *The Daily Telegraph*, p. 32.
5. Kerr, S. (1996, July 22). Risky business: The new pay game. *Business Week*, pp. 93–96; Gupta, N., Jenkins, G. D., Jr., & Mitra, A. (1995). The case of the invisible merit raise: How people see their pay raises. *Compensation and Benefits Review, 27*(3), 71–76.
6. Conlin, M., & Berner, R. (2002, February 18). A little less in the envelope this week. *Business Week*, 64–66.
7. Sweeney, P. (2000, June 14). Counting the till, then trolling for new accounts. *New York Times*, p. C11.
8. Work week. (1996, April 2). *Wall Street Journal*, p. A1.
9. Buchanan, L. (2001, October 1). Managing one-to-one. *Inc.*, 82–90.
10. Gilster, P. A. (2001, January). Online incentives sizzle—and you shine. *Workforce*, 44–47.
11. Poe, A. C. (2003, February). Keeping hotel workers. *HRMagazine*, 91–93.
12. Frase-Blunt, M. (2001, August). What goes up may come down. *HRMagazine*, 85–90; The outlook. (2001, November 5). *Wall Street Journal*, p. A1; Conlin, M., & Berner, R. (2002, February 18). A little less in the envelope this week. *Business Week*, 64–66.
13. Marks, S. J. (2001, June). Incentives that really reward and motivate. *Workforce*, 108–114.
14. Conlin, M. (2002, February 25). The software says you're just average. *Business Week*, 126.
15. Bloom, M. (1999). The art and context of the deal: A balanced view of executive incentives. *Compensation and Benefits Review, 31*(1), 25–31.
16. Del Franco, M. (2002, November). Don't drop those incentives yet. *Catalog Age*, 29.
17. Daniels, C. (1999, November 22). "Thank you" is nice, but this is better. *Fortune*, 370.
18. Knowlton, C. (1990, April 9). 11 men's million-dollar motivator. *Fortune*, 65–68.
19. Winter, I. (1997, June 2). Personal communication.
20. Knez, M., & Simester, D. (2002, February). Making across-the-board incentives work. *Harvard Business Review*, 16–17.
21. Novak, C. J. (1997, April). Proceed with caution when paying teams. *HRMagazine*, 73–76.
22. Balu, R. (2000, December). Bonuses aren't just for the bosses. *Fast Company*, 74–76.
23. Duncan, W. J. (2001, Summer). Stock ownership and work motivation. *Organizational Dynamics*, 1–11.
24. Boyle, M. (2001, January 22). Keep your (stock) options open. *Fortune*, 155–158; Armour, S. (1999, July 23). Watching the stock clock. *USA Today*, p. B1.
25. O'Hara, T. (2001, July 16). Options with an uncertain value. *Washington Post*, p. E12.
26. Conlin, M., & Berner, R. (2002, February 18). A little less in the envelope this week. *Business Week*, 64–66.
27. Harrington, A. (1999, October 11). Saying "we love you" with stock options. *Fortune*, 316.

28. Larson, J. (1999, March 3). Small valley firms earn big results with ESOPs. *Arizona Republic*, pp. E1–E2.
29. Arndt, M., & Bernstein, A. (2000, March 20). From milestone to millstone? *Business Week*, 120–122.
30. Jones, T. (1995, September 18). Fast slide on flip side of success. *Chicago Tribune*, sect. 4, pp. 1–2.
31. Hirsch, J. S. (1995, May 2). Avis employees find stock ownership is mixed blessing. *Wall Street Journal*, pp. B1, B4.
32. Lardner, J. (1999, March 1). OK, here are your options. *U.S. News and World Report*, 44.
33. Benefits survey. (2002). *Society for Human Resource Management*.
34. Benefits survey. (2002). *Society for Human Resource Management*; Employers help workers achieve balance in life. (1998, November). *HRFocus*, S3.
35. Greene, K. (2001, March 29). Firms try again to help workers with elder care. *Wall Street Journal*, pp. B1, B6.
36. O'Toole, R. E., & Ferry, J. L. (2002). The growing importance of elder care benefits for an aging workforce. *Compensation and Benefits Management, 18*(1), 40–44.
37. Yandrick, R. M. (2001, November). Elder care grows up. *HRMagazine*, 72–77; O'Toole, R. E., & Ferry, J. L. (2002). The growing importance of elder care benefits for an aging workforce. *Compensation and Benefits Management, 18*(1), 40–44.
38. Greene, K. (2001, March 29). Firms try again to help workers with elder care. *Wall Street Journal*, pp. B1, B6.
39. Goodspeed, L. (2000). Providing employee perks without breaking the bank. *Boston Business Journal, 20*(44), p. 8.
40. Geary, L. H., & Powe, M. J. (2001, December). Corporate America's best benefits. *Money*, 140–147; Frase-Blunt, M. (2002, December). Time to redo your benefits? *HRMagazine*, 73–75.
41. U.S. Chamber of Commerce. (1997). *Employee benefits*. Washington, DC: U.S. Chamber of Commerce.
42. O'Connell, N. L. (2001). Rewarding employees with psychic income pays long-term dividends. *Benefits Quarterly, 17*(3), 7–21; Hutchins, J. (2002, March). How to make the right voluntary benefit choices. *Workforce*, 42–48.
43. O'Connell, N. L. (2001). Rewarding employees with psychic income pays long-term dividends. *Benefits Quarterly, 17*(3), 7–21.
44. Kerr, S. (1996, July 22). Risky business: The new pay game. *Fortune*, 94–96.
45. Frase-Blunt, M. (2002, December). Time to redo your benefits? *HRMagazine*, 73–75.
46. Katz-Stone, A. (2001). Cafeteria-plan options lead to a smorgasbord of issues. *Boston Business Journal, 21*(37), p. 37.
47. Hom, D. (1996). How Pitney Bowes broadens benefit choices with value-added services. *Compensation and Benefits Review, 28*(2), pp. 60–66.
48. Hutchins, J. (2002, March). How to make the right voluntary benefit choices. *Workforce*, 42–48.
49. Kuzmits, F. E. (1998). Communicating benefits: A double-click away. *Compensation and Benefits Review, 30*(5), pp. 60–64.
50. Gemus, J. V. (2001). Clicking into benefits. *Bests Review, 102*(7), pp. 128–129.
51. Lawler, E. E., III. (1981). *Pay and organization development*. Reading, MA: Addison-Wesley.
52. Dunham, K. (2001, May 1). Employers ease bans on workers asking "What do they pay you?" *Wall Street Journal*, p. B10.

53. Can a company prohibit employees from talking about their pay? (2001, July/August). *Cost Management Update*, 3–4; *NLRB v. Main Street Terrace Care Center*. (2000). 218 F.3d 531 (6th Cir.).

54. Pfeffer, J. (1998, May/June). Six dangerous myths about pay. *Harvard Business Review*, 108–119.

55. Dunham, K. (2001, May 1). Employers ease bans on workers asking "What do they pay you?" *Wall Street Journal*, p. B10

56. Markels, A. (1998, April 9). Blank check. *Wall Street Journal*, p. R11.

57. Dunham, K. (2001, May 1). Employers ease bans on workers asking "What do they pay you?" *Wall Street Journal*, p. B10.

58. Fox, A. (2002, July). Companies can benefit when they disclose pay processes to employees. *HRMagazine*, 25.

8

Helping Employees
Manage Their Careers

T he previous chapter covered the wide range of financial rewards that managers use to motivate and retain their employees. This chapter's focus is a little less tangible. Its focus is on employee career management—how organizations can help employees navigate through the various stages of their careers.

You might be surprised that a chapter on career management is included in this book. After all, the business press has recently been emphasizing do-it-yourself careers. Designing a successful career is increasingly seen as the responsibility of the individual employee, and not the organization. However, wise managers are attentive to the different needs demonstrated by employees at different career stages. Surveys frequently indicate that career development and opportunities for growth are among the most important features that employees consider when choosing to join, or remain with, an employer.[1] If you understand how employee needs are likely to change over the course of the career, you'll be able to design human resource systems that are responsive to those needs. So let's start with an overview model that describes the typical person's career development.

CAREER DEVELOPMENT STAGES

People progress through a predictable sequence of stages as they move through a career. At each stage, people tend to have a particular developmental need or concern that dominates their attention. Table 8.1 describes these career stages, and the primary developmental issue associated with each.[2] I've presented the developmental concerns as a series of questions that summarize the issues preoccupying people at each stage.

The earliest career stage is called *Growth*, and usually precedes a person's actual entry or involvement in the workforce. During this first stage, the challenge is developing a sense of self: What am I good at? What do I like to do? This generalized self-knowledge prepares people for getting involved in work activities. As people develop greater confidence in their ability to get things done and make decisions, they are also developing work habits and attitudes toward work.[3] Once a person has established a sense of self, he or she can adopt a longer term perspective and develop broader career goals. During the *Exploration* stage, people develop preferences about alternative career options and learn what kinds of training might be required for those careers.[4] Once a person has identified a fit between the self-concept developed in the Growth stage and the career options identified in the Exploration stage, he or she begins to make a conscious career choice. The individual completes the necessary training, secures a position in the chosen occupation, and moves into the *Establishment* stage of his or her career.[5]

During the Establishment stage, a person is primarily concerned with becoming more competent and becoming an expert in the chosen occupation. People in this stage are establishing their personal reputations, and therefore tend to be self-focused. In other words, they are more concerned about developing their own skills and talents than reaching out to teach others. As a person transitions into the next stage, *Maintenance*, he

TABLE 8.1

Career Development Stages[6]

The Stage	The Developmental Question	Traditional Ages
Growth	Who am I?	Before 14
Exploration	What do I want to do?	14–24
Establishment	How can I get better?	25–44
Maintenance	How can I share what I know?	45–65
Disengagement	How do I get out of this?	Post–65

or she may experience a *midcareer crisis*. "Crisis" is a misleading term—for me, it always evokes a mental picture of Edward Munch's "The Scream." But the midcareer crisis isn't necessarily a traumatic experience.[7] The term refers to a critical reassessment often associated with a turning point in career development. After doing something for a while, it's natural to take a little time to reflect on that choice and develop a plan for the future.[8] Some people will be re-energized by this assessment and invest additional energy and resources in their chosen career direction. Some people will choose to embark on a new career direction—and recycle through Exploration and Establishment by specifying a new career choice, finding a new position in that career, and advancing within it.[9] Still others will remain on their chosen career path but experience a leveling-off in terms of their emotional investment. One typical outcome of the midcareer reassessment is a greater attention to the development of other people. If the Establishment stage is characterized by a me-focus (a focus on developing one's own skills and talents), then the Maintenance stage is characterized by a shift to an other-focus (a focus on developing other people's skills and talents).

The final career stage is called *Disengagement*. The critical challenge during this career stage is transitioning out of the chosen career. During this stage, people are looking ahead and thinking about what they will do when they stop doing what they've been doing. This doesn't necessarily mean that they become less productive at work. It just means that they devote more attention to developing other interests—in travel, in gardening, in grandchildren, or maybe in another career entirely.

Career stages look nice and neat when they are displayed in an orderly sequence like that shown in Table 8.1. From personal experience, you and I both know that real-life careers can be a lot messier. Now, you've probably noticed that column of Traditional Ages in Table 8.1, and maybe it's even starting to make you a little edgy ("I'm 50 years old and I'm still trying to establish myself in my career!" "I'm only 23 and I'd like to disengage right now!"). Relax! First, those age estimates are only rough parameters, even under ideal circumstances. Second, those age estimates describe how people move through these stages in a "traditional" career. When I say "traditional," I mean the way people thought about careers in the 1950s, which is when the whole idea of a "career" came to be part of the common parlance. At that time, people entered the workforce anticipating a lifetime of employment with one employer[10] and it was common for a person to spend his or her entire worklife in a single department of one organization. Organizations offered these employees promotion-based career systems designed to meet the needs of employees moving through the Establishment and Maintenance stages. Let's see how a promotion-based career system works.

THE TRADITIONAL MODEL: PROMOTION-BASED CAREERS

Take a moment to picture the typical organization. If you were to draw that organization, what geometric shape would it have? Probably your mental picture had a rough pyramid shape—a relatively tall structure, with a lot of people clustered at the lower levels and a select few at the top. Now picture an entry-level employee starting a job at the base of this pyramid. How will this employee move through the organization as his or her career progresses?

In a promotion-based career, people move into higher and higher levels of the organization as they progress through the career stages. Organizations establish *job ladders* that provide a clear sequence of promotions, from the entry level to the highest management levels. As people acquire skills and experience in lower level jobs, they are promoted into positions offering more responsibility (and accompanied by greater organizational rewards). In a promotion-based career system, employee movement tends to be linear and vertical so that employees either move up, or they don't move at all.

The promotion-based career system was the dominant career model operating when the baby boomer generation (a label used to describe employees born between 1946 and 1964) embarked on their organizational careers. During the 1970s and 1980s, when baby boomers were entering the Establishment stage of their careers, U.S. organizations were expanding and adding many new positions. This was very convenient for the boomers, because a steady diet of promotions up the organizational ladder gave them plenty of opportunity to expand their skill sets and develop competence in their chosen fields. Eventually, of course, the promotions had to end. Given the pyramid shape of the typical organization, there were only a limited number of upper level positions available. However, for many baby boomers, the promotions slowed just as they were transitioning into the Maintenance stage of their careers. Remember that during the Maintenance stage, employees often choose to invest less energy and resources into their career. Employees in this career stage may be more interested in making a contribution in their current job rather than taking on the new responsibilities and challenges associated with a job at the next level.

In general, this traditional promotion-based system does a good job of meeting employee needs during the Establishment and Maintenance stages. But it's not perfect. A promotion-based career model can be associated with two distinct problems: the *Peter Principle* and *plateauing*.

The Peter Principle

Laurence J. Peter observed the following principle: People in organizations are promoted to their level of incompetence.[11] The Peter Principle is a common problem in promotion-based careers. Promotions are based on a person's past performance, but performance in one job may not predict performance in the next. Take Susan, a talented marketing employee. Susan performed so well as an entry-level employee that she was promoted into her boss's job when the position became vacant. She did very well in that job, too. So when a position at the next level opened up, she was promoted again. Unfortunately, Susan is a poor fit to this job. Her performance is weak, and she's been told she's unlikely to be promoted again. Susan has been promoted to her level of incompetence—a sad situation for Susan and the organization. The Peter Principle is especially likely to occur during periods when organizations are experiencing rapid growth. In an effort to fill positions quickly, people may be promoted before they have had a chance to grow into their previous positions.

Plateauing

Plateauing is the polar opposite of the Peter Principle. In the Peter Principle, people are promoted into positions for which they are poorly suited. In plateauing, people are unable to be promoted into positions for which they would be well suited.[12] That was Mark's experience. He performed very well as an entry-level accountant. However, all of the positions at the next level were already filled. None of the people occupying those positions are anywhere near retirement, and so Mark faces the prospect of spending a long stretch working in a job he no longer finds interesting or challenging. If employees are not able to meet their needs for growth and development on the job, they are likely to become frustrated and demotivated. Eventually, they may leave the organization.

THE DEMISE OF THE TRADITIONAL CAREER

The promotion-based career system is no longer the dominant career model operating in today's organizations. Organizations can no longer promise employees the rapid promotion rates that the baby boomers enjoyed during the Establishment stage. Plateauing has become a serious problem for organizations, and it's being driven by several factors. First, most organizations are not in a major growth period right now. Second, organizations have made considerable efforts to downsize and reduce organizational levels, which results in fewer managerial positions for people to get promoted into.[13] Finally, organizations are increasingly adopting flexible organizational structures that involve more self-directed teams and a general move away from organizational hierarchies.[14] As a result of these changes, organizations need to legitimize career paths that offer alternatives to the traditional promotion-or-bust model. If yesterday's career was best described as "hierarchical," then today's career is increasingly de-scribed as "boundaryless"[15] and "protean."[16]

New careers call for new career management. In the traditional frame-work, organizations were usually the ones driving the employee's career. Organizations brought new employees in, trained and developed them, and nurtured the careers of those who were most promising.[17] Today, em-ployees are expected to play a more active role. Unfortunately, many orga-nizations have interpreted this change as meaning that they have no responsibility for employee career development—they've shifted the *entire* responsibility onto the employees' shoulders. That's like throwing employ-ees into the deep end of the pool and expecting them to be Olympic class swimmers. It's not surprising that many employees feel uncertain about what organizations really expect from them and are becoming increasingly cynical about what they can expect in return.[18]

However, some organizations are making a serious effort to engage em-ployees in an active collaborative effort to manage their careers (see Box 8.1 for examples). These organizations recognize that people need to adjust their expectations about continuous upward mobility—and recognize their own responsibility to educate employees about career options. With the right kinds of effort, these initiatives can be successful, because employees themselves are becoming more open to alternatives to the traditional pro-motion-based model as a way of balancing work and nonwork needs.[19]

CAREER DEVELOPMENT STAGES AND THE NEW CAREER

Take another look at the career development stages in Table 8.1. If people no longer have traditional careers, do the career development stages still apply? In a word, yes. In today's work environment, people's careers have become increasingly a succession of "mini-stages."[20] As people move across organizations, product areas, technologies, and functions they still move through the Establishment–Maintenance–Disengagement se-quence. But, they may move through this sequence multiple times during their work lives and at an accelerated rate. A person who makes a dramatic career shift, for example, may need to return to an earlier stage of career development that he or she had already progressed past in the original ca-reer choice. In fields characterized by rapid change (e.g., high technology or computer fields), the cycles may be particularly short; people may quickly establish themselves as an expert in a new technology, and just as quickly tire of the experience and be ready to move on. The career develop-ment stages are still operating, but they are becoming more and more dis-connected from chronological age.

One of the things that distinguishes the career management programs described in Box 8.1 from traditional career management is their focus on the *entire* career cycle. Notice that several of these programs are designed to help the employees disengage from one career and initiate another— even across employers! That's revolutionary in the traditional world of career management, where organizations were only concerned about an employee's career as long as that career was being played out inside the organization's four walls. However, in the new career model, employees make major career shifts within the same company, or exit and reenter the company at different career stages (remember our discussion of "boomerangs" in chap. 3?).

BOX 8.1

Career Management as a Partnership
Between Employer and Employee

✖ NYNEX Corp., the regional Bell holding company for New York and New England, offers financial managers a career management module that encourages financial managers to take an active role in their career development. Managers begin with a self-assessment of their personal values and skills. Managers then confer with their immediate superiors to determine how their self-ratings of skills compare with the superior's assessment. After the discussion, a development program for the employee is agreed upon—the program often includes major career changes, and not necessarily within NYNEX.[21]

✖ Raychem Corp in Menlo Park, CA, established an in-house "career maintenance" center where employees mull advancement strategies, update resumes, and receive interview pointers—for jobs inside *and* outside the company.[22]

✖ Several major corporations—including AT&T, DuPont, and Johnson & Johnson—have formed the Talent Alliance, a sweeping collaboration on career management and job matching that is making ambitious pledges to employees in member corporations. It's a nonprofit alliance that promises a comprehensive career management program—from testing to training to gaining access to a broad job pool.[23]

✖ New hires at Sun Microsystems receive in their orientation packets information about Sun's Career Resilience program. The program began in 1991 as an outplacement service but now offers a full range of assessment and counseling services to help people in the internal labor market—and for those who want out, an introduction to the independent Career Action Center down the road in Palo Alto.[24]

✖ Chase Manhattan Bank's Career Vision program offers employees confidential self-assessment tests; training in skills like project management, teamwork, and finance; and career advisers who help them plan training, get project assignments, or even change departments.[25]

As the supervising manager, you play a key role in your employees' career development. Alignment Strategies Inc. interviewed former employees and found that the key reason they gave for leaving jobs was the lack of a quality relationship with their supervisor. But because they didn't want to burn any bridges or leave negative impressions, most exiting employees cited better salaries or better opportunities elsewhere as reasons for leaving.[26] Your employees will value the opportunity to discuss their careers, but you'll need to take the initiative. You need to schedule regular career development discussions with the employees you supervise. Encourage them to discuss their career goals. Be honest about the requirements needed to achieve those goals and develop plans to meet them.

Let's pick up your role at the point where you are most likely to enter an employee's career—the exploration stage.

Managing Employees in the Exploration Stage

Employees who are in this early career stage are not fully committed to any one career path. Employees in this career stage value the opportunity to experiment, so they may be particularly interested in an organization's ability to provide training opportunities and expose them to different jobs. Organizations that aren't willing to provide that kind of flexibility to employees during the Exploration stage may find themselves operating as a revolving door. In 2001, fully 76% of surveyed MBAs reported that they planned to stay with their first employer for less than 5 years.[27]

How do organizations provide opportunities to experiment? They provide mechanisms that allow employees to "try on" a job before making a commitment. For example, new employees at SAS Institute, a software developer in Carey, North Carolina, start off with 8 weeks of boot camp, where they learn about the company, the technology, and general business skills (e.g., time management). Employees then spend several more weeks rotating among various work teams until they identify those that best suit their needs and interests.[28] Another method of providing opportunities to experiment without commitment is through internship programs (discussed briefly in chap. 3, when we talked about different recruiting strategies). In the past, internship programs were dominated by college students, but today's interns include plenty of older people. These older interns might be veterans of an earlier career, making a fresh start in a second or third career. Whereas only 5% of internships were open to folks past their college years in 1995, according to career information company vault.com, that number has now climbed to 20%.[29]

Managing Employees in the Establishment Stage

Remember that employees transition from Exploration to Establishment once they identify their chosen career. Here's where you, the supervising manager, make two important contributions to the employee's career. First, you have a major impact when you give the employee his or her initial assignments. Research suggests that employees who are given challenging assignments at the start are more successful 5 to 7 years down the road.[30] Early career challenges give the employee a feeling of psychological success—and initiate a cycle in which the newcomer seeks out even greater challenges and achieves more success.[31]

Second, you can help your employees expand their skill set. Employees in the Establishment stage are looking for ways to develop expertise and competence; they want the opportunity to hone their skills. Are there ways that you can meet this need without promotions? Sure—lots of them, but you may need to think creatively.

Lateral and Downward Moves.   The traditional model of career development assumed that skills are nurtured within a particular functional area (e.g., accounting or marketing). However, an alternative approach is to enhance employee skill development through cross-functional assignments. Mobil Oil, for example, has a global leadership program that rotates employees through different functional areas as a way of preparing employees for future leadership positions.[32] Cross-functional opportunities are also offered in the banking industry. For example, a bank might move a commercial loan officer to the trust department or to consumer banking. The employee is still using financial skills but dealing with different clients.

Employees can develop new skills by being transferred to different locations or departments. Wal-Mart, for example, transfers employees to new stores (to learn startup skills), larger stores (that offer greater responsibility), and/or stores in different geographic locations (to learn regional differences in customer preferences), just to provide a different kind of work experience. These lateral moves might be international. More and more companies, Intel and American Greetings among them, are sending U.S. employees overseas for specific projects that last anywhere from 3 months to a year.[33] Or lateral moves might include short-term stints at another company. Dow Chemical sent one of their employees on a 2-year stint to show Nalco Chemical a few things about environmental and safety operations. In exchange, Dow got a Nalco employee to share his expertise in sales and marketing with Dow's Advanced Cleaning Systems Business. The move helped the companies to share expertise and to save money because they don't have to hire experts of their own.[34]

Cross-functional moves might even include a step *down* in the organizational hierarchy. An employer, for example, might suggest that an employee transfer to another department that offers more upward mobility—in the long run. However, the responsibilities are so different across departments that the employer wants to minimize risk by moving the employee into a lower position on the organizational chart.[35]

Now, place yourself in the shoes of an employee in the Establishment stage of his career. He's highly motivated. He's working hard, but there's no promotion in sight. Now the boss comes and says "Great news! You're getting transferred to another department. It might look like a demotion, but trust me—it's a terrific opportunity." Downward moves and lateral moves are likely to be met with skepticism by employees who expect a more traditional career path, and organizations need to be proactive to legitimize them as valid career opportunities. You may need to show employees that lateral and downward moves *are* valued. Corning, for example, offers a 5% pay raise for lateral moves. GATX (a Chicago-based transportation, warehousing, and financial services firm) sometimes gives managers making a lateral move a one-time bonus equivalent to about a month's pay.[36] At some organizations, employees who are moved to lower level positions on the organization chart retain their original job titles. You may also need to offer employees a safety net. At Heublein, transferred employees have the option of returning to their old jobs if the new one proves to be inappropriate or unsatisfying.

Externship Programs.   Externship programs are another way that organizations are trying to build in more challenge and skill development opportunities for employees during the Establishment stage of their careers. These programs are becoming popular in the consulting industry. In an externship program, consultants take a full-time operational role at a client company for 6 to 24 months. For example, at Mercer (a management consulting firm) a consultant worked on an Internet strategy for Hallmark Cards. Because he wanted to see how the strategy unfolded, he moved to Hallmark to oversee the implementation.[37] Externship programs are an opportunity for employees to see a project through to fruition or to gain operating experience in a particular industry.

Dual Career Tracks.   The traditional career offers only one path to career success—progression up a job ladder into upper level management. But, not every employee makes a good manager. Not every employee wants to be a manager. And yet, historically, being a manager has been the only way employees were able to earn organizational rewards.

One way that organizations avoid plateauing employees during the Establishment career stage is to develop dual career tracks. One track is the traditional ladder leading to upper level management; the second is an alternative ladder for technical or sales employees. These alternative paths offer tracks that parallel managerial tracks but don't involve managing other people. Dual career paths are especially common in sales, banking, and the health industries. For example, South Texas Veterans' Health Care System offers a clinical track for employees who want to continue hands-on nursing. Instead of advancing into nursing management, employees on this alternative "clinical track" advance into positions that offer the same prestige as their management counterparts. Similarly, EDS offers a technical track for employees who want to emphasize their technical skills. The title EDS Fellow is awarded to the corporation's most innovative thought leaders; employees with that title are recognized as industry experts and have the same earning potential as EDS executives.[38]

Some organizations have had terrific success with dual career tracks, and others have been less successful. Dual career tracks are often established that offer only a few rungs on the alternative ladder, which only postpones the plateauing problem. Also, the alternative ladder may match the salaries associated with the managerial ladder, but it may not offer some of the other organizational rewards (e.g., stock options) associated with managerial positions. Therefore, the alternative track may not have the same credibility or attractiveness as the traditional management track.

Manager's Checkpoint

Use the following questions to see whether your organization would benefit from developing strategies to meet the needs of employees in the Establishment stage of their careers:

- Has the promotion rate for employees been slow or stalled? Are employees in the Establishment stage leaving the organization at an increased rate? (If your answer to these questions is yes, your organization may be experiencing a "brain drain" resulting from the plateauing of promising employees. That suggests you want to investigate some alternatives to a traditional promotion-based system.)
- Would my organization benefit from more generalists in upper level management positions? (The traditional promotion-based system encourages the development of functional specialists, while lateral and downward moves can encourage the development of generalists.)

- Have I been promoting employees into management who might prefer to maintain hands-on involvement in technical work or sales? (If the answer is yes, you may have employees who would benefit from the development of a dual career track.)

Managing Employees in the Maintenance Stage

Remember that employees in the Maintenance stage of their careers frequently become more other-directed.[39] In the traditional promotion-based career model, these employees might have enjoyed the Maintenance stage of their careers in upper management positions where they would supervise and train members of their staff. However, because promotions have slowed, many employees in the Maintenance stage of their careers may not be in managerial positions. How can you meet their needs to make a contribution to other people?

Mentoring Opportunities. Frequently, Maintenance needs can be met by encouraging employees to mentor employees in earlier career stages. A mentor is a more senior employee who coaches, advises, and encourages individuals at a lower organizational level. Mentors make two distinct contributions to their protégés' careers: First, they can directly impact the protégé's career advancement by sponsoring the protégé for organizational opportunities and coaching the protégé in job skills. Second, they can provide psychological support. Encouragement, pep talks, and a supportive shoulder can greatly enhance the protégé's overall career satisfaction.

Mentoring relationships have been shown to be beneficial for both the mentor and the protégé. For the protégé, mentoring has been associated with higher salaries, faster promotion rates, and greater career satisfaction.[40] But there are substantial benefits to the mentor as well, including the fulfillment of passing on hard-earned wisdom to the next generation.[41]

Now, here's the challenge for organizations. Given that mentoring relationships are so clearly beneficial, how can we make sure that these mentoring relationships develop? Most mentoring relationships develop informally. A person in the Maintenance stage makes a psychological connection with someone in the Establishment stage. That connection is often sparked by similarities between the two people. Maybe the Establishment-stage employee graduated from the same college as the Maintenance-stage employee, or grew up with a similar family background. This means that employees who are different from the typical Maintenance-stage employee can be left out of these spontaneous relationships.

To overcome this problem, organizations (including Avon, MTV, Xerox, and General Electric) are increasingly offering formal mentoring programs that directly match younger managers with more seasoned mentors who offer different sets of talents and experiences.[42] The early research on these programs suggests that they offer many of the same benefits as informal mentoring relationships,[43] but formal mentoring assignments might need some additional managerial involvement and oversight. For example, you can't assume that everyone automatically makes a good mentor. Some Maintenance employees may need training about how to cultivate a protégé's talents, and both parties may need help in establishing relationship boundaries and learning how to manage conflicts.[44] You'll need to help the mentor and protégé to establish goals for their relationship, and monitor their progress. If the relationship is not working, you'll be able to detect and correct the problems or, if necessary, re-assign the protégé to a new mentor.[45] And don't assume that a mentoring relationship has to last forever. Some organizations build effective mentoring relationships that last only 6 to 9 months—just long enough for the partnership to transfer key skills.[46]

Just as organizations provide tangible rewards to employees taking on risky career moves (e.g., making lateral or downward moves), organizations may need to demonstrate to employees that their participation in mentoring is a valued contribution. For example, Netcentives (a web-based marketing startup) encourages new hires to select any senior executive who they'd like to have as a mentor. Netcentives then rewards the senior executive with stock options for serving as a mentor.[4147]

Mentoring programs, by the way, aren't limited to managerial careers. Stalcorp (the name stands for the steel, aluminum, and copper industrial components the company manufactures) started a mentoring program to address a retention problem among their manufacturing employees. In the press department, where the metal is shaped and formed, senior employees make sure that protégés can read gauges and blueprints and are clear on safety procedures. Mentors get $250 if new hires stick around for 90 days and do well, and another $250 if they're there after 6 months—a nice chunk of change for the mentor, who generally makes around $10 an hour.[48]

Sabbaticals.   The other challenge for employees as they enter the Maintenance stage of their careers is the reappraisal—that midcareer "crisis," as it's commonly called. Employees in the Maintenance stage need time to reflect on their career direction and make decisions about the future. Organizations are trying to meet this need by giving employees sabbatical opportunities. Sabbaticals are paid or unpaid leaves that give the employee time off to pursue other interests. For example, an employee at Greenpages, an $83-million company in Kittery, Maine, took several months off to hike the Appalachian trail—and returned charged up and more productive.[49] The director of furniture services at Wells Fargo took time off to train for and compete in a swimming championship—and returned refreshed and ready to get back to work.

Sabbatical policies may be very liberal or very restrictive. Mutual-fund researcher Morningstar allows all employees a 6-week, paid sabbatical every 4 years to do whatever they choose. Xerox, in contrast, lets U.S. employees who have been with the company at least 3 years take off for 12 months with pay, but they must work for a nonprofit organization with which they are already affiliated.[50] But why would an organization provide sabbaticals at all? Well, remember that employees moving into the Maintenance stage of their careers are already engaging in this reassessment process—whether you provide a sabbatical or not. In the absence of a sabbatical policy, employees who feel driven to engage in this kind of reassessment may have no choice but to quit in order to have the time and resources to explore other interests.

Sabbaticals may be perceived as costly to the organization. After all, the organization is paying a salary and not getting any immediate return. Therefore, many human resource management experts speculated that sabbaticals would be abandoned during recessions. However, sabbaticals have actually proven to be very popular during short-term economic downturns because they provide a way for organizations to reduce salary costs while retaining valued employees. For example, the consulting firm Accenture needed to cut costs. One strategy they used was to offer sabbaticals to employees. Employees got only 20% of their salary (representing substantial salary savings for Accenture) for a leave that lasted from 6 to 12 months. Employees were even permitted to take another job during their leave, as long as they didn't work for an Accenture competitor.[51] Many employees chose to spend their sabbatical volunteering for a nonprofit group, giving Accenture positive public relations.[52]

Manager's Checkpoint

The following questions might help you to decide whether a formal mentoring program or a sabbatical program would be valuable to your organization:

- Do I have a large proportion of employees in the Maintenance career stage who are not supervising other people? (Supervisory responsibilities give employees in the Maintenance career stage the opportunity to develop and mentor other people. Employees not in supervisory positions may need organizationally sponsored opportunities to develop mentoring relationships.)

- Do I have more diversity (in terms of employee gender, racial or ethnic background, or other demographic variables) among my recent hires than among my long-term employees? (If yes, you may need to be concerned that informal mentoring relationships may not develop. A formal mentoring program may help to establish relationships between employees at different career stages.)

- Do employees in the Maintenance career stage seem "burned out" or bored with their current responsibilities? (If yes, employees may benefit from a sabbatical that gives them an opportunity to recharge and reevaluate their career goals. This respite may help the organization to retain a valuable employee through the midcareer crisis.)

Managing Employees During the Disengagement Stage

In the traditional career, employees moved into the Disengagement stage after a long history with their employer. Organizations often seem to have a love-hate relationship with these long-time employees. During bad labor markets, organizations try to hold onto these employees for as long as possible. During good labor markets, organizations seem to want to push them out the door.

Early Retirement Programs.   Early retirement programs are designed to speed up the traditional transition from full-time work to retirement. Early retirement packages offer retirement incentives to employees who elect to retire during a "window" period; employees who do not retire during that period do not receive the incentives. Most commonly, the company adds some number of years to employees' age and/or tenure. For example, the organization might offer a 5–5 program in which 5 years are added to an employee's age, and 5 years are added to an employee's organizational service. Under this plan, an employee who is 50 years old could opt for early retirement and receive benefits he or she otherwise would not be eligible for until 5 years later.

Organizations often initiate early retirement programs in an effort to reduce the salary costs associated with senior employees. If employees have already started the psychological and emotional work of disengaging from their career, they may be ready to retire and pursue alternative activities. Early retirement programs can also open up promotion opportunities and ease plateauing problems at lower levels of the organization. As a result, an early retirement program targeted to Disengagement-stage employees may help organizations to meet the needs of these employees as well as employees in earlier career stages. But early retirement programs are very tricky to manage. Organizations have difficulty predicting how many employees are likely to take advantage of early retirement opportunities. If too many senior level employees retire, leaving too many open positions, organizations end up replacing their plateauing woes with the Peter Principle.

Phased Retirement Programs.   In the traditional retirement system, an employee in the Disengagement stage can be employed full-time one day, and fully retired the next. Many retirees are psychologically or financially unprepared to make this abrupt transition. *Phased retirement* is a broad term used to describe arrangements in which employees at, or near, traditional retirement age *gradually* reduce their work hours and job responsibilities. People are already creating their own phased retirement on an informal basis by retiring from one job, and going to work part time for someone else. A formal phased retirement lets an organization maintain a relationship with its own retirees instead of completely severing the tie. According to a recent study by Watson Wyatt Worldwide, about 16% of U.S. organizations offer some kind of phased retirement, and another 28% have plans to start in the next few years.[53]

One option might be for an employee to retire, then be hired back for part time or temporary work. The employee might be given shorter hours, or a part-time work schedule. At Wrigley, one option for full employees who are 2–3 years away from retirement is to move progressively from 40 hours per week down to 30 hours and then to 20 hours. This gives the organization some lead time for filling the employee's job and training a replacement. Aerospace Corp. gives employees several options for phased retirement, including part-time work, consulting, and a 3-month unpaid leave of absence that lets employees try out full retirement to see if they like it. If they don't, they can return to full-time employment without any loss of benefits. The most popular option is to become a "retiree casual." With management approval, these workers retire—with pension and medical benefits—and then are rehired to work up to 999 hours per year, the maximum allowed while retaining pension benefits.[54]

Manager's Checkpoint

The following questions might help you to decide whether early retirement or phased retirement programs might be useful in your organization:

- Do I have employees who are nearing retirement age and blocking the advancement of more junior people? What is the relative size of these two groups? (Employees who are nearing retirement age may be interested in an early retirement package that speeds up their disengagement. But watch out—if there are too many employees eligible for early retirement, you may not have enough junior employees to fill their positions.)

- Is my organization suffering from "pipeline" problems that will make it difficult to fill upper level positions? (If yes, a phased retirement program might help to keep senior employees in the job past traditional retirement ages.)

WHAT'S NEXT?

In this chapter, we took the long view. We examined the relationship you have with your employees over the entire career cycle. Like any relationship, the employer–employee relationship will have its ups and downs. In the next chapter, we'll focus on the downs and discuss disciplinary actions in organizations.

FOR FURTHER READING

Graig, L. A., & Paganelli, V. (2000). Phased retirement: Reshaping the end of work. *Compensation and Benefits Management, 16*(2), 1–9.
Ibarra, H. (2002, December). How to stay stuck in the wrong career. *Harvard Business Review,* 40–47.
Joinson, C. (2001, May). Employee, sculpt thyself … with a little help. *HRMagazine,* 60–64.
Warner, F. (2002, April). Inside Intel's mentoring movement. *Fast Company,* 116–120.

MANAGER'S KNOT 8.1

"My company has adopted a philosophy that emphasizes the role of the employee in career management. How can I encourage my employees to take responsibility for managing their own careers?"

Start by making sure that your employees have all the information they need to plan their careers within the organization. For example, is your organization planning to grow in certain areas, and shrink in others? This kind of candid information will help employees to understand the long-term opportunities that exist within the company. Then take a close look at your employee performance appraisal process. Are employees receiving honest performance feedback, so that they can see how their skills and capabilities are perceived within the organization? Providing information on these two dimensions will help employees to assess their own fit within the organization. You might also consider providing access to other career management resources that give employees the opportunity to assess their own skills and career goals.

MANAGER'S KNOT 8.2

"My company does a great job of recruiting college graduates. But lately I've noticed that my best performers don't stick around as long as I'd like. I know that they are frustrated by a lack of advancement opportunities. I don't see a lot of opportunity for promotions for about 10 years, when many of the senior managers will be retiring. How can I maintain motivation among the junior people in the meantime?"

Your question describes a common dilemma in organizations. In earlier decades, organizations expanded rapidly and promoted people quickly, so now management ranks tend to be filled with a cohort of people in a limited age range. That means advancement opportunities have slowed down, but it also means that big groups of managers will be retiring simultaneously. Your new hires are in the Exploration and Establishment stages of their careers, and they may respond positively to chances to broaden their skills even in the absence of promotional opportunities—especially if these skill-building opportunities are accompanied by tangible organizational rewards (including pay raises). Think about project work, cross-functional moves, externships, and other ways that lower level employees can experiment and develop new skills. In 10 years, when the current managers begin to retire, you'll have a cohort of talented people to replace them who have a broad understanding of all the different areas of your business.

MANAGER'S KNOT 8.3

"My problem's personal. I'm a department manager in a large manufacturing organization. I've been doing this job for about eight years, and frankly, I'm bored with it. I'm good at what I do—I just don't find it that interesting any more. I don't think I'm seen as having the potential to move into top management, but I don't want to stay in this job forever, either."

Your reaction is not at all surprising. After 8 years in one job, you may be entering the reappraisal period many people experience at the midpoint of the career cycle. The question to consider (and it's a big one!) is whether you want to try and reinvent your current job, or disengage and begin the career cycle anew. Both of those sound like big steps, but either one may be possible even within your current employer. For example, is there a way to build mentoring responsibilities into your current job that might introduce a new interesting dimension? Would you be interested in a lateral move to a different product or department within the company?

ENDNOTES

1. Cappelli, P. (2000, Jan-Feb). A market-driven approach to retaining talent. *Harvard Business Review*, 103–111; Olesen, M. (1999, October). What makes employees stay. *Training and Development*, 48–52.
2. Super, D. E. (1957). *The psychology of careers*. New York: HarperCollins; Super, D. E. (1984). Career and life development. In D. Brown, L. Brooks, & Associates (Eds.), *Career choice and development* (pp. 192–234). San Francisco: Jossey-Bass; Super, D. E., Savickas, M. L., & Super, C. M. (1996). The life-span, life-space approach to careers. In D. Brown, L. Brooks, & Associates (Eds.), *Career choice and development* (3rd ed., pp. 121–178). San Francisco: Jossey-Bass.
3. Super, D. E., Savickas, M. L., & Super, C. M. (1996). The life-span, life-space approach to careers. In D. Brown, L. Brooks, & Associates (Eds.), *Career choice and development* (3rd ed., pp. 121–178). San Francisco: Jossey-Bass.
4. Savickas, M. L. (2002). Career construction: A developmental theory of vocational behavior. In D. Brown & Associates (Eds.), *Career choice and development* (4th ed., pp. 149–205). San Francisco: Jossey-Bass.
5. Super, D. E., Savickas, M. L., & Super, C. M. (1996). The life-span, life-space approach to careers. In D. Brown, L. Brooks, & Associates (Eds.), *Career choice and development* (3rd ed., pp. 121–178). San Francisco: Jossey-Bass.
6. Super, D. E. (1957). *The psychology of careers*. New York: HarperCollins; Super, D. E. (1984). Career and life development. In D. Brown, L. Brooks, & Associates (Eds.), *Career choice and development* (pp. 192–234). San Francisco: Jossey-Bass; Super, D. E., Savickas, M. L., & Super, C. M. (1996). The life-span, life-space approach to careers. In D. Brown, L. Brooks, & Associates (Eds.), *Career choice and development* (pp. 121–178). San Francisco: Jossey-Bass.
7. Lachman, M. E., Lewkowicz, C., Marcus, A., & Peng, Y. (1994). Images of midlife development among young, middle-aged and older adults. *Journal of Adult Development, 1*, 201–211.
8. Boyatzis, R., McKee, A., & Goleman, D. (2002, April). Reawakening your passion for work. *Harvard Business Review*, 5–11.
9. Super, D. E., Savickas, M. L., & Super, C. M. (1996). The life-span, life-space approach to careers. In D. Brown, L. Brooks, & Associates (Eds.), *Career choice and development* (3rd ed., pp. 121–178). San Francisco: Jossey-Bass.
10. Mirvis, P. H., & Hall, D. T. (1994). Psychological success and the boundaryless career. *Journal of Organizational Behavior, 15*, 365–380; Hall, D. T., & Mirvis, P. H. (1995). The new career contract: Developing the whole person at midlife and beyond. *Journal of Vocational Behavior, 47*, 269–289.
11. Peter, L. J., & Hull, R. (1996). *The Peter Principle*. Cutchogue, NY: Buccaneer Books.

12. Tremblay, M., Roger, A., & Toulouse, J. (1995). Career plateau and work attitudes: An empirical study of managers. *Human Relations, 48,* 221–237; Veiga, J. F. (1981). Plateaued versus non-plateaued managers' career patterns, attitudes and path potential. *Academy of Management Journal, 24,* 566–578.

13. Miles, R. E., & Snow, C. C. (1996). Twenty-first century careers. In M. B. Arthur & D. M. Rousseau (Eds.), *The boundaryless career* (pp. 97–115). New York: Oxford University Press.

14. Colby, A. G. (1995, June). Making the new career development model work. *HRMagazine,* 150–152.

15. Arthur, M. B., & Rousseau, D. M. (1996). The boundaryless career as a new employment principle. In M. G. Arthur & D. M. Rousseau (Eds.), *The boundaryless career* (pp. 3–20). New York: Oxford University Press.

16. Hall, D. T., & Moss, J. E. (1998, Winter). The new protean career contract: Helping organizations and employees adapt. *Organizational Dynamics,* 22–37.

17. Thite, M. (2001). Help us but help yourself: The paradox of contemporary career management. *Career Development International, 6*(6), 312–317.

18. Feldman, D. C. (2000). The Dilbert syndrome: How employee cynicism about ineffective management is changing the nature of careers in organizations. *American Behavioral Scientist, 43,* 1286–1300; Mirvis, P. H., & Hall, D. T. (1994). Psychological success and the boundaryless career. *Journal of Organizational Behavior, 15,* 365–380.

19. Feldman, D. C. (2002). Stability in the midst of change: A developmental perspective on the study of careers. In D. C. Feldman (Ed.), *Work careers: A developmental perspective* (pp. 3–26). San Francisco: Jossey-Bass.

20. Hall, D. T., & Mirvis, P. H. (1995). The new career contract: Developing the whole person at midlife and beyond. *Journal of Vocational Behavior, 47,* 269–289; Hall, D. T., & Mirvis, P. H. (1996). The new protean career: Psychological success and the path with a heart. In D. T. Hall (Ed.), *The career is dead—long live the career* (pp. 15–45). San Francisco: Jossey-Bass.

21. McConville, D. J. (1995, April). Moving up sideways. *Across the Board, 32*(4), 37–41.

22. Graham, E. (1995, October 31). Their careers: Count on nothing and work like a demon. *Wall Street Journal,* pp. B1, B7.

23. Lancaster, H. (1997, March 11). Companies promise to help employees plot their careers. *Wall Street Journal,* p. B1.

24. Stewart, T. A. (1995, March 20). Planning a career in a world without managers. *Fortune,* 72–80.

25. Stewart, T. A. (1995, March 20). Planning a career in a world without managers. *Fortune,* 72–80.

26. Dixon-Kheir, C. (2001, January). Supervisors are key to keeping young talent. *HRMagazine,* 139–142.

27. Koudsi, S. (2001, April 16). MBA students want old-economy bosses. *Fortune,* 407–408.

28. Olesen, M. (1999, October). What makes employees stay. *Training and Development,* 48–52.

29. Jeffrey, N. A. (2002). Boomers become interns to experience new jobs. *Wall Street Journal Online.* Retrieved July 12, 2002, from wsj.com

30. Habermas, T., & Bluck, S. (2000). Getting a life: The emergence of the life story in adolescence. *Psychological Bulletin, 126,* 748–769.

31. Hall, D. T. (1996). Protean careers of the 21st century. *Academy of Management Executive, 10,* 8–16.

32. Branch, S. (1998, November 9). You hired 'em. But can you keep 'em? *Fortune*, 247–250.
33. Fisher, A. (1997, January 13). Six ways to supercharge your career. *Fortune*, 46–48; McConville, D. J. (1995, April). Moving up sideways. *Across the Board, 32*(4), 37–41.
34. Work week. (1994, April 12). *Wall Street Journal*, p. A1.
35. Lloyd, J. (2001, October 12). Moving down the career ladder. *Business Journal-Milwaukee*, p. 15.
36. McConville, D. J. (1995, April). Moving up sideways. *Across the Board, 32*(4), 37–41.
37. Silverman, R. E. (2000, November 7). Mercer tries to keep employees through its externship program. *Wall Street Journal*, p. B18.
38. Joinson, C. (1997, October). Multiple career paths help retain talent. *HRMagazine*, 59–64.
39. Kram, K. E. (1985). *Mentoring at work*. Glenview, IL: Scott, Foresman; Levinson, D. J. (1978). *The seasons of a man's life*. New York: Knopf.
40. Burke, R. J. (1984). Mentors in organizations. *Group and Organization Studies, 9*, 353–372; Dreher, G. F., & Ash, R. A. (1990). A comparative study of mentoring among men and women in managerial, professional, and technical positions. *Journal of Applied Psychology, 75*, 539–546; Dreher, G. F., & Cox, T. H. (1996). Race, gender, and opportunity: A study of compensation attainment and the establishment of mentoring relationships. *Journal of Applied Psychology, 81*, 297–308; Fagenson, E. A. (1989). The mentor advantage: Perceived career/job experiences of protégés vs. non-proteges. *Journal of Organizational Behavior, 10*, 309–320.
41. Van Collie, S. (1998, March). Moving up through mentoring. *Workforce*, 36–42; Ragins, B. R., & Scandura, T. A. (1999). Burden or blessing? Expected costs and benefits of being a mentor. *Journal of Organizational Behavior, 20*, 493–509.
42. Loeb, M. (1995, November 27). The new mentoring. *Fortune*, 213.
43. Chao, G. T., Walz, P. M., & Gardner, P. D. (1992). Formal and informal mentorships: A comparison on mentoring functions and contrast with nonmentored counterparts. *Personnel Psychology, 45*, 619–636; Wilson, J. A., & Elman, N. S. (1990). Organizational benefits of mentoring. *Academy of Management Executive, 4*(4), 88–94.
44. Segal, J. A. (2000, March). Mirror-image mentoring. *HRMagazine*, 147–166.
45. Segal, J. A. (2000, March). Mirror-image mentoring. *HRMagazine*, 147–166.
46. Warner, F. (2002, April). Inside Intel's mentoring movement. *Fast Company*, 116–120.
47. Dahle, C. (1998). Mentor-centives. *Fast Company, 17*, p. 188.
48. Smith, A. K., Perry, J., Dillon, S., & Smart, T. (2000). Charting your own course. *U.S. News and World Report, 129*(18), 56–65.
49. Caggiano, C. (1998). Time off for good behavior. *Inc., 20*(10), 115.
50. Gutner, T. (2001, November 19). The pause that refreshes. *BusinessWeek*, 138.
51. Dunham, K. J. (2001, June 19). Employers seek ways to lure back laid-off workers when times improve. *Wall Street Journal*, pp. B1, B16.
52. Mallory, M. (2001, October 28). Volunteering cost-cutters: Temporary switch of jobs can help firms cut expenses. *Atlanta Journal and Constitution*, p. 1R.
53. Graig, L. A., & Paganelli, V. (2000). Phased retirement: Reshaping the end of work. *Compensation and Benefits Management, 16*(2), 1–9.
54. Hirschman, C. (2001, December). Exit strategies. *HRMagazine*, 52–57.

IV

Organizational Discipline and Exit

9

Disciplining Employees

We'd all like to have the perfect employer–employee relationship— you know, the one where the employee does everything right, goes the extra mile in fulfilling responsibilities, and never needs to be disciplined. But, in fact, managers are frequently called on to take disciplinary action to correct employee behavior. In this chapter, I'll lay out some general parameters to keep in mind when disciplining employees. I'll describe some alternatives to consider when designing disciplinary systems and discuss some current hot issues in employee discipline. And I'll provide some pointers to consider when discussing disciplinary issues with employees.

DISCIPLINE IN ORGANIZATIONS

Picture this scene: A small child reaches out a hand to a hot burner on a kitchen stove. A vigilant adult warns the child: "Don't touch! It's hot!" But overcome by curiosity, the child reaches again—and is immediately rewarded by a burned finger. This childhood incident illustrates three basic principles of discipline in organizations. Together, these principles form the *Hot Stove Rule*. First, disciplinary action should always be preceded by a warning. It's the organization's responsibility to communicate the operating rules, as well as the consequences of violating those rules. An employee should never be surprised by a disciplinary action. Second, disciplinary action should immediately follow the wrongdoing. The longer the delay between the employee behavior and the punishment, the less behavior change that is likely to result. And, finally, discipline should be enforced consistently, in an impersonal and unbiased way. The stove doesn't care who it burns—young, old, male, female. In the same way, the severity of disciplinary action in organizations should depend on the severity of the offense, not the personal characteristics of the employee. Thinking about the *Hot Stove Rule* will help you to establish and apply disciplinary procedures that are both effective and fair. There are two basic forms of disciplinary procedures in organizations (progressive discipline and positive discipline) and both are based on the principles inherent in the Hot Stove Rule.

Progressive Discipline and Positive Discipline Approaches

Virtually all unionized employers and most nonunionized employers use some variation of a *progressive discipline* procedure. In a progressive discipline approach, the organization develops a series of disciplinary "steps." The first offense committed by an employee may evoke a relatively mild disciplinary reaction from the organization, but as employee offenses accumulate, the disciplinary response of the organization becomes progressively more severe.

The left side of Table 9.1 illustrates a typical progressive discipline procedure. The exact number of steps will vary across organizations, but most systems will begin with an informal verbal warning and eventually progress (in the extreme) to termination. Let's say, for example, that your organization requires all employees to start work at 8 AM. One of your employees, Jane, arrives at work at 8:20 AM. The first time this happens, you give Jane a verbal warning. The second time Jane arrives late, you issue a written warning that is placed in Jane's personnel file. The third time Jane arrives late, she is suspended without pay. And the fourth time Jane arrives late, she is terminated.

TABLE 9.1
Progressive and Positive Discipline Approaches

	Progressive Discipline	Positive Discipline
First offense	Verbal warning	Verbal reminder
Second offense	Written warning	Written reminder
Third offense	Suspension without pay	Decision-making day
Final offense	Termination	Termination

In this example, Jane's repeated violation of the company's policy on work hours is the impetus that advances the disciplinary process. However, employee behavior is rarely identical from one event to the next. One of the challenges for managers is deciding whether later offenses are "similar enough" to an initial offense to warrant a more severe disciplinary action. Suppose you have an employee who, within a 1-month period, has violated your organization's safety rules 10 times, but he has violated a *different* rule each time. Are these 10 offenses similar enough to be treated as the same kind of offense? Certainly. The employee's behavior is not tied to any one individual safety rule—his behavior shows a general disregard for the organization's policies on safety. It would be unreasonable to expect the organization to maintain a separate disciplinary sequence for every safety rule it has on the books. To deal with this problem, organizations often "bundle" related offenses into more general categories. These categories might include violations of company policies or procedures, performance problems, conduct infractions, and absenteeism or tardiness.[1] Repeated offenses within a category will advance the employee through the disciplinary process, but offenses in different categories initiate separate disciplinary sequences. Because the employee's safety rule violations all constitute the same type of offense, each violation advances the disciplinary process. However, an employee with a history of absenteeism should have that problem disciplined separately from performance issues.

Bundling also helps organizations to make decisions about the seriousness of offenses, and the starting point of the disciplinary process. Whenever possible, the disciplinary procedure should start at the beginning to ensure that the organization has provided timely warnings to the employee and sufficient opportunity to change course (remember the Hot Stove Rule!).[2] Starting with a verbal warning is clearly appropriate when the organization is addressing employee absenteeism or performance problems. However, it would be irresponsible if the organization responded to more serious offenses with a verbal warning. Policy violations or conduct infractions may initiate the disciplinary process at the written warning stage. And if the behavior is sufficiently egregious (e.g., theft, violent behavior), termination may be appropriate even for a first offense.[3]

The right side of Table 9.1 illustrates an alternative approach to addressing Jane's tardiness problem, *positive discipline*. At first glance, you may not see very great differences between the progressive and positive discipline approaches. Both approaches establish a series of steps that describe how the organization reacts to employees who violate organizational expectations. But in fact, the philosophies behind the two approaches are miles apart from one another. Progressive discipline is a punishment-based approach; it gives managers a set of hammers they can use to pound out the problematic behavior, each hammer bigger and heavier than the one before. When employees change their behavior, they do so in order to avoid more serious punishments in the future. You might get the behavior change you want, but the change may be accompanied by some emotional baggage. Employees are likely to respond to progressive discipline with anger and resentment, leading to a "me vs. them" attitude that causes further problems down the road.[4]

In contrast, positive discipline is a participative approach to discipline. In a positive discipline system, the organization and the employee form a partnership, and both parties are assumed to share an interest in changing the employee's behavior. In the first steps of a positive discipline approach, the verbal and written warnings are replaced with reminders. What's the difference between a *warning* and a *reminder*? A warning in a progressive discipline approach alerts the employee that, if the problem behavior continues, future punishment will be forthcoming. A reminder in a positive discipline system is focused on making sure that the employee understands the organizational rule, and why it is on the books. Instead of warning Jane about the consequences of her actions, a manager using positive discipline would remind her of the company policy on work hours and ask for her agreement to solve the problem.[5]

The most controversial step in a positive discipline approach is the decision-making day. At the point where a progressive discipline system would suspend the employee without pay, a positive discipline system offers the employee a decision-making day—usually with full pay. It's this "fully-paid" bit that managers often have trouble accepting. After all, Jane has violated organizational policy not once, but multiple times! Why should she be given a day at leisure? The point of offering the employee a decision-making day is to demonstrate the organization's commitment to helping the employee solve the problem. By giving the employee paid time off to reflect on his or her behavior, the organization is making a tangible gesture of support. In some systems, employees are asked to return from the decision-making day with a written plan for changing their behavior. For example, Jane might return from her decision-making day with a list of changes designed to ensure that she arrives at work on time: buying a clock with a more reliable alarm, developing a car pool arrangement to reduce her dependence on public transportation, switching shifts to accommodate her child-care needs. This written plan becomes a contract with the company—either Jane lives up to the agreement or the relationship will end.[6] As a result, both the progressive and positive discipline systems culminate in the same final step: If Jane continues to arrive late to work, she will be terminated.

Positive discipline systems are less common than traditional progressive discipline systems, but organizations that do take a positive approach to discipline report a great deal of success. Organizations that use positive discipline report fewer terminations, fewer disciplinary complaints, and less employee turnover.[7] Take Frito-Lay, for example. An unhappy employee at Frito-Lay developed a creative way to express his frustration with the company. He began writing obscene messages on potato chips with a felt-tip pen, and slipping them back into the packaging process. You can imagine the public relations nightmare this caused for Frito-Lay, as more and more customers opened up their bags of chips to find these cheeky messages. Frito-Lay's managers took immediate action. Under Frito-Lay's progressive discipline system, anyone caught tampering with the potato chips was punished. But things got worse, not better. More workers joined in the message-writing campaign. Consumer complaints poured in. As the employee problems increased, managers took more disciplinary action—but harsher punishment only led to more employee misbehavior. In a 9-month period, 58 out of 210 employees were fired. In desperation, Frito-Lay switched to a positive discipline approach. In the year following the switch, terminations dropped to 19; and, in the second year following the switch, only 2 employees were terminated.[8]

The choice between the progressive and positive approaches to discipline is one that you need to make within the context of the larger organizational culture. You may find that a traditional progressive discipline system conflicts with the goals of your other human resource management systems. If you've made an effort to develop your employees and involve them in day-to-day decision making, you may be sending a conflicting message when you impose unilateral punishments as a way of correcting behavior. Remember the distinction made in chapter 6 between acting as a judge and acting as a coach in the performance appraisal process? The same distinction applies here. Progressive discipline systems emphasize your role as a judge—your primary responsibility is determining when the rules have been broken, and meting out appropriate punishments. In contrast, positive discipline requires a coach style. It's hard to say which system is more challenging for a manager. On the one hand, coaching an employee through the disciplinary process requires considerable patience and interpersonal skills. It may be easier, in the short run at least, to play the judge. But wouldn't you rather go into a disciplinary meeting having the opportunity to pledge your support and commitment to helping the employee change? In the long run, that approach may result in more productive working relationship.

Manager's Checkpoint

Use the following questions to decide which discipline system is right for your needs:

- Is my workplace one in which employee behavior is heavily regulated, either by union rules or by government legislation? (In heavily regulated environments, it may be more practical to employ a progressive discipline approach, because you will need to maintain detailed disciplinary records for outside agencies.)
- Is my organizational culture one that encourages active employee participation in on-the-job activities? (If your organizational culture is very participative, a top-down progressive discipline approach may be a poor fit.)
- What is the demographic composition of my workforce? Am I employing highly educated, highly skilled employees? (Highly educated, highly skilled employees may find a progressive discipline approach particularly in conflict with their professional identities.)
- Have I made a substantial investment in my employees in terms of recruiting, training, and development activities? (If you've made a substantial effort in identifying and developing good employees, you'll want to protect that investment by engaging in positive discipline, rather than risk an adversarial relationship resulting from progressive discipline.)

Dispute Resolution Procedures

In any discipline system, employees may at times feel that a disciplinary action was undeserved. Disciplinary actions that are seen as unfair impact not just the disciplined employee, but the entire workforce (see Box 9.1 for examples). Many organizations now offer employees the opportunity to contest disciplinary procedures that they think are unfair. Why should an organization make dispute resolution procedures available? These systems serve several important purposes. First, providing opportunities for employees to appeal disciplinary decisions demonstrates that the organization is committed to fair treatment. Dispute resolution procedures can foster an atmosphere of trust and confidence in management—a sense that management will try to do the right thing.[9] Second, organizational dispute resolution procedures reduce an employee's need to take legal action

---

BOX 9.1
Coworkers Respond to Employee Discipline

✖ When the *Australia Post* disciplined a worker for displaying too many photographs at her workplace, sympathetic coworkers showed support by bringing photos to work to protest company rules limiting personal items on their desks.[10]

✖ After the September 11 terrorist attacks on New York, NCCI Holdings Inc. of Boca Raton, Florida, enforced a policy against displaying political and religious symbols at work and ordered employees to remove American flags from their desks. Employees leaked word of the policy onto the Internet and the company was deluged with thousands of irate phone calls and e-mails from all over the country.[11]

✖ After overhearing his boss reprimand a 66-year-old coworker so severely that she burst into tears, a 19-year-old burger flipper initiated what may be the first-ever strike against a McDonalds franchise. Along with 15 coworkers, the employee picketed the restaurant for 5 days until the franchise owner gave in to most of the group's requests, including a requirement that managers attend "people skills" workshops.[12]

---

if he or she feels unfairly treated, which saves time and money. A legal dispute that results in a decision favoring the company can easily cost up to $100,000 in legal fees, and the price tag can be much higher if the company is required to pay damages to the employee bringing the complaint. One company estimates that its legal costs shrunk by 90% over a 4-year period after it began offering internal dispute resolution procedures as an alternative to litigation.[13] Finally, if an employee's complaint cannot be resolved through the organization's dispute resolution procedure and does go to court, having a dispute resolution procedure can offer the employer legal protection. Courts tend to look favorably on organizations that have made a proactive effort to ensure that employees are fairly treated.

Organizations use a wide variety of dispute resolution procedures. These systems have one thing in common—a third party (someone not directly involved in the disciplinary action) is available to review the case. But the systems vary in terms of who that third party might be (see Box 9.2 for examples).

Step-Review System.   In this dispute resolution system, an employee's appeal is reviewed by successive layers of management. Employees are encouraged to first discuss their complaint with their manager. If the dispute is not resolved, employees can then bring the complaint to the next level of supervision in their department. If the dispute is still not set-

---

BOX 9.2
Alternative Dispute Resolution Procedures

✖ Bank of America offers employees a three-step "Let's Talk" procedure. In Step One, employee complaints are heard within an organizational unit and discussions may involve the local human resource manager. In Step Two, employees may put their complaints in writing and submit them to a senior manager of their division. If the decision at this stage is unsatisfactory, employees may then address their concerns to a corporate senior executive.[14]

✖ Darden Industries Inc., the Orlando, Florida, company that owns the Red Lobster and Olive Garden restaurant chains, uses peer review to resolve disputes. Employees who think that they have been unfairly disciplined present their views to a three-person panel. The panel has the authority to overturn management decisions and can award damages to employees.[15]

✖ After being involved in very public disputes with employees claiming race discrimination, Coca-Cola appointed the company's first ombudsperson as part of a companywide diversity initiative. The *Wall Street Journal* predicts that the demand for people to fill ombudsperson positions will increase as more companies cope with corporate ethics problems.[16]

✖ The U.S. Postal Services hires neutral outside mediators to resolve employee disputes. Before the mediation program was introduced, Postal Service employees who were involved in a dispute with their boss had no choice but to file claims with outside agencies like the EEOC, and resolution of these grievances could take years. In the first 22 months of full operation of the mediation program, complaints to outside agencies dropped by 30%.[17]

✖ Employees at Philip Morris who want to pursue claims of unfair disciplinary action are encouraged to take the dispute to arbitration. But in order to ensure that employee rights are maintained in the process, employees receive financial assistance from the company through the company's Dispute Resolution Benefits Plan—enabling employees the financial means to hire their own legal counsel.[18]

---

tled, employees may have the opportunity to have their complaint heard at upper management levels.[19]

Open Door Policy. Open Door systems offer employees greater flexibility in who can hear their complaints. In this dispute resolution system, an employee's appeal can be reviewed by anyone in management—the employee is free to choose someone who they perceive will give them a fair hearing. This system is designed to reduce the risk an employee might feel in bringing forward a complaint and to encourage open communication between an employee and a management representative.[20]

Peer Review.   In this dispute resolution system, complaints are reviewed by employee committees. In contrast to the Step-Review and Open Door options in which reviews are exclusively conducted by management personnel, these committees include a mix of management and nonmanagement representatives. Companies using peer review generally ask employees to volunteer their services. These employees receive training in company policy, fair employment laws, and conflict resolution before they hear a case.[21]

Ombudsperson.   In this dispute resolution system, the organization has established an organizational position with the responsibility for hearing employee complaints. The person occupying this position may be impartial, but sometimes the ombudsperson's role is explicitly defined as advocating for the aggrieved employee; the ombudsperson's job is to balance the power discrepancy between the employee and management. The ombudsperson serves as a mediator between the employee and the organization. After reviewing the case, the ombudsperson makes recommendations to the company and the employee. Many organizations have ombudspersons, but individuals with this job title vary dramatically in terms of their power and authority. In many organizations, the ombudsperson's recommendations are nonbinding—management can choose to ignore the ombudsperson's advice. In other organizations, the ombudsperson reports directly to top level management and has considerable authority to enforce decisions.

Mediation.   Mediation uses a third party to guide the employee and the company toward a mutually beneficial resolution. The mediator's role is similar to that of a relationship counselor. The mediator helps the company and the employee identify the key issues and discuss the conflict. The mediator doesn't make the decision directly. Instead, the mediator helps the company and the employee decide for themselves how to resolve the conflict and on what terms.[22] Companies can either train their own employees to work as mediators or hire outside mediators as needed from national mediation and arbitration firms.

Arbitration.   In this dispute resolution system, an arbitrator from outside the organization is brought in to hear the dispute. The arbitrator hears from both sides of the case and then resolves it by rendering a specific decision or award. Arbitrators usually are experienced employment attorneys or retired judges.[23] In "nonbinding" arbitration, either side may reject the arbitrator's decision—for example, the employee may choose to file a legal complaint. In "binding" arbitration, the company and the employee agree beforehand that they will accept the arbitrator's final decision, whatever it is.

Historically, arbitration was offered to employees as a voluntary alternative to litigation—it was the employee's choice whether to pursue a complaint through arbitration or through the court system. However, some organizations now have a policy of *mandatory arbitration*. When arbitration is mandatory, individuals sign arbitration agreements as a condition of employment.[24] These agreements stipulate that employees must arbitrate disputes instead of suing the company. The U.S. Supreme Court has upheld employers' rights to require mandatory arbitration of its workers,[25] but the legal endorsement has not erased the controversy surrounding these systems. Because mandatory arbitration programs reduce employee choice, they tend to be viewed with suspicion by employees.[26] Mandatory systems may be seen as unfairly favoring the employer's side in a dispute.

In practice, most organizations that insist on mandatory arbitration offer employees other internal grievance options as well. Employees usually pursue these alternative dispute resolution strategies first, so very few cases ever make it to arbitration. In fact, a survey published by the American Arbitration Association reveals that the vast majority of companies with mandatory arbitration programs have not yet arbitrated a single dispute.[27]

Designing a Dispute Resolution System. As you can see, there are several options you can choose from in designing a dispute resolution procedure. Keep in mind that some of these options may be combined. For example, some organizations offer a Step-Review System in which the final step is going to an outside arbitrator. The choice among dispute resolution systems depends on a variety of factors (including the number of disputes you expect to have and the resources you have available for resolving them). But, regardless of the system you implement, it's important that the system contain two critical elements. First, employees' reactions will be most positive if they feel the system has allowed them sufficient opportunity for "voice"—that is, the opportunity to tell their side of story.[28] Second, employees' reactions will be most positive if they recognize the decision maker as fair and impartial.[29]

Manager's Checkpoint

Use the following questions to decide what type of dispute resolution system is right for your needs:

- What is the current level of trust within the organization? Are management personnel viewed as fair and impartial? (If management is distrusted, a dispute resolute system that relies heavily on managerial judgments may be viewed with suspicion. In these situations, a Peer Review system or an Ombudsperson might be preferable.)

- How many complaints are likely to be heard in the system? (The answer to this question depends both on the size of the organization and the amount of disciplinary action taken. If you anticipate a large number of employee complaints, it may be worthwhile to invest in permanent systems for managing these grievances, such as establishing an Ombudsperson position or Peer Review panels. However, if few complaints are anticipated, these might be best handled through outside mediators or arbitrators as situations arise.)

- What kinds of resources do I have for training employees? (All managers should be trained in conflict management skills. However, Peer Review panels require that nonmanagement personnel receive considerable training as well. In contrast, Arbitration and Mediation systems give you the option of hiring those skills from outside on an as-needed basis.)

EMPLOYEE DISCIPLINE: GRAY AREAS

Regardless of which disciplinary procedure you use, one of the challenges you face is defining what is a disciplinable offense. Most organizations have some basic rules and policies they spell out in the employee handbook. Violations of these rules are clearly areas in which disciplinary action is likely to follow. These might include rules about work schedules, attendance, productivity standards, or health and safety. However, there are many gray areas—areas in which managers would like to control employee behavior. Let's consider a few of these controversial areas and discuss whether you can discipline these activities.

Employee Drug Use

Estimates suggest that drug abuse in the United States costs employers from $75 billion to $100 billion per year.[30] If that number seems high, consider all the factors that go into it: employee absenteeism, reduced productivity, on-the-job accidents. In one study conducted by the Substance Abuse and Mental Health Services Administration, American adults who reported abusing drugs or alcohol were more likely to have missed 2 or more days of work in the past month due to illness or injury, which translates into an absenteeism rate 78% higher than the absenteeism rate for nonabusers. A report by the National Institute on Drug Abuse found that substance-abusing workers were one third less productive than nonusing workers. And another study by the U.S. Postal Service found that substance abusers were involved in 55% more accidents and experienced 85% more on-the-job injuries than nonusers.[31]

Many employers would like to control these costs by screening employees for drug use, and disciplining those who are found to be using illegal drugs. A variety of drug testing methods are now available. These procedures look for evidence of drug use in samples of employee urine, blood, or hair. One study of American Management Association members found that about 92% of companies conducting drug tests were using urine samples, 15% used blood sampling, and only about 2% used hair sampling (some companies reported using multiple methods).[32] The relative popularity of these alternative methods reflects, in part, their cost to the employer. Urinalysis is the cheapest form of drug testing (about $35 per test), whereas a hair analysis can cost nearly twice as much.[33] Unfortunately, urinalysis is also one of the least reliable methods of detecting illegal drugs; over-the-counter cold medications or poppy seeds can sometimes trigger a positive drug test. As a result, it's a good idea (and sometimes explicitly required by law, depending on the state in which you operate) to confirm a positive urinalysis test with a second, more reliable test before taking any disciplinary action against an employee.

In addition to differences in cost, drug tests differ in the type of drugs they are likely to identify, and over what time period the test is effective. Urinalysis, for example, is more likely to identify marijuana users, whereas hair sampling is more likely to identify users of hard drugs.[34] Urinalysis and blood sampling generally detect drug use during the previous week, and hair sampling can detect drug use going back a month or more.[35]

Regardless of whether urine, blood, or hair samples are used, the most effective deterrent to employee drug use is random testing. In random drug testing, employers identify which employees will be tested by drawing a random sample from the workforce. Employees cannot predict when they will be sent for a drug test, so employees are unable to "game" the test by limiting drug use only during testing periods. Drug testing within the private sector generally falls under the jurisdiction of state law, and states vary tremendously in their support for random drug testing. For example, the California state constitution contains an individual right to privacy clause that has been applied to drug testing, so it's hard for employers to implement random testing in that state. In general, state laws provide employers more latitude for implementing random drug testing for employees who work in safety-sensitive positions (e.g., employees who operate heavy equipment or transport passengers) than employees in positions where safety is less of an issue (e.g., employees who work at desk jobs).[36]

The alternative to random testing is to limit drug tests to situations in which there is "reasonable cause." For example, if you've noticed that an employee is making an excessive amount of mistakes and behaving erratically, this might constitute sufficient cause to order a drug test. If your company implements reasonable cause testing, managers need to be trained to recognize the signs of potential drug abuse: bloodshot eyes, frequent sniffling, tremors, mood swings, lapses in concentration.[37] Any one of these characteristics may be symptomatic of some other cause (e.g., a cold, stress), so managers need to be able to identify constellations of these symptoms in conjunction with behavioral indicators (e.g., performance problems) before sending employees to be tested.

Because drug testing is extremely controversial, some organizations are trying to control the effects of drug use without directly testing for drugs. For example, Old Town Trolley of San Diego, a company that runs sightseeing tours in the San Diego area, requires drivers to play a video game before they are declared fit for work. When the game is successfully completed, the driver receives a pass that gives the dispatcher the green light to assign the driver to a trolley.[38] Ion Implant also uses video games to ensure that truck drivers are able to operate vehicles. A driver can't turn the truck's ignition until he or she completes the game and receives a receipt saying the driver is fit to drive. These testing strategies make sure that employees who do not have fast enough reflexes or sufficient hand–eye coordination are not put in situations where they might endanger themselves or other people. Besides identifying employees who are not ready to perform their jobs because of drug use, these tests also identify employees who are not fit for work for other reasons (e.g., employees who are suffering from a medical problem or who are distracted by personal issues).

Whatever decisions your organization makes about drug testing—whether to test, when to test, how to test—these decisions should be clearly described in a policy available to employees. The policy should clearly explain the organization's drug testing procedures and the disciplinary procedures that might follow positive drug results.[39]

Employee E-Mail and Internet Use

A survey by the career Web site vault.com found that 10% of U.S. employees receive more than 20 personal e-mails at work each day, and 13% of employees spend over 2 hours a day surfing nonbusiness sites on the Internet.[40] These electronic activities take time, and some employers are concerned about this lost productivity. In addition, companies worry that they could be held liable if employees use company resources to circulate racist or sexist material and create a hostile environment for women or members of minority groups.[41] Increasingly, organizations want to monitor employee electronic activities, and tools are readily available to assist in this monitoring. Software can identify which employees are the most active on the Internet and which Web sites they visit, including pornography, shopping, and job-hunting sites.[42] Employee e-mail can be stored and reviewed for inappropriate content.

According to the American Management Association, about 78% of American companies now monitor their employees' electronic communications. About 63% monitor Internet access, and 47% review employee e-mail.[43] These monitoring activities can lead to disciplinary action against employees. Xerox, for example, uses software that records every Web site employees visit, and every minute they spend at each site. One day, Xerox notified 40 employees working in locations across the United States that they were being fired for surfing to forbidden Web sites (many of which were pornographic).[44] The *New York Times*, Dow Chemical, General Motors, and Edward Jones and Co. have fired employees for sending e-mail containing inappropriate jokes or pornographic images.[45]

A variety of courts have unambiguously ruled that, because employers own the computer equipment in their workplace, employers have the right to monitor their use and discipline employees who misuse computer resources. This right is based on a federal law called the Electronics Communications Privacy Act. According to this law, an employer is prohibited from intentionally intercepting an employee's electronic communications *unless* the monitoring is done for a legitimate business purpose, such as customer service or for maintenance or repair. That "legitimate business purpose" exemption gives employers wide latitude to monitor employee activities that might interfere with organizational productivity or might violate equal opportunity laws. This exemption even applies to e-mail the employee sends from home, if the employee is using company-owned equipment or software.[46] As a result of these unambiguous rulings, employees cannot expect privacy in their electronic communications at work—even if the company assures them of that right. In one well-publicized case, Pillsbury had assured employees that their e-mail was private. But when Pillsbury management intercepted an e-mail from an employee to his supervisor blasting company managers and threatening to "kill the back-stabbing bastards," the employee was fired. The employee claimed that he had been wrongfully terminated and tried to sue Pillsbury, but the court threw out the case.[47]

What's the bottom line? As an employer, you are within your rights if you choose to monitor employees' electronic activities and take disciplinary action in response to inappropriate use of e-mail or the Internet. You probably aren't even required to warn employees that they are being monitored.

Only one state (Connecticut) requires employers to tell employees that their electronic activities are being monitored.[48]

However, before you start surreptitiously monitoring your employees' electronic activity, consider the consequences. Secretly monitoring employees' communications may help you to identify a few bad apples who are misusing company resources, but at the same time it can create a sense of distrust and betrayal when employees learn that management has been "spying" on them. A better approach is to make electronic monitoring part of a larger effort to educate employees about appropriate Internet use and the consequences of misuse. Start with a clear organizational policy outlining what use of e-mail and the Internet is and is not permitted. Your employees may be confused about what is acceptable behavior and what isn't. Is informal networking with peers at other companies categorized as personal or professional? Is the occasional message to a friend or family member OK or strictly forbidden? Where does your company draw the line? DHL Systems, for example, established a company policy on e-mail that clearly indicates that e-mail is not to be used for any discriminatory or harassing messages, while giving employees the green light on using e-mail for occasional nonbusiness use.[49] Similarly, Boeing's policy specifically allows employees to use faxes, e-mail, and the Internet for personal reasons—as long as the employee's usage is of reasonable duration and frequency and doesn't cause embarrassment to the company.[50]

Then make sure that employees are aware of your company's policy— and remind them of the policy on a regular basis. Xerox, for example, flashes a message on the screen every time employees log on, telling employees not to use the Web for anything but work.[51] Before BellSouth employees can log on to their computers, they must click "OK" to acknowledge a message warning them against the misuse of e-mail and the Internet.[52] These warnings are consistent with the Hot Stove Rule, because they remind employees about company policy regarding Internet usage. Research suggests that warning employees that their behavior is being monitored is one of the most powerful ways to influence the perceived fairness of these systems.[53]

Employee Behavior Outside the Workplace

So far, we've focused on issues related to disciplining employees for behavior in the workplace. But, what about behavior that takes place at home or other nonworkplace locations? Some employers argue that their employees' off-the-job behavior (such as smoking, drinking alcohol, or engaging in extreme sports) can affect on-the-job outcomes. Even if these behaviors are legal, they can result in lost workdays, lower productivity, and higher health insurance costs. To control these costs, some companies will only hire applicants who agree to avoid these behaviors off-the-job—and discipline employees who violate the policy once hired. Most company policies focus on off-duty smoking behavior. Turner Broadcasting will not hire smokers and regularly monitors employees for compliance. St. Cloud, Florida, requires applicants for city jobs to swear they've been tobacco-free for a year. New hires can't smoke or dip, and they can be tested to make sure they're not cheating.[54] The acceptability of disciplining employees for legal behavior outside the workplace depends very much on the state in which you operate. Some states limit the employer's right to base employment decisions on legal behavior that occurs outside the workplace. More than 20 states have passed laws that protect smokers, and a few have laws that protect any legal activity.[55] However, even when these disciplinary actions are legal, monitoring employee behavior outside the workplace can be difficult to do, and may be viewed as an invasion of privacy.

TALKING WITH EMPLOYEES ABOUT DISCIPLINARY ISSUES

Until this point, we've discussed the overall structure of discipline in organizations: Developing the disciplinary system, designing a grievance procedure, deciding on what will be a disciplinable offense. But disciplining employees is not an arm's-length activity. One of the hardest parts is directly talking with employees about their problematic behavior.

Disciplinary discussions should take place as soon as possible after the infraction occurs—remember the Hot Stove Rule! One of the most common mistakes that managers make is delaying disciplinary discussions. Act quickly. It's much better to clarify (and solve) the problem before it gets completely out of hand.

Let's assume that this is the first time you've had to discipline an employee about a particular offense. During this first discussion, you want to clearly describe the infraction and why it is unacceptable (a violation of company policy). Be specific and behavioral, so the employee understands exactly what behavior needs to change: "John, you arrived late for work this morning. We expect all employees to start work at 8AM." "Jennifer, it's a safety requirement that all employees wear hard hats in the construction area. You were in that area without your hard hat." Don't assume that the employee is already aware of the misconduct. The employee may have chosen to ignore the organizational policy about work hours or safety equipment—but it's also possible that the employee is completely unaware of, or misinterpreting, the policy.

During this first discussion, you should set a deadline for corrective action and be clear about what correction means. Jennifer should immediately start wearing her hard hat, and John should arrive on time tomorrow. But other infractions may require a longer time period before improvement can be observed.[56] Emphasize that it's the employee's responsibility to correct the problem, but this doesn't mean you can't express your willingness to help. Jennifer may not be wearing her hard hat because she was unable to find one that fit properly, which suggests that the organization needs to do a better job of making safety equipment available.

Be sure that you keep a record of this discussion. Make a note of the employee's name, the date, and time of the discussion. If handled well, this one discussion may put an end to the issue. However, if the problematic behavior does continue, you'll need to document that the earlier steps in a progressive or positive sequence have been followed according to your company's discipline policy. Don't skip any steps.[57]

If this isn't the first time you've disciplined an employee for the same offense, you'll want to remind the employee of the previous times this issue has been addressed. Make sure that the employee understands the company disciplinary policy—and what will happen if the behavior continues.

Don't be surprised if employees become emotional or defensive during disciplinary meetings. Even when your goal of improving behavior is completely well-intentioned, being disciplined can be uncomfortable and unpleasant for the employee. There is one important thing to know: Employees may ask if someone (a coworker) can accompany them to a disciplinary meeting. The National Labor Relations Board has historically recognized that unionized workers have the right to representation during disciplinary meetings, and later court decisions have extended the same right to nonunion employees.[58] There is no obligation to suggest to an employee that he or she be accompanied by a coworker. However, if the employee makes the request, you should allow him or her to find a colleague to be present before continuing a discussion.[59]

Manager's Checkpoint

The following questions might help you to prepare for a disciplinary discussion:

- Have I identified the specific company rules and policies that the employee's behavior violated? Am I prepared to explain the impact that the employee's behavior has on the workplace, including effects on coworkers or customers?
- Have I reviewed the company's policy on discipline, so that I know the appropriate action to take with respect to the offense?

- Have I reviewed the employee's file to learn about previous disciplinary actions?
- Am I prepared to describe the problem in behavioral terms, without making any personal attributions about the employee's character?

WHAT'S NEXT?

The last step in a progressive discipline or a positive discipline sequence is termination. In the next chapter, we'll discuss what managers need to know before terminating an employee for either disciplinary or nondisciplinary reasons.

FOR FURTHER READING

Falcone, P. (1999, November). Adopt a formal approach to progressive discipline. *HRMagazine*, 55–59.

Fowler, A. (1996, November 21). How to conduct a disciplinary interview. *People Management*, 40–42.

Grote, D. (2001, September/October). Discipline without punishment. *Across the Board*, 52–57.

McCabe, D. M., & Rabil, J. M. (2002). Administering the employment relationship: The ethics of conflict resolution in relation to justice in the workplace. *Journal of Business Ethics, 36*, 33–48.

MANAGER'S KNOT 9.1

"My organization has a very strict attendance policy. If employees are sick, they are required to call in first thing in the morning to explain their absence. If employees are taking vacation, they are required to request the time off at least a week in advance. I have one employee who has been violating this policy on a regular basis—he'll call in midday and explain that 'something has come up' and he needs to take a personal day. The problem is, he's my star performer. How can I address this problem without demotivating him?"

Remember the Hot Stove Rule—disciplinary action should be consistent and fair, without regard for the personal characteristics of the employee. Bending the rules for this employee sends a message to his coworkers that absences are tolerated for some but not others. But a disciplinary discussion doesn't have to be demotivating. Schedule a discussion with this star performer. Make sure that he knows the policy, and understands the effect that his behavior is having on the workplace. Your behavior can set the tone for a positive discussion.

MANAGER'S KNOT 9.2

"I supervise a group of customer service employees. One employee has lately been bringing less than her full potential to work. She hasn't done anything that directly violates any company rules, but she's been a bit short with customers. I don't think her behavior is severe enough to prompt disciplinary action—and yet I fear that leaving this behavior unchecked could cause problems down the road."

Managers are frequently faced with this kind of problem. Often employee behavior falls into an ambiguous gray area—the behavior doesn't violate any explicit company rules, but nonetheless the behavior is problematic. Rather than treating this as a disciplinary problem, it might be better handled as part of the performance management process. Clarify for the employee your expectations about interacting with customers, and explain that these expectations are part of what you consider to be "good performance." If her behavior fails to improve, you can later take disciplinary action in response to her failure to meet performance standards, knowing that you made every effort to make sure that the employee had knowledge of those standards.

MANAGER'S KNOT 9.3

"Recently I've had a lot of problems with employees calling in sick on Monday morning. I suspect that they are partying too hard on the weekends. Is it time for me to start a drug testing program?"

Before taking such a dramatic step, stop and take a closer look at the problem. First, what is your company's policy on absences due to illness? When organizations have strict use-it-or-lose it policies, employees sometimes respond very rationally by using their full allotment. Are there incentives in the system for employees to avoid taking sick days (e.g., the opportunity to convert unused sick leave into vacation time, or the opportunity to carry unused sick leave into the following year)? Sometimes disciplinary problems are actually problems with the management system in disguise. Second, why do you think that the attendance problem is related to drug use? Have you observed other evidence of employee drug use (e.g., erratic behavior, increased accidents)? If the problem is limited to Monday morning attendance, look at other causes before turning to drug testing. However, if you continue to believe that your attendance problems are associated with drug use, carefully review your state's law on drug testing and get professional help (from lawyers and human resource professionals) in designing the program.

ENDNOTES

1. Falcone, P. (1998, November). Adopt a formal approach to progressive discipline. *HRMagazine*, 55–59.
2. Falcone, P. (1998, November). Adopt a formal approach to progressive discipline. *HRMagazine*, 55–59.
3. Baskin, M. (1999, March). Avoiding legal pitfalls in the disciplinary process. *Association Management*, 81.
4. Falcone, P. (1998, November). Adopt a formal approach to progressive discipline. *HRMagazine*, 55–59; Atwater, L. E., Waldman, D. A., Carey, J. A., & Cartier, P. (2001). Recipient and observer reactions to discipline: Are managers experiencing wishful thinking? *Journal of Organizational Behavior, 22*, 249–270.
5. Sunoo, B. P. (1996, August). Positive discipline—Sending the right or wrong message? *Personnel Journal*, 109–110.
6. Sunoo, B. P. (1996, August). Positive discipline—Sending the right or wrong message? *Personnel Journal*, 109–110.
7. Campbell, D. N., Fleming, R. L., & Grote, R. C. (1985, July/August). Discipline without punishment—at last. *Harvard Business Review*, 162–178.
8. Grote, D. (2001, September/October). Discipline without punishment. *Across the Board*, 52–57.
9. Seeley, R. S. (1992, July). Corporate due process. *HRMagazine*, 46–49.
10. Dubecki, L. (2002, July 17). Australia Post workers decorate desks to support colleague. *The Age*, 7.
11. Carlton, J. (2001, September 18). Despite reversal of no-flag policy, NCCI faces an angry public. *Wall Street Journal*, p. A12.
12. Fields-Meyer, T., & Sweeney, W. (1998, May 18). McHoffa. *People Weekly*, 137.
13. Caudron, S. (1997, May). Blow the whistle on employee disputes. *Workforce*, 50–57.
14. Seeley, R. S. (1992, July). Corporate due process. *HRMagazine*, 46–49.
15. Jacobs, M. A. (1998, January 20). Red Lobster tale: Peers decide fired waitress's fate. *Wall Street Journal*, pp. B11, B16.
16. Maher, K. (2002, March 12). Budding career. *Wall Street Journal*, p. B10.
17. Meece, M. (2000, September 6). The very model of conciliation. *New York Times*, p. C1.
18. Caudron, S. (1997, May). Blow the whistle on employee disputes. *Workforce*, 50–57.
19. Bohlander, G. W., & White, H. (1988). Building bridges: Nonunion employee grievance systems. *Personnel, 65*, 62–66.
20. Caudron, S. (1997, May). Blow the whistle on employee disputes. *Workforce*, 50–57; McCabe, D. M. (1990). Corporate nonunion grievance procedures: Open door policies—a procedural analysis. *Labor Law Journal, 41*, 551–557.
21. McCabe, D. M., & Rabil, J. M. (2002). Administering the employment relationship: The ethics of conflict resolution in relation to justice in the workplace. *Journal of Business Ethics, 36*, 33–48.
22. Wittenberg, C., Mackenzie, S., Shaw, M., & Ross D. (1997, September). And justice for all. *HRMagazine*, 131–137.

23. Caudron, S. (1997, May). Blow the whistle on employee disputes. *Workforce*, 50–57.
24. Hirschman, C. (2001, July). Order in the hearing! *HRMagazine*, 58–64.
25. *Circuit City Stores v. Adams*. (2001). U.S. No. 99-1379.
26. Hirschman, C. (2001, July). Order in the hearing! *HRMagazine*, 58–64.
27. Caudron, S. (1997, May). Blow the whistle on employee disputes. *Workforce*, 50–57.
28. Shapiro, D. L., & Brett, J. M. (1993). Comparing three processes underlying judgments of procedural justice: A field study of mediation and arbitration. *Journal of Personality and Social Psychology, 65*, 1167–1177; Conlon, D. E. (1993). Some tests of the self-interest and group-value models of procedural justice: Evidence from an organizational appeal procedure. *Academy of Management Journal, 36*, 1109–1124.
29. Shapiro, D. L., & Brett, J. M. (1993). Comparing three processes underlying judgments of procedural justice: A field study of mediation and arbitration. *Journal of Personality and Social Psychology, 65*, 1167–1177; Blancero, D., & Dyer, L. (1996). Due process for non-union employees: The influence of system characteristics on fairness perceptions. *Human Resource Management, 35*, 343–359.
30. Bahls, J. E. (1998, February). Drugs in the workplace. *HRMagazine*, 81–87.
31. Ferraro, E. F. (2000, January). Is drug testing good policy? *Security Management*, 165–166.
32. Armour, S. (2001, July 16). Accused workers challenge drug-test results in court. *USA Today*, p. 1B.
33. Work week. (1996, April 30). *Wall Street Journal*, p. A1.
34. Overman, S. (1999, August). Splitting hairs. *HRMagazine*, 42–48.
35. Curry, S. R. (1997, June 23). The brave new world of drug testing. *Fortune*, 163.
36. Flynn, G. (1999, January). How to prescribe drug testing. *Workforce*, 107–109.
37. Flynn, G. (1999, January). How to prescribe drug testing. *Workforce*, 107–109.
38. Maltby, L. L. (1990). Put performance to the test. *Personnel, 67*(7), 30–31.
39. Vaugh, S. (2001, June 3). Career challenge: Firms looking closer at costs of addiction. *Los Angeles Times*, p. W1.
40. Cohen, A. (2001, Summer). Worker watchers. *Fortune/CNET Technology Review*, 70–80.
41. Bosses spy on their employees more often than many think. (1997, May 23). *Chicago Tribune*, sect. 3, p. 2; Armstrong, L. (2000, July 10). Someone to watch over you. *Business Week*, 189–190; Carrns, A. (2000, February 4). Prying times. *Wall Street Journal*, pp. A1, A8.
42. McCarthy, M. J. (1999, October 21). Now the boss knows where you're clicking. *Wall Street Journal*, pp. B1, B4.
43. Work week. (2001, April 17). *Wall Street Journal*, p. A1.
44. Guernsey, L. (1999, December 16). The web: New ticket to a pink slip. *New York Times*, p. G1; Armstrong, L. (2000, July 10). Someone to watch over you. *Business Week*, 189–190
45. Wingfield, N. (1999, December 2). More companies monitor employees' e-mail. *Wall Street Journal*, p. B8; GM suspends porn surfers. (2000, December 20). *Toronto Star*, p. A4.
46. Guernsey, L. (1999, December 16). The web: New ticket to a pink slip. *New York Times*, p. G1.
47. Brown, E. (1997, February 3). The myth of e-mail privacy. *Fortune*, 66.
48. Husted, B. (2001, July 22). Surf the net at work if you will—but your boss may be watching. *Atlanta Journal and Constitution*, p. 1P.

49. Greengard, S. (1996, May). Privacy: Entitlement or illusion? *Personnel Journal*, 74–88.
50. McCarthy, M. J. (1999, October 21). Virtual morality: A new workplace quandary. *Wall Street Journal*, pp. B1, B4.
51. Guernsey, L. (1999, December 16). The web: New ticket to a pink slip. *New York Times*, p. G1.
52. McCarthy, M. J. (1999, October 21). Virtual morality: A new workplace quandary. *Wall Street Journal*, pp. B1, B4.
53. Ambrose, M. L., & Alder, G. S. (2000). Designing, implementing, and utilizing computerized performance monitoring: Enhancing organizational justice. *Research in Personnel and Human Resources Management, 18*, 187–219; Hovorka-Mead, A. D., Ross, W. H. Jr., Whipple, T., & Renchin, M. B. (2002). Watching the detectives: Seasonal student employee reactions to electronic monitoring with and without advance notice. *Personnel Psychology, 55*, 329–362.
54. Tse, K., & Foust, D. (2002, April 15). At risk from smoking: Your job. *BusinessWeek*, 12.
55. Hirschman, C. (2003, February). Off duty, out of work. *HRMagazine*, 51–56.
56. Ramsey, R. D. (1998, February). Guidelines for the progressive discipline of employees. *Supervision*, 10–12.
57. Fowler, A. (1996, November 21). How to conduct a disciplinary interview. *People Management*, 40–42.
58. Work week. (2001, November 20). *Wall Street Journal*, p. A1; Roberts, V. (2001, December). Court upholds extending Weingarten rights to nonunion workers. *HR News*, 13.
59. Redeker, J. R. (1989). *Employee discipline: Policies and practices*. Washington, DC: Bureau of National Affairs.

10

Ending the Employment Relationship

Now it's time to shift our attention to the end of the employment relationship. How you say goodbye can have a huge impact on how you feel about yourself as a manager, how the terminated employee feels about the organization he or she is leaving, and how the employee's coworkers feel about remaining employed by the organization. When terminations are inevitable, how can they be conducted in ways that minimize negative aftereffects? In this chapter, I'll describe some legal issues associated with employee terminations, so you're clear about how to conduct terminations that are legally enforceable. But conducting terminations the right way is not just about staying inside the law. I'll talk about extra steps that some organizations take in downsizing situations. These steps are not legally required, but they can help ease the burdens of the employees who are let go. I'll also tell you how to prepare for the termination interview, in which you tell employees that the relationship is over.

EMPLOYMENT AT WILL

Go out to any city street and start interviewing men and women. Ask them this question: "When can an employee lose his or her job?" Chances are you'll hear two types of answers. First, people generally understand that employees can lose their jobs because of poor performance—a failure to meet company standards for the job, or a failure to follow company rules. This kind of termination is one that occurs *"for just cause."* Second, people also recognize that companies sometimes experience financial difficulties that result in downsizing the workforce. In downsizing terminations, people get fired so the company can save money, even if the individual employees have been performing well. Those are two good reasons why people lose jobs.

What the person on the street doesn't always recognize is that an organization doesn't generally need a *good* reason to fire an employee.[1] In fact, the prevailing philosophy in the United States is that an employer has the right to end an employment relationship at any time, with no notice, for *no* reason at all. This principle is called *employment at will.* Employment at will is created whenever there is no specification about how long an employment relationship will last. Less than 15% of the U.S. workforce is covered by union contracts that specify the length of an employment relationship, how the relationship can be severed, and how the relationship can be extended. Another 10%–15% of the U.S. workforce is employed with individual contracts that specify similar elements. That leaves about 70%–75% of the workforce who are *employed at will*, meaning that the relationship can be terminated at any time by either party.[2]

Employment at will is a common law doctrine—that means it's a legal principle that has evolved over time through common usage. Advocates of employment at will believe that this principle balances the power distribution between the employer and employee. An employee working without a written contract is free to terminate the relationship and move to another employer at any time. (As an employee, you might reasonably question the extent of this "freedom." An employee's options may be limited by family obligations or economic conditions, for example.) Businesses successfully argued that employers ought to have similar rights. If an employee is employed "at will," they can be fired on a moment's notice for any legitimate business reason—or for no reason at all.[3] Employment at will is recognized by all U.S. states except for Montana. In Montana, employees can *only* be fired for just cause (e.g., poor performance, violation of company rules).[4] In the remaining states, as long as the termination does not violate other laws (e.g., federal laws prohibiting discrimination), the employer can end the employment relationship without just cause.

Many students who graduated in spring 2001 learned about employment at will the hard way. As the U.S. economy shifted from boom to something closer to bust, many companies reassessed their hiring needs. Companies that had hired college seniors and MBA students in January

2001 (scheduled to start after May 2001 graduations) reneged on the offers a few months later. Because the new hires were employed at will with no contract specifying length of employment, they could be fired at any time—even before they started work! This action was perfectly legal, but it wasn't very popular with the students who thought that they had a job locked in after graduation. To make amends, some companies offered "apology" or "reverse hiring" bonuses (see Box 10.1)—essentially paying the students to stay away.[5]

BOX 10.1

Fired Before You Start!!![6]

The company	What they offered
Cisco Systems	90 days pay, plus outplacement services
Intel	Signing bonus plus two months pay
Nortel Networks	Bonuses in excess of $1,000
Dell Computer	One month's pay; expense reimbursement to interns

---

Most U.S. states, while accepting the general principle of employment at will, also recognize certain exceptions to the principle. These exceptions define situations in which employees *cannot* be terminated at the will of the employer. If an employee is terminated in these situations, the termination constitutes a *wrongful discharge* and the employee can bring a suit against the employer. Wrongful discharge suits are very expensive for employers. It costs the average employer approximately $80,000 to mount a legal defense in a wrongful discharge suit—and that's if the employer wins![7]

The exceptions to employment at will are defined at the state level, so they vary a bit from state to state. However, most states recognize some form of these three exceptions to employment at will: violation of public policy, implied contract, and implied covenant of good faith.

Violation of Public Policy

The first exception to employment at will applies to situations in which employees are terminated when they are trying to do something for the public good. It's in the public's interest that citizens serve on a jury when called, so a clerical employee should not be terminated if she is absent from work due to jury duty. It's in the public's interest that employees report employers who engage in unsafe practices, so a doctor should not be terminated if he refuses to approve for human testing a drug that he believes is dangerous. In these examples, the employee's behavior is motivated by an urge to assist the public—terminating an employee in these circumstances would constitute a wrongful discharge.

A wrongful discharge case involving PeopleSoft received a great deal of attention in the business press. The employee bringing the suit had discovered that PeopleSoft was terminating and losing minority employees at approximately three times the rate it was reporting these numbers to the federal government. The employee's suit alleged that she was terminated after bringing this discrepancy to management's attention, because the actual figures would have threatened contracts that PeopleSoft had with the federal government. See how the exception works? It's in the public interest that employees report situations in which employers do not comply with federal regulations. So an employee should not be terminated if she "blows the whistle" on an employer who is not in compliance. In this case, a jury awarded the employee more than $5 million, which is one of the largest whistle-blowing awards seen so far.[8]

Implied Contract

A second exception to employment at will occurs when employees have an *implied contract* with their employer. In these cases, there is no formal written contract, but the employer has nonetheless made promises about the conditions under which employment would be terminated. An employee alleging wrongful discharge might present two types of evidence of an implied contract. First, the employee might argue that agents of the company (e.g., recruiters, supervisors) made verbal promises about the conditions under which employment would be terminated. For example, if a recruiter promised "as long as you perform, you'll always have a job with us," that verbal statement might be construed as a promise that employees will only be terminated for just cause.[9] Second, the employee might present written documents such as employee handbooks. The description of disciplinary procedures in employee handbooks has, in some cases, been interpreted as suggesting that employees could only be fired after some form of "due process" or "progressive discipline" was followed (remember the discussion in the previous chapter about progressive discipline?).[10] To avoid this interpretation, many organizations now explicitly state in their employee handbooks and other employment documents that they are an "at will" employer, and the provision of progressive discipline does not change that status.[11]

Implied Covenant of Good Faith

The third exception to employment at will covers situations in which employers were found to act in bad faith. If an employer appears to have acted with malice, and deliberately planned the timing of a termination to ensure that the employee cannot collect a bonus or other benefits, the termination might constitute a wrongful discharge. In one of the early cases establishing this exception, an employee had been promised a two-part bonus. The employee collected the first part of the bonus when he made a sale, and the second part was to be collected when delivery was made to the customer. Firing the employee before the delivery date constituted a violation of the employee's expectation that the employer would act in good faith.[12] More recently, some former employees have sued dot-coms for wrongful discharge, claiming they were fired so the company could avoid issuing stock options or prevent employees from exercising or cashing in the options. In other words, they are accusing the dot-coms of acting in bad faith.[13]

Manager's Checkpoint

Use the following questions to decide whether an employee can be terminated at will:

- Did the employee know that he or she was employed at will? (You may want to include this information in offer letters and reinforce the message in other written documentation.)
- Has the employee been engaged in any activities that might be interpreted as acting in the public's interest? (Look for situations in which the employee has engaged in civic duties or whistle-blowing efforts. Terminations in these situations might be construed as public policy violations.)
- Has anyone in the organization made any verbal or written promises to the employee? Is there any language in the employee's offer letter or employee handbook that limits the employer's ability to terminate at will? (Verbal or written promises made by organizational representatives, or communicated in organizational documents, might be construed as an implied contract.)
- Will the termination limit the employee's access to bonuses or benefits to which he or she is otherwise entitled? (Terminations in these situations might be construed as violations of an implied covenant of good faith.)

TERMINATIONS IN A DOWNSIZING CONTEXT

Terminating an employee is never fun, but some situations are easier than others. If an employee isn't performing well, or isn't able to follow organizational policies, then terminating the relationship may be the best decision for both the employee and the organization. Carrying an unproductive employee, or continually monitoring and disciplining infractions, saps the strength of the overall organization; everyone may breathe a collective sigh of relief when the employee is gone. The situation is different for managers terminating employees in a downsizing context. In downsizing situations, you may need to terminate employees who have been good performers, or who have been loyal to the organization for a long time. Unfortunately, there's a very good chance that you'll be involved in a downsizing situation at least once during your managerial career. Today's organizations are diligently monitoring costs, and acting quickly before rising costs get out of hand, so layoffs are occurring even during good economic periods.

However, downsizing is a very risky business. Cut too few employees and you'll see little effect on bottom-line savings. Cut too deeply and you'll find yourself in a hiring binge when the economy improves.[14] If the downsizing process isn't handled correctly, valued employees may jump ship. And the entire process will be watched closely by the downsizing "survivors"—the people who escaped the downsizing axe (at least this time). Research suggests that the post-downsizing morale of these survivors is very much affected by how the terminated employees are treated during the downsizing effort.[15] It's important that survivors feel that the downsizing effort was fairly managed, because the future success of the company depends on their motivation and good will. The amount of work after a downsizing effort is likely to remain the same, but the survivors are asked to put in longer hours and shoulder much of the work that used to be performed by their former coworkers.[16]

Downsizing aftershocks may last years after the actual terminations are made, so the decision to downsize can't be made lightly. Before deciding to terminate any employees, consider whether alternative cost-cutting methods will do the job instead. Organizations usually investigate a variety of strategies such as reduced overtime, shortened work weeks, salary reductions, and other forms of belt tightening before terminating employees (see Box 10.2 for some examples of organizational cost cutting).

This chapter's focus, however, is on terminations. Let's assume that the decision has been made: The company is going to downsize. There are two important issues to consider. First, what criteria will be used to make these termination decisions? And second, what can the organization do to ease the pain of the employees who are being terminated?

BOX 10.2

Cost-Cutting Alternatives

✗ Cutting back on perks: At Maurice Villency Inc., a New York luxury goods and furniture company, employees gave up free baseball tickets, food during meetings, and free coffee cups.[17]

✗ Cutting back on travel costs: Telecommunications-equipment maker Lucent Technologies Inc. asked employees to stay in budget hotels and fly coach on all but very lengthy business trips.[18]

✗ Pay cuts: Agilent, a high-tech spin-off from Hewlett-Packard, cut pay 10% for all employees, from the CEO down.[19]

✗ Reduced work weeks: Discount brokerage firm Charles Schwab Corp. asked 26,000 employees to take three Fridays off in one calendar month to help cut pay costs.[20]

✗ Involuntary vacations: The Chicago consulting firm DiamondCluster International furloughed 200 workers for 6 months with partial pay and mandated 2 weeks of unpaid vacation for everyone else.[21]

✗ Employee attrition: Intel Corp., facing a steep slowdown in demand for its computer chips, chose to fill only critical positions such as engineers and technical workers when workers left—leaving other positions vacant.[22]

✗ Employee buyouts: Procter & Gamble asked for volunteers from its nonmanufacturing workforce to take advantage of a buyout package. Employees who took the buyout were eligible for benefits including severance pay, health care, outplacement assistance, and retraining reimbursement, depending on how long they were with P&G.[23]

Termination Criteria

The first challenge for organizations in a downsizing effort is to decide on the criteria to identify which employees will be terminated. Organizations have considerable flexibility in selecting downsizing criteria, so long as the criteria do not have an adverse impact on members of a particular group (remember the discussion of adverse impact in chap. 2?).[24] Historically, organizations have usually based downsizing decisions on seniority, so the most recently hired are the first employees to go. This can be seen as fair in many situations, but it can be problematic for the organization if those recent hires have cutting-edge skills that the company needs in the future. As a result, there has been a shift away from seniority as the sole criterion to a new emphasis on performance and skills.[25]

Organizations who base downsizing decisions on employee performance use the employees' performance appraisal history as a basis for terminations.[26] This strategy can ensure that the employees who leave are those who contribute the least to the organization. Unfortunately, many organizational performance appraisal systems are not up to this task (see the discussion of performance appraisal in chap. 6). If your performance appraisal system was designed to identify which employees were eligible for bonuses or promotions, you may find that the system is able to make finer distinctions at the top end of the workforce than at the bottom. Employees may also see this as an attempt by management to repackage downsizing decisions as terminations with just cause—companies generally do not offer severance pay or other benefits if they base the downsizing decisions on performance appraisals.[27]

When organizations use skills as the criteria for terminations, the emphasis is more on future potential than on past performance. The terminations are likely to be accompanied by a major restructuring of the remaining work, so the critical question is whether employees possess the skills needed to perform the post-downsizing jobs. Organizations that adopt this strategy subject individual employees to thorough competency assessments. These competency assessments frequently include not only technical skills, but also leadership and teamwork skills.[28]

Easing the Pain

The law places very few burdens on the manager in termination situations. In most cases (I'll tell you about one major exception a little later), the only legal requirement is that companies pay terminated employees for the work they completed up to the time of termination—that's it! When an employee is being terminated for performance or disciplinary reasons, it makes sense to send them packing. But downsizing situations are different. These may be good performers who are being let go. When employees are terminated to cut costs, organizations often offer severance pay or other benefits that help to ease the employee's transition out of the organization—benefits that are usually not offered to employees who are terminated with just cause.

Advance Notice.   The Worker Adjustment and Retraining Notification Act, more commonly known as the WARN Act, requires that organizations provide advance notice to employees in certain downsizing situations. This is a federal law that went into effect in 1989. If the company has more than 100 employees, and is conducting mass layoffs that will affect 50 or more full-time employees within a 30-day period, the company must give employees being laid off 60 days advance notice. The WARN Act was originally developed for old economy manufacturing situations, but it is increasingly being applied to new economy white-collar downsizing situations.[29] Any firm, regardless of their business, needs to be aware of the WARN Act before initiating large-scale terminations.

Even if advance notice is not legally required, it's something that you want to consider offering your employees. Researchers investigating layoffs report that the more advance notice employees receive, the fairer they see the layoff procedure.[30] Organizations often don't like to give employees advance notice that their jobs are being eliminated. Managers worry that employees will not be productive, and will spend their remaining time job hunting. But keeping downsizing plans under wraps can cause considerable distress if the news leaks out and employees are caught by surprise. Warning employees that layoffs are coming can offer a worthwhile trade-off: you may create some short-run anxiety and lose a few hours of productivity, but give employees time to prepare themselves emotionally and financially.[31]

Some companies have done a great job of giving employees time to adjust to the downsizing news. 3Com, for example, gave their employees the formal 60-day notice required by the WARN Act, but the company also gave employees permission to stay home during that 60-day period and use the time to search for new jobs.[32] DaimlerChrysler AG's U.S. unit used a wide array of internal outlets to communicate details of its plans when it laid off 20% of its work-force over a 3-year period. The big car manufacturer kept employees informed through an internal television network, daily newsletter, and bimonthly magazine.[33]

Severance Benefits.   Severance pay is a continuation of the employee's pay that extends beyond the termination date.[34] It's intended to "tide employees over" until they find steady employment. Paying severance is not required by law. However, so many employers (about 80% of U.S. companies) offer severance pay in downsizing situations that it has come to be expected by employees, especially among those who work for large companies.[35]

The most common formula for calculating severance pay is to offer nonmanagerial employees one week's salary for every year of service to the company; two weeks' salary per year is typical for managerial employees.[36] However, there is some evidence that the severance pay is becoming less generous than in the past: In the first quarter of 2002, discharged managers and executives averaged 8 weeks of severance pay, down 33% from the 12 weeks of severance pay their counterparts received in the first quarter of 2001.[37] More generous severance packages may be appropriate if you expect employees to be unemployed for an extended period. Research suggests that the relation between the amount of severance received and the perceived fairness of a layoff is stronger for terminated employees who remain unemployed for longer periods of time.[38]

Outplacement Services and Educational Benefits.   Long-term employees who are downsized may need considerable coaching and retooling to be competitive in the current labor market. Some of the terminated employees may have worked for you for many years and haven't updated their resumes or tested the employment waters in a long time. Do they know current salaries? Have they considered relocating? Do they know how to negotiate?

Some organizations offer outplacement services and/or educational benefits to help terminated employees find new jobs. Outplacement services might include workshops on successful interviewing, resume preparation advice, and job leads. For example, Motorola hosted a job fair (in conjunction with its outplacement-counseling firm) with more than 40 local employers as a way of helping terminated employees find new opportunities.[39] United Technologies, a manufacturing company, went the education route instead. United Technologies covered tuition and books for terminated workers to pursue courses at any accredited educational institution for one year following their departure.[40] And BankBoston created a Transition Assistance Program for people whose jobs disappeared after its 1996 merger with BayBank. The program offered terminated employees technical assistance and financial support in starting their own businesses, educational grants for job retraining, 3-month paid internships with noncompeting companies, and community-service stipends equivalent to as much as half their salary for work in nonprofit organizations.[41]

Manager's Checkpoint

The following questions might help you to decide whether you should make proactive efforts to ease the transition for downsized employees:

- Is my downsizing situation subject to the advance notification requirement of the WARN Act? (If your downsizing will affect 50 or more employees, you may be required to give employees 60 days notice. If not, you may still want to consider providing as much advance notice as possible to give employees the opportunity to prepare for the transition.)
- What are the norms in my industry? (If employees generally receive severance pay in your industry when companies downsize, employees are likely to expect these benefits.)
- Do I expect the terminated employees to find work quickly? (The longer you expect your terminated employees to remain unemployed, the greater their need for severance pay.)

- What's the average job tenure of the employees I am terminating? What level of skills do they possess? (Employees who have worked for you for a long time, and employees with limited skills, are most in need of outplacement benefits.)

TELLING EMPLOYEES IT'S OVER

There's no shortage of horror stories when it comes to termination. One employee was fired on Take Our Daughters to Work Day—he and his daughter were escorted out of the building.[42] Another employee was ordered to fire his own father, only to be fired himself a few weeks later.[43] And still another employee returned from his 2-week honeymoon to find a FedEx envelope waiting at his home telling him his job had been eliminated days earlier.[44] Are these extreme stories? Absolutely. Are they unusual? Not really.

The quality of treatment an employee receives at termination is the single most important factor determining whether that employee considers filing a wrongful discharge suit against his or her employer—nearly twice as important as *any* other factor, including the quality of treatment the employee received during their organizational tenure.[45] In other words, the way the termination interview is handled is critical. Telling an employee that he or she has been terminated is never going to be easy. However, the news can be communicated in humane ways that preserve the employee's dignity. Many organizations now recognize how important it is that managers know how to give employees the bad news and offer training programs that teach managers how to terminate employees.[46] Before reading on, try answering the following questions:

- *Who* should tell an employee that he or she is being terminated?
- *When* (what day, and what time of day) should an employee be told that he or she is being terminated?
- *Where* should an employee be told that he or she is being terminated?
- *How* should an employee be told that he or she is being terminated?

Who Should Tell?

The answer here is (hopefully) obvious. Terminating employees is part of your job as the supervising manager—it's not something that should be passed to upper management or to the human resource department. If the employee is being terminated for just cause, you have the necessary information about previous problems that led to this step. If the employee is being terminated in a downsizing situation, you should explain the situation to the employee. A third party (e.g., a representative from human resources) may be present, but it's your responsibility to communicate the news.[47]

When Should Employees Be Told?

Most managers postpone telling employees about the termination until Friday at 5 PM. They put it off as long as possible, and then breathe a sigh of relief that the difficult conversation is over and rush home. There's no good time to tell someone they are being let go, but Friday afternoon is the worst option! Place yourself in Karen's shoes. It's Friday afternoon, 5:15 PM, and the boss has just told Karen not to come in on Monday. Karen goes to her usual after work happy hour and complains to her buddies about the callous treatment she's received from her employer. Then she goes home and tells her spouse, who immediately starts worrying aloud about how the next month's bills will be paid. Everywhere she turns, Karen is surrounded by people who are outraged and upset by the company's decision—while she is still coping with her own feelings about the termination. In their efforts to be supportive, Karen's family and friends fan the flames of her anger. She stews about the firing all weekend and Monday morning calls her lawyer to see if she can sue her former employer.

Now consider an alternative scenario: Karen gets fired on Monday at 8:30 AM. None of her family and friends are free until the evening. Karen spends several hours thinking about her life. She's still angry and upset about the firing, but the longer she thinks about it, the more she realizes that the former job wasn't a good fit. She develops a plan to start looking for work in a different industry. In preparation, she buys a newspaper for the classified ads, and makes up a list of employment agencies to visit the next day. By the time she has to explain her situation to family and friends, she's come to grips with the situation and has an action plan in mind. Karen is certainly not happy about being fired, but she is better able to cope with it.[48]

Where Should Employees Be Told?

Most managers call employees into their office to tell them the bad news. That's not always a good idea. Even under the best of circumstances, telling an employee that he or she has been fired is a tremendously emotional experience for everyone involved. Suppose the employee becomes angry and refuses to leave your office? Suppose the employee crumbles and starts to cry? An alternative solution is to have the discussion in a neutral place—a private conference room, for example, or a vacant office. After breaking the news, you can leave the room—giving the employee a few precious moments of privacy to pull himself together before facing his coworkers.[49]

HOW SHOULD EMPLOYEES BE TOLD?

In general, terminations should be communicated face-to-face, one-on-one. This is probably the most important message you will ever have to communicate to an employee. Giving the message face-to-face and one-on-one demonstrates that you appreciate the gravity of the situation and respect the employee enough to commit your personal time to ensuring that the message is accurately communicated.

There are, however, exceptions to this general principle—you need to know your company culture. In some companies, e-mail is consistently used to inform employees of important changes, and in some circumstances, it may be appropriate to use e-mail to tell employees about termination decisions. For example, Amazon.com called an in-person meeting to announce job cuts, but some telecommuters weren't able to attend. To ensure that the telecommuters weren't left out of the communication loop, the news was sent electronically to them once the meeting was underway.[50] Discovery Communications had employees working all over the world. In order to ensure that all employees had the information in the shortest time possible, they let employees know they were being fired by sending an e-mail message—heading off rumors and misinformation.[51] E-mail is no substitute for face-to-face communication, but in some organizational contexts it may be part of the communication process.

Similarly, there may be circumstances in which it is appropriate to terminate employees in a group rather than one-on-one. In some downsizing situations, companies are eliminating entire divisions or units. Conveying the information to the whole group makes it clear that the company is not using downsizing as an excuse to get rid of individual employees. This group level meeting should be followed by a series of meetings with the individual employees who are affected.

The Termination Meeting

How long does it take to tell an employee that he or she has been terminated? Is your answer 30 minutes? 60 minutes? In fact, termination meetings should usually last only 15 minutes or less.[52] There are only three things you need to do during this meeting: Present the fact that the employee no longer has a job, explain why (is it a disciplinary decision? A downsizing situation?), and plan the next step.

That sequence might sound easy, but it isn't. It's harder than you might expect to tell someone that they've been fired. Managers like to soften the blow by using indirect language that can be misinterpreted by the employee:

Manager: Your project is winding down.

Employee: Oh, we're ramping up a new project.

Manager: We no longer need you in Sales.

Employee: Oh, I'm being transferred over to Manufacturing.

Be especially careful of terms like "layoff," which might be interpreted by the employee as a short-term situation in which the employee will be brought back later.[53]

The termination meeting is not the time to discuss performance issues at length. If the termination is a result of disciplinary action, and you've followed your organization's progressive or positive discipline procedures, these issues have been discussed in detail in earlier meetings. Even if the termination comes as a surprise (as it might in a downsizing situation), keep the discussion brief. Just hearing that they've been terminated is going to evoke a strong emotional reaction. It's going to be hard for a terminated employee to process any additional details or information. That's why planning the next step is so important. The employee should leave the termination meeting with a "next step" clearly in mind. This might be meeting with outplacement to plan a job search, or contacting HR to arrange for delivery of a final paycheck. This "next step" provides a clear point of contact with the organization so the employee can ask any questions that haven't yet been addressed.

Manager's Checkpoint

Use the following questions to prepare for the termination meeting:

- Have I identified a suitable place and time to conduct the termination meeting? (Neutral, private locations are best. Give the employee time to come to grips with the news before having to face coworkers or family.)
- Have I outlined what I want to say during the meeting? (Convey the news of the termination, and the reasons for it, clearly and unambiguously. Planning a script and rehearsing what you want to say will help to ensure a smooth accurate delivery.)
- Do I know the "next step?" (The employee should know whom to contact to ask questions or to make additional arrangements.)

WHAT'S NEXT?

We've now worked our way through the entire employment life-cycle—from welcoming employees into the organization to saying good-bye as they leave. But there are a few important issues that we haven't addressed. In the next chapter, we'll revisit equal opportunity law and discuss a manager's responsibilities with respect to sexual harassment in the workplace.

FOR FURTHER READING

Bayer, R. (2000, September/October). Termination with dignity. *Business Horizons*, 4–10.

Falcone, P. (1999, May). A legal dichotomy? *HRMagazine*, 110–120.

Falcone, P. (2001, April). Give employees the (gentle) boot. *HRMagazine*, 121–128.

Stuller, J. U. (1997, January). You'll be hearing from my lawyer. *Across the Board*, 32–38.

MANAGER'S KNOT 10.1

"I have an employee who has repeatedly violated company policy on work hours and absenteeism. I followed my company's progressive discipline policy, and told Lucy that she was being fired. She wasn't surprised—we've talked about her attendance problems on multiple occasions. But Lucy asked if she could resign rather than being fired. Should I let Lucy resign?"

Sometimes managers do allow employees to resign rather than being fired. This option can allow the employee to save face, and avoid having to disclose in future interviews that they were fired. However, the decision to let Lucy resign comes at a cost. It can send an inconsistent message to the rest of the staff, who expected to see Lucy's behavior disciplined in a way consistent with the organizational policy. In general, it's a good idea to follow your organization's policy all the way through to the final step (termination) rather than setting precedents for future exceptions. If you do decide to give Lucy the option of resigning, you should explain what information you will be providing to prospective employers who might call and ask for employment references.

MANAGER'S KNOT 10.2

"I've learned recently that I'm going to need to reduce the size of my workgroup as part of a company-wide downsizing initiative. It's clear to me which employee should go—Richard is clearly my lowest performer,

and he doesn't have the same level of skill as my other employees. Here's my dilemma—I have enough money in the budget to hire Richard back on a part-time, temporary basis. It wouldn't hurt to have an extra pair of hands on some of our bigger projects, and I'm sure Richard would appreciate the income. Good idea or bad?"

Managers often try to "soften the blow" by generating ideas about how to give terminated employees short-term work. But before you decide to rehire Richard on a part-time basis, think about how your offer is likely to be viewed. One concern is that Richard might interpret your gesture as providing hope for the future ("If I do a really good job on this project, maybe she'll hire me back on a full-time basis"). Also, your part-time offer will limit the amount of time that Richard has available to pursue other opportunities and make a more permanent move. In general, it's better for terminations to send a clear, unambiguous message to employees that the relationship is over.

MANAGER'S KNOT 10.3

"My company is going through a major downsizing effort and I'm going to have to tell several of my staff that they are being let go. Headquarters has sent me a script that I'm supposed to use. But I feel false using a script. These are people I've known for years, and it breaks my heart to see them go."

Using a script doesn't have to be false. This is clearly going to be an emotional time for everyone. You owe it to your employees to clearly convey the information they need to move on. Rehearsing a script and role playing the meeting will help you to do that. Using a script doesn't mean that you can't express any emotion or that you can't make minor changes that seem more natural to your own communication style. But the script will ensure that you consistently convey the same information to each of the affected employees—without glossing over any important information, skipping any steps, or providing unnecessary filler. You may find the script to be a great asset during this difficult time.

ENDNOTES

1. Kim, P. T. (1997). Bargaining with imperfect information: A study of worker perceptions of legal protection in an at-will world. *Cornell Law Review, 83*(1), 106–161; Kim, P. T. (1998). An empirical challenge to employment at will. *New Zealand Journal of Industrial Relations, 23*(2), 91–103.
2. Siegel, M. (1998, October 26). Yes, they can fire you. *Fortune*, 301; Dunford, B. B., & Devine, D. J. (1998). Employment at will and employee discharge: A justice perspective on legal action following termination. *Personnel Psychology, 51*, 903–934.
3. Falcone, P. (1999, May). A legal dichotomy? *HRMagazine*, 110–120.
4. Heller, M. (2001, May). A return to at-will employment. *Workforce*, 42–46.

5. Silverman, R. E. (2001, February 27). As the economy slows, job offers get rescinded. *Wall Street Journal*, pp. B1, B14.
6. Goodin, D. (2001, May 4). Graduating students weigh new job incentive: Money to stay away. *Wall Street Journal*, pp. B1, B4.
7. Joel, L. G., III. (1996). *Every employee's guide to the law*. New York: Pantheon.
8. Sandburg, B. (2001, August 17). Hard day for PeopleSoft. *The Recorder*, 1.
9. *Pugh v. See Candies, Inc.* (1981). 116 Cal. App. 3d 311, 171 Cal. Rept. 917.
10. Falcone, P. (1999, May). A legal dichotomy? *HRMagazine*, 110–120; *Toussaint v. Blue Cross & Blue Shield* (1980). 408 Mich. 579, 292 N. W.2d 880.
11. Falcone, P. (1999, May). A legal dichotomy? *HRMagazine*, 110–120.
12. *Fortune v. National Cash Register.* (1977). 373 Mass. 96, 364 N.E.2d 1251.
13. Alexander, K. (2000, November 24). Lost stock options give rise to suits over job termination. *Los Angeles Times*, p. C1.
14. Kuczynski, S. (1999, June). Help! I shrunk the company! *HRMagazine*, 40–45.
15. Brockner, J. (1990). Scope of justice in the workplace: How survivors react to co-worker layoffs. *Journal of Social Issues, 46*, 95–106; Brockner, J., Tyler, T. R., & Cooper-Schneider, R. (1992). The influence of prior commitment to an institution on reactions to perceived unfairness: The higher they are, the harder they fall. *Administrative Science Quarterly, 37*, 241–261; Brockner, J., Konovsky, M., Cooper-Schneider, R., Folger, R., Martin, C., & Bies, R. J. (1994). Interactive effects of procedural justice and outcome negativity on victims and survivors of job loss. *Academy of Management Journal, 37*, 397–409.
16. Hymowitz, C. (2002, October 22). Getting a lean staff to do "ghost work" after layoffs. Retrieved from http://online.wsj.com
17. Dunham, K. J. (2002, March 19). The Jungle. *Wall Street Journal*, p. B4.
18. Lublin, J. S. (2001, January 4). As more companies end little perks, critics call moves petty, pointless. *Wall Street Journal*, pp. B1, B4.
19. Raphael, T. (2001, September). Hold the line on salaries and benefits. *Workforce*, 38–44.
20. Roman, M. (2001, February 12). Schwab: Thank God it's just Friday. *Business Week*, 44.
21. Geller, A. (2001, September 24). Employers push workers to stay home. *Arizona Republic*, pp. D1, D2.
22. Williams, M. (2001, February 21). Intel to trim jobs through attrition and defer raises. *Wall Street Journal*, p. B6.
23. Nelson, E. (2001, June 12). Job-cut buyouts favored by P&G pose problems. *Wall Street Journal*, pp. B1, B10.
24. Connell, D. S. (2001). RIF a la carte: Using reported cases to develop effective reduction-in-force criteria. *Employee Relations Law Journal, 27*(3), 7–47.
25. Armour, S. (2001, March 19). New economy changes how firms face layoffs. *USA Today*, p. B1.
26. Connell, D. S. (2001). RIF a la carte: Using reported cases to develop effective reduction-in-force criteria. *Employee Relations Law Journal, 27*(3), 7–47.
27. Berenson, A. (2001, March 21). Laid off or fired? *International Herald Tribune*, p. 9; Hymowitz, C. (2001, October 30). Firms that get stingy with layoff packages may pay a high price. *Wall Street Journal*, p. B1.
28. Connell, D. S. (2001). RIF a la carte: Using reported cases to develop effective reduction-in-force criteria. *Employee Relations Law Journal, 27*(3), 7–47.
29. Warner, M. (2001, January 22). Pity the poor dot-commer (a little bit). *Fortune*, 40.
30. Brockner, J., Konovsky, M., Cooper-Schneider, R., Folger, R., Martin, C., & Bies, R. J. (1994). Interactive effects of procedural justice and outcome negativity on victims and survivors of job loss. *Academy of Management Journal, 37*, 397–409.

31. Boyle, M. (2001, March 19). The not-so-fine art of the layoff. *Fortune*, 209–210.
32. Murray, M. (2001, March 13). Waiting for the ax to fall. *Wall Street Journal*, pp. B1, B12.
33. Dunham, K. J. (2001, March 13). The kinder, gentler way to lay off employees. *Wall Street Journal*, pp. B1, B10.
34. Fisher, A. (2002, February 18). What does it take to get a man-sized salary? *Fortune*, 148.
35. Work week. (2002, January 8). *Wall Street Journal*, p. A1.
36. Fisher, A. (2002, February 18). What does it take to get a man-sized salary? *Fortune*, 148; Hirschman, C. (2001, April). The kindest cut. *HRMagazine*, 48–53.
37. Managers, executives now commanding only eight-weeks severance pay, on average. (2002, September). *Managing Benefits Plans*, 9.
38. Wanberg, C. R., Bunce, L. W., & Gavin, M. B. (1999). Perceived fairness of layoffs among individuals who have been laid off: A longitudinal study. *Personnel Psychology, 52*, 59–84.
39. Dunham, K. J. (2001, March 13). The kinder, gentler way to lay off employees. *Wall Street Journal*, pp. B1, B10.
40. Sullivan, A. (1999, July 28). Company to offer laid-off workers education benefits *Wall Street Journal*, p. B10.
41. Kanter, R. M. (1997, July 21). Show humanity when you show employees the door. *Wall Street Journal*, p. A22.
42. Daughter there as dad gets fired. (1995, May 6). *Chicago Tribune*, p. 10.
43. Eiben, T. (1996, June 10). Never fire your father. *Fortune*, 66.
44. Lee, J. (2001, February 21). Discarded dreams of dot-com rejects. *New York Times*, p. C1.
45. Lind, E. A., Greenberg, J., Scott, K. S., & Welchans, T. D. (2000). The winding road from employee to complainant: Situational and psychological determinants of wrongful-termination claims. *Administrative Science Quarterly, 45*, 557–590.
46. Dunham, K. J. (2001, March 13). The kinder, gentler way to lay off employees. *Wall Street Journal*, pp. B1, B10.
47. Karl, K. A., & Hancock, B. W. (1999). Expert advice on employment termination practices: How expert is it? *Public Personnel Management, 28*(1), 51–62; Boyle, M. (2001, March 19). The not-so-fine art of the layoff. *Fortune*, 209–210.
48. Jones, D. (1996, February 16). Managers study up for downsizings. *USA Today*, pp. B1, B2; Labich, K. (1996, June 10). How to fire people and still sleep at night. *Fortune*, 65–72.
49. Labich, K. (1996, June 10). How to fire people and still sleep at night. *Fortune*, 65–72.
50. Modern pink slips: E-mail is bad news. (2001, February 26). *USA Today*, p. D3.
51. Dunham, K. J. (2001, March 13). The kinder, gentler way to lay off employees. *Wall Street Journal*, pp. B1, B10.
52. Gerlin, A. (1995, April 26). Seminars teach managers finer points of firing. *Wall Street Journal*, pp. B1, B11.
53. Mamis, R. A. (1995, January). Employees from hell. *Inc.*, 50–57.

V

Day-to-Day Concerns in Human Resource Management

11

Controlling Sexual Harassment in the Workplace

In chapter 2 you learned about Title VII of the Civil Rights Act, one of the most important EEO laws that managers need to know. In this chapter, I'll focus on one particular application of Title VII: sexual harassment. One of your responsibilities as a manager is to ensure that your workplace is free from harassment. I'll review the legal definition of sexual harassment, and I'll summarize what we've learned from recent court cases about how an organization can defend itself against sexual harassment claims. But, in this chapter, I'll go beyond the legal requirements and talk about the proactive steps you can take to create a workplace in which all employees (both men and women) can work without experiencing negative behaviors or consequences due to their sex.

WHY WORRY ABOUT SEXUAL HARASSMENT?

Research documenting the prevalence of harassment in the workplace generates some pretty scary figures. Surveys indicate that anywhere from 40% to 90% of working women have been sexually harassed at work.[1] Why such a wide range? The variation in the reported rates of harassment reflects two differences among sexual harassment surveys. First, there are real differences in sexual harassment rates depending on the organizational context.[2] You might find, for example, that the average female employee reports fewer incidents of sexual harassment in a workplace with relatively equal numbers of men and women, but more incidents in a male-dominated workplace with a culture that has traditionally not supported women. Second, variations in reported rates of harassment sometimes reflect how the researchers asked their questions. Asking people point-blank whether they have experienced sexual harassment tends to elicit fewer affirmative responses then a series of questions about specific on-the-job experiences (e.g., "Are pornographic materials displayed in your workplace?" "Has anyone in your workplace touched you in a way that made you feel uncomfortable?"). We see much higher rates of reported harassment when researchers explicitly ask respondents about nonverbal types of harassment (e.g., sexual graffiti in the workplace) and harassment perpetuated by coworkers.[3]

However, even if the actual rates of sexual harassment are closer to the low end of that range, it's still a problem with serious consequences. People who are targets of sexual harassment at work experience a wide variety of negative symptoms. These symptoms include both psychological reactions (e.g., lowered self-esteem, more depression, higher stress) and physiological ones (e.g., gastrointestinal disturbances, inability to sleep, fatigue, nausea, weight loss).[4] And as you can imagine, a person who is stressed and fatigued is unlikely to be able to perform well on the job—the experience of sexual harassment is also associated with greater absenteeism and lower productivity.[5] Further, these negative reactions kick in at a relatively low threshold. It's not just severe harassment that has detrimental effects. Even relatively mild harassment has been associated with emotional distress, stress-related health problems, and greater susceptibility to physical illness.[6]

Although many women experience sexual harassment on the job, few ever report the problem to officials either inside or outside their company.[7] Most targets of harassment try to avoid the harasser or simply tolerate the situation as best they can. That might surprise you. Why wouldn't someone who is being harassed, and beginning to suffer some of the related consequences such as stress, immediately march into a manager's office and demand that the situation be corrected? Many victims of harassment say that they chose to do nothing because they didn't think the organization would do anything in response to their complaint.[8] They fear retaliation; the harassment might get worse if coworkers learn that they have complained about the mistreatment. It's this reluctance to come forward with complaints that makes sexual harassment such a difficult problem for managers to address. That's why, in this chapter, we'll be focusing on the proactive efforts you can initiate to develop a culture that encourages people to act on sexual harassment as soon as it occurs—so that the problem can be addressed promptly and effectively.

SEXUAL HARASSMENT AS DEFINED BY EEO LAW

You'll remember from chapter 2 that Title VII of the CRA prohibits discrimination based on sex and other personal characteristics. More specifically, Title VII says that it is illegal to "fail or refuse to hire or to discharge any individual" or to discriminate in the "compensation, terms, conditions, or privileges of employment" on the basis of any employee's or applicant's race, color, religion, sex, or national origin. Do you see the words "sexual harassment" anywhere? No, you don't. In fact, you could read the entire text of the CRA and you won't find the term there either.

Sexual harassment has not always been associated with the CRA. In fact, the term "sexual harassment" wasn't even part of the legal vocabulary until the late 1970s.[9] In the very first cases of sexual harassment that made their way into the legal system, judges thought that sexual harassment fell outside the scope of the CRA. Some of these early cases involved very extreme sexual behaviors (including situations where female subordinates were raped by their bosses). While the courts agreed that these were outrageous acts, they didn't think sexual harassment really fell under the umbrella of employee civil rights.

Over time, the courts and the EEOC have concluded that sexual harassment is a *kind* of sex discrimination, because harassment is a condition of employment that is placed on members of one sex but not the other. Both the courts and the EEOC agree that sexual harassment is a violation of Title VII of the CRA, and managers have a responsibility to educate employees about sexual harassment and protect employees from sexual harassment.

Notice that I said "employees" in general, and not just "female employees." You'll remember from chapter 2 that Title VII protects men *and* women from sex discrimination. That protection extends to sexual harassment too. The EEOC receives about 16,000 sexual harassment claims each year,[10] and claims filed by men now account for more than 13% of that number.[11] These claims include men who are harassed by women (remember the harassment experienced by Michael Douglas' character in the movie *Disclosure?*), but also men who are harassed by other men.[12]

This is how the EEOC defined sexual harassment in 1980: "unwelcome sexual advances, requests for sexual favors, and other verbal or physical conduct of a sexual nature."[13] There are several important elements in that definition.

First, notice the emphasis on *unwelcome behaviors*. Title VII does not prohibit *all* sexual behavior in the workplace—only those behaviors that are unwelcome.[14] If a person perceives sexual advances or other sexual behaviors directed toward him or her as "unwelcome," then those behaviors are harassment.[15] It doesn't matter whether the person initiating the behavior didn't mean to be harassing, or was only kidding around—it's still harassment.

This emphasis on the target's perceptions is one of the things that makes sexual harassment difficult to control in organizations. You're a manager, not a mind reader! How are you supposed to know whether or not someone will perceive something as unwelcome? Hold onto that thought—we'll come back to it in a few minutes. But first, look at the problem from the EEOC's perspective. Why would the EEOC choose to include the word "unwelcome" in their definition, rather than other words like "involuntary?" Try a thought experiment: Are there any situations in which you might agree to sexual advances even if you found the advances to be unwelcome? Not a difficult experiment, is it? Suppose the person making the advances is your boss—someone with a great deal of power over your work life. The EEOC wanted to ensure that their definition of sexual harassment would encompass situations in which someone who agreed to an unwelcome sexual advance (making it look like a consensual relationship) would still have legal recourse.

Second, don't be misled by the EEOC's use of the term *sexual* in that 1980 definition. In recent cases, the definition of sexual harassment has been broadened to include a variety of "sex-based harassment," including harassment that doesn't include *any* sexual activity or language, but is directed at employees because of their sex.[16] In one legal case, a supervisor regularly referred to an employee as a "dumb ass woman."[17] No one, not the supervisor, the subordinate, or the judges who heard the case, thought the supervisor intended the phrase "dumb ass woman" as a sexual advance. However, the phrase was a negative term directed only at women, and therefore, it constituted sexual harassment.

Now that you've got a general idea of what constitutes sexual harassment, we need to make an additional distinction. There are two different kinds of sexual harassment: *quid pro quo* harassment and *hostile environment* harassment.

Quid Pro Quo Harassment

We'll start with the easier-to-understand, more straightforward form of sexual harassment, called quid pro quo harassment. Quid pro quo is a Latin phrase meaning, literally, "this for that." It describes harassment situations in which someone asks for sexual favors in exchange for something (e.g., a promotion or a raise). Because this form of sexual harassment assumes that the harasser has something to offer, by definition the harasser is someone in a position of authority who controls important resources (e.g., a manager who makes promotion decisions or a supervisor who decides daily task assignments). Sexual harassment cases of this type are generally not very controversial. If you were to take a poll on any American street corner, most people would agree that you shouldn't have to sleep with the boss to advance in your career.

A person bringing a sexual harassment claim to court (i.e., the plaintiff in a sexual harassment case) would have to demonstrate that his or her work outcomes (e.g., a promotion, raises) were directly associated with the sexual behavior. If a plaintiff can establish that he or she experienced a *tangible loss* (e.g., failed to get promoted or receive a pay raise) as a result of not complying with sexual demands made by a supervisor, then the employer is seen as responsible—regardless of whether the employer knew about the supervisor's conduct![18] In legal terminology, this is called *strict liability*, and it applies whenever a person with organizational authority is the harasser. The supervisor (or other organizational authority) acts on behalf of the employer, so when the supervisor engages in sexual harassment, the law sees the employer as the responsible party.[19] (That's why it's especially important that supervisors receive training on sexual harassment issues. More on this later.)

Hostile Environment Harassment

The other form of harassment is hostile environment harassment. This type of harassment occurs when people in the workplace (e.g., supervisors, coworkers, or customers) act in ways that interfere with a person's work performance or create an intimidating, hostile, or offensive working environment. Were you surprised to see "customers" included in that definition? It's an important point—organizations aren't just responsible for sexual harassment initiated by their own employees. They are also responsible for sexual harassment initiated by customers, clients, or vendors. For example, a Pizza Hut franchise was held liable for $200,000 in compensatory damages plus nearly $40,000 in attorney's fees and costs because it failed to prevent two of its customers from sexually harassing a waitress.[20]

In making a hostile environment harassment claim, the plaintiff would not have to show that the sexual behavior in the workplace had any tangible effects on raises or promotions. Instead, the plaintiff would provide evidence that the work environment was a hostile or offensive one. Here's where things get a little tricky. You're not going to get perfect agreement across people on the exact point at which an environment becomes hostile or offensive. As a result, hostile environment cases tend to be more controversial than quid pro quo cases—one person's hostile environment is another person's horseplay.[21]

People's perceptions of a hostile environment are influenced by lots of personal characteristics, including age, religion, and national origin.[22] However, the most consistent differences in perceptions of a hostile environment are observed between men and women.[23] In general, women seem to be more sensitive to the implications of sexual behavior in the workplace, and are more likely to label sexual behavior as harassment.[24] Here's an example: In a national survey, 75% of men said that they would be flattered by sexual advances in the workplace (15% said they would be offended). But 75% of women said that they would be offended by the same type of advance.[25] It's that mind reader problem again—if everyone has a different idea about what constitutes a hostile environment, how will we ever know what kinds of behavior are OK, and what kinds are not OK?

Once a sexual harassment complaint gets into the legal system, it's up to a U.S. judge to decide whether or not a person has experienced a hostile environment. Box 11.1 lists some of the specific behaviors and events that judges in recent cases have said were part of a hostile environment. Sometimes, when I show managers that list of behaviors, they throw their hands in the air and say "anything can be sexual harassment!" But that's not the case—we all know, and courts recognize, there are some outliers out there. There are some people who are hypersensitive and see sexual harassment at the drop of a hat. Everything *isn't* sexual harassment. Those behaviors in Box 11.1 constitute sexual harassment when they are "sufficiently severe and pervasive that a *reasonable person* would find the environment to be hostile." In some U.S. courts, however, a slightly different standard is applied. Recognizing that men and women often disagree in their interpretations of sexual harassment,[26] some courts use a gender-specific *reasonable woman* perspective in deciding whether a hostile environment is created.[27] In these courts, a hostile environment is created when a female

---

BOX 11.1
A Hostile Environment Might Include:

Sexual comments, jokes, or innuendos

Sexually oriented phone calls, letters, or e-mails

Requests for dates or sexual relations

Comments about an employee's body or physical appearance

Staring at an employee's body parts or making sexual gestures

Physical contact, including unwelcome touching, grabbing, pinching, or rubbing

Requirement that employees wear sexually provocative work uniforms

Pornography and sexual graffiti

plaintiff alleges conduct that a reasonable woman would consider sufficiently severe or pervasive to alter conditions of employment.

What does that reasonable person (or in some courts, the reasonable woman) look for in deciding whether a hostile environment was created? The EEOC suggests that there are a number of important dimensions to consider. First, we need to look at the frequency and severity of the behavior. A reasonable person is unlikely to think that one single sexual joke (even one in very bad taste) created a hostile environment. However, an ongoing pattern of sexual jokes might create a hostile environment, and even one case of serious sexual assault probably creates one. Second, the EEOC suggests that behavior that is physically threatening or humiliating to the employee is likely to cross the line into sexual harassment. If a reasonable person would feel endangered or personally humiliated by the behavior, a hostile environment is created. Finally, the EEOC suggests that behavior that directly interferes with a person's job performance probably constitutes sexual harassment. If people in the work environment engage in hazing behavior (e.g., hiding equipment, or damaging an employee's workspace) that interferes with the person's ability to do his or her job, they are probably creating a hostile environment.

By the way, this idea of a hostile environment is not unique to sexual harassment. Courts recognize the idea of hostile environments in other areas of discrimination (e.g., race, disability, religion) as well.[28] Hostile environment conditions violate Title VII of the CRA because they place conditions on one type of person (e.g., a person of a particular race or religion, or a person with a disability) that are not placed on others. It's the manager's responsibility to ensure that employees do not encounter a hostile environment on the job as a result of any of the personal attributes protected by equal opportunity law.

As I mentioned earlier, employers experience strict liability when supervisors engage in quid pro quo harassment. Strict liability also applies to hostile environment harassment if a supervisor is responsible for creating the hostile environment. However, if the hostile environment is created by other people in the workplace (e.g., coworkers or clients), the organization may be able to mount an *affirmative defense.*[29]

Affirmative Defense in Hostile Environment Cases.   The affirmative defense to hostile environment claims of sexual harassment has two critical steps. The first step is for the employer to show that "reasonable care" was used to prevent and correct sexual harassment behavior. Reasonable care includes, for example, evidence that an antiharassment policy was in place, that all employees were informed of the policy, and that the policy was consistently enforced by the organization.[30] Demonstrating that your organization made efforts to create a harassment-free environment, that you acted promptly in response to complaints, and that harassers have been disciplined for inappropriate behavior, could all operate in your favor if your organization ever has to defend itself against a harassment claim in the courts.

In the second step, the employer would show that the employee claiming harassment unreasonably failed to take advantage of the preventive or corrective opportunities provided by the employer.[31] So, if your organization had an accessible, user-friendly complaint system in place, and your employee failed to use it, that's another point in your favor.

The courts' recognition of the affirmative defense represents a very recent and very dramatic shift in the way judges review sexual harassment cases. In the past, judges have been very supportive when employees bypassed internal complaint systems. Those internal systems were frequently biased and unresponsive, and employees often had little recourse but to complain directly to the EEOC. However, organizations are making greater investments in designing effective internal complaint systems, and courts are increasingly giving organizations credit for their proactive efforts. Best of all, the complaint system that is your strongest defense in court is the same complaint system that will probably keep you out of court in the first place! In the second half of this chapter, I'll explain how you can develop an organizational culture that is most likely to minimize sexual harassment risks. But first let's do a process check and make sure you're comfortable with what we've discussed so far.

Manager's Checkpoint

Now that you've read about Title VII and its application to sexual harassment, use the following questions to make sure you understand how sexual harassment is defined and know what your responsibilities are in controlling sexual harassment:

- What's the difference between quid pro quo and hostile environment sexual harassment? (Quid pro quo harassment involves an exchange of job outcomes for sexual favors; a hostile environment is created by the actions of other people in the workplace, even if these actions have no direct impact on the employee's job outcomes.)
- What does strict liability mean in the context of sexual harassment? (An organization is always responsible for the behavior of its authorities. It is legally liable for quid pro quo or hostile environment harassment initiated by organizational supervisors or managers.)

- What is an affirmative defense in sexual harassment? (An organization may be able to defend itself against some hostile environment claims by demonstrating that it took reasonable care to protect employees from harassment, and that the complaining employee unreasonably did not take advantage of the resources provided by the organization).

DEVELOPING A ZERO TOLERANCE ORGANIZATIONAL CULTURE

The affirmative defense discussed in the first part of this chapter is all about employers defending themselves against sexual harassment complaints. However, many of the recommended components of that defense will also contribute to an organizational culture that minimizes the negative effects of sexual harassment, and eventually reduces the likelihood of complaints. These cultures are frequently described as *zero tolerance* cultures.[32] Zero tolerance means that unacceptable behavior will not be tolerated—under any circumstances.

A zero tolerance culture with respect to sexual harassment includes three critical components: a sexual harassment policy, a system for hearing and investigating complaints, and a sexual harassment awareness training program. We'll discuss each of those components below. You'll also want to review Box 11.2 for examples of specific strategies that organizations are using to create zero tolerance cultures. It's not easy to create a zero tolerance culture; on the contrary, it takes a lot of work. But it can be done. If you need some inspiration, one place to look is the Mitsubishi automotive plant in Normal, Illinois. Yes—Mitsubishi. The same Mitsubishi that gained notoriety because of its abusive treatment of female employees in the 1990s is now a zero tolerance workplace. How did it make the switch? By attending to the same three components we're discussing here. Mitsubishi developed a strongly worded policy on harassment, actively investigated employee complaints (and took disciplinary action when the investigation indicated that the policy had been violated), and trained all employees in discrimination issues—with refresher courses every 2 years.[33]

Sexual Harassment Policy

The first step in developing a zero tolerance organizational culture is adopting a strongly worded sexual harassment policy using plain and simple language that even the least educated employee can understand.[34] The sexual harassment policy should be separate and distinct from other organizational antidiscrimination policies. Effective sexual harassment policies include the following information: definitions of quid pro quo and hostile

---

BOX 11.2

Proactive Efforts to Reduce Sexual Harassment in the Workplace

* When American Home Shield Corporation decided to train its employees in preventing sexual harassment, it faced enormous scheduling difficulties. The difficulties were overcome by introducing an online training course that includes pop-up videos, quizzes and federal harassment law, music, and voiceovers. The company reports that the online training was a cheaper and more time-efficient alternative to traditional classroom training—and with online training, it's easy to track when employees take it. However, online training needs to include periodic tests to ensure that employees understand the material and aren't just clicking their way through the training content.[35]

* At Los Angeles-based Sizzler International, all managers must take a test before sexual harassment training to see where they fall on the sexual harassment knowledge continuum. Then they go through training, which involves a video and a workshop. Afterward, they take a posttest. If they miss 2 out of 14 questions, they must complete the training again. If they again fail the posttest, management considers termination.[36]

* Chemical giant Dupont was one of the first U.S. organizations to sponsor sexual harassment education workshops. In addition to providing ongoing training, Dupont also operates a harassment hotline. Employees can contact the hotline 24 hours a day, 365 days a year, to report harassment concerns.[37]

---

environment harassment, with examples of each type; a description of the procedures for making complaints; and a pledge that complaints will be taken seriously and promptly investigated. It's also a good idea to include in the policy the consequences of policy violations (e.g., discipline and possibly termination). Finally, the policy should make clear that the organization prohibits any employee from retaliating in any way against anyone who has voiced concerns about sexual harassment.

In describing the kinds of behaviors that might violate company policy, the behaviors in Box 11.1 are a good starting point. You'll recall that these behaviors *might* constitute sexual harassment, if a reasonable person found them sufficiently severe or pervasive. However, organizations trying to create a zero tolerance culture often go a step further and explicitly prohibit all of these behaviors in the workplace. One author uses the analogy of the 55 mph speed limit.[38] There are plenty of highways in the United States with speed limits higher than 55 mph, but the driver who sticks with 55 will never get a speeding ticket. In the same way, individual judges and courts might find a certain degree of sexual behavior in the workplace acceptable—but, if your company policy prohibits all sexual behavior and consistently takes action against it, you'll never have to worry about employee behavior crossing the line into illegal sexual harassment. You'll learn about, and be able to correct, problematic behaviors long before they escalate into sexual harassment as defined by the legal system.

Once you've got the written policy, you also need to make sure that the policy is widely available and easily accessible. Many organizational policies get buried in employee handbooks, but you want employees to have direct and immediate access to this one. For example, the policy can be posted conspicuously throughout the organization, including the cafeteria and employee break rooms. It can be distributed with employee paychecks. It can be routinely reviewed in company meetings and training programs. To document that employees are aware of the company policy, many organizations have employees sign an acknowledgment that they have received a copy of the policy and understand it.

The Complaint System

Alongside the policy, you need a system for receiving and investigating employee complaints about sexual harassment. It's especially important for these complaint procedures to provide options to the employee about who can hear their complaint. It is not acceptable to have complaints heard only by the employee's immediate supervisor because the immediate supervisor may be the person engaging in the problematic behavior.[39] Many organizations allow complaints to be heard by human resource management, by affirmative action officers, or by anyone in a management position. Some organizations also ensure that both men and women in the organization can receive complaints. It may be embarrassing or difficult for an employee to discuss a sexual harassment complaint with someone of the opposite sex.[40]

Moreover, the complaint system should not impose any obstacles for a person who believes he or she is being harassed. You want a system that is easy to use. Now, ironically, an accessible complaint system paired with a strongly worded policy against sexual harassment may generate a sharp increase in complaints at first. You have to keep reminding yourself that this is a good thing. You *want* to hear complaints, because you want to handle them before they get into the legal system. When it comes to sexual harassment, no news is *not* good news.

When a complaint is received, it should be quickly investigated. The investigator may or may not be the same person receiving the initial complaint. In fact, many organizations outsource the investigation, and ask an external investigator to interview both the person bringing the complaint and the person who is accused of violating company policy. The choice between an internal and an external investigator is a tough one. On the one hand, an external investigator may be viewed as more neutral and more objective—and, therefore, more fair by both parties. On the other hand, an internal investigation may benefit from the knowledge the investigator has about the organization's structure and culture. The critical thing is that the investigator have sufficient credibility and not be uncomfortable in discussing sensitive topics.

The EEOC has produced a document (available at eeoc.gov) that offers guidance about the questions employers should ask during an investigation of harassment.[41] For example, the guidelines suggest that investigators ask the person bringing the complaint how he or she reacted to the harassment and how he or she would like to see the situation resolved. The investigator should also ask whether there are witnesses to the behavior, or any available documentation. These questions can help the investigator prepare to discuss the incident with the accused. When the investigator meets with the accused party, the investigator will ask for the accused party's response to the allegations, and try to collect additional relevant information.

Most people who complain about harassment just want it to be stopped, and that is the organization's key responsibility—stopping harassment.[42] If the investigation has found that company policy on harassment has been violated, disciplinary action might be required (see chap. 9 on disciplining employees). However, many harassers may not be aware that their behavior was unwelcomed by others. They may genuinely have intended their behavior to be flattering or joking. These individuals are making bad assumptions about what workplace behavior is acceptable, and those assumptions are better corrected through education than through punishment. Whatever choice is made (discipline or education), the remedial action should be taken promptly and be consistent with the severity of the harassment.

Training

The third component of a zero tolerance culture is education and training. All employees should be trained to recognize signs of sexual harassment.[43] Remember that different people will find different types of behavior offensive, so the purpose of the training is to produce a common understanding of what behaviors fall outside of the *organization's* definition of what is acceptable. Effective training can eliminate the "mind reader" problem I referred to earlier in this chapter. If the training describes specific inappropriate behaviors, there's no need to wonder whether or not someone else *might* find them offensive.

Some training should be included in the initial orientation of new employees. This ensures that, from the very beginning of the employment relationship, employees know where the company stands on the issue of sexual harassment.[44] Additional training should be conducted on a regular basis (e.g., annually) to ensure that employees remain familiar with the company's sexual harassment policy. New court rulings are continually clarifying the definition of sexual harassment, and ongoing training is the best way to ensure that this new information is cascading down the organization.

A wide range of videos are available for use in these training programs.[45] Training videos can be an effective way to illustrate the behaviors that illustrate the behaviors that constitute sexual harassment.[46] However, effective training programs supplement the video information with active learning techniques such as small group discussions or role-play techniques.[47] By using a combination of training techniques, you can ensure that employees have benefited from understanding what sexual harassment is, but have also developed behavioral skills for responding to harassment. For example, the training should teach employees how to communicate to a person who is engaging in harassment that his or her behavior is unwelcome.[48] And employees should be very clear on the "next step" (e.g., knowing to whom harassment should be reported) should the inappropriate behavior persist.

The training given to nonmanagement and management employees may be very similar. However, separate training should be conducted for supervisors so that they know how to prevent and/or correct harassment. The supervisor needs to know what to do with the complaints that come forward.[49]

Manager's Checkpoint

The following questions might help you to ensure that you've taken proactive steps to create a zero tolerance culture regarding sexual harassment in your organization:

- Does my organization have a strongly worded policy on sexual harassment that clearly defines sexual harassment? (Make sure that the policy is jargon-free and includes specific examples of both quid pro quo and hostile environment harassment.)
- Are all employees aware of the policy? (The policy should be easily accessible to all employees.)
- Is there a system ready to receive and investigate complaints? Are there any obstacles that would limit an employee's ability to bring a complaint forward? (The best complaint system is one

that provides employees with alternative channels and the opportunity to bypass the usual chain of command.)

- Have employees been trained so that they understand sexual harassment and the organizational policy? (All employees should be trained to recognize sexual harassment and know how to take action against it. But employees with supervisory responsibilities will need additional training to know how to respond to complaints.)

WHAT IF IT'S TRUE LOVE?

With all of this concern about sexual harassment, you may be wondering whether organizational policies are regulating Cupid out of business. Today's employees put in long hours and frequently socialize with their coworkers. Some of those coworkers are likely to fall in love and engage in truly consensual romantic relationships. For example, Bill Gates, the CEO of Microsoft, married a midlevel executive at his own company. And it's not just the managers who are engaging in romantic relationships at work. In a recent poll, 47% of employees said that they had been involved in an office romance.[50] How can organizations distinguish between these consensual relationships and the nonconsensual relationships prohibited by EEO law? This is a real sticky situation, because even a consensual relationship could turn into a sexual harassment incident down the road.[51]

Historically, organizations have taken one of two options regarding romantic relationships in the workplace. One option is to turn a blind eye and hope that any romantic relationships that develop won't turn sour and devolve into harassment. Most organizations take this option—the majority of U.S. organizations have no formal policy on office romances.[52] The second option is to explicitly prohibit dating relationships among employees. Some organizations prohibit all romantic relationships between coworkers,[53] while others only prohibit supervisor–subordinate romances.[54] There are virtually no legal limits on the employer's ability to prohibit romantic relationships, even away from the workplace.[55] So, if you so choose, you can establish an organizational policy prohibiting romantic relationships and take disciplinary action against employees who violate the policy. But do you really want to take this stand? Do you want to be the employer who outlawed true love?

However, you may not need to make this choice, because a third option is beginning to emerge. Some organizations are establishing policies that stop short of prohibiting romantic relationships, but ask the couple to report the relationship to the company. If the relationship is between a manager and an employee he or she supervises, the company may revise the chain of command to eliminate any conflicts of interest. IBM, for example, used to warn managers that they risked losing their jobs if they had a romance with a subordinate. But now managers and subordinates can be romantically involved as long as the manager comes forward and agrees to stop supervising the subordinate.[56] In organizations taking this middle road, employees are often asked to sign *consensual relationship agreements* (also called love contracts). The primary purpose of these agreements is to remind employees of their rights and obligations and to provide the employer with documentation that the employees were engaged in a consensual relationship that does not violate the company's sexual harassment policy.[57]

WHAT'S NEXT?

In this chapter, I addressed one particular managerial challenge—controlling sexual harassment in the workplace. EEO law, in general, places certain requirements on managers to educate their employees and reduce the risk of discrimination. However, the largest benefits occur when managers try not to just comply with the minimal requirements of EEO law, but engage in proactive efforts to create environments in which employees can work productively without fear of harassment. In the next chapter, I'll turn to another EEO law, the ADEA, and discuss the challenges (and benefits) associated with managing older workers.

FOR FURTHER READING

Bland, T. S., & Stalcup, S. S. (2001). Managing harassment. *Human Resource Management, 40*(1), 51–61.

Janove, J. W. (2001, November). Sexual harassment and the three big surprises. *HRMagazine*, 123–130.

Kosanovich, W. L., Rosenberg, J. L., & Swanson, L. (2002, Summer). Preventing and correcting sexual harassment: A guide to the Ellerth/Faragher affirmative defense. *Employee Relations Law Journal, 28*(1), 79–99.

Talbot, M. (2002, October 13). Men behaving badly. *New York Times Magazine*, 52–57, 82, 84, 95.

MANAGER'S KNOT 11.1

"I work in HR at a bank, and I recently learned that one of our senior managers is dating a teller. By all accounts, this is a voluntary, consensual relationship. Still, should I be concerned about sexual harassment claims resulting from their relationship?"

As a third party, it's going to be very difficult for you to gauge whether or not the relationship is consensual. But the more important question is whether the bank has educated employees so that *they* can tell the difference in their own relationships. Does your organization have a policy on sexual harassment? Have employees received training about sexual harassment, and do they know how to report complaints? If your organization has a policy, a complaint process, and a training program in place, you can be more confident that employees can distinguish between consensual romantic relationships and unwelcome sexual behaviors.

MANAGER'S KNOT 11.2

"I've got a real problem on my hands. One of our team leaders is verbally abusive to his team members—yelling, swearing, things like that. Most of the complaints I'm hearing come from female staffers, but when I investigated the situation, I learned that he's just as likely to launch into a verbal attack on his male team members as the female ones. If there's no evidence that the team leader is treating people differently based on their sex, it's not sexual harassment, is it?"

It may not be sexual harassment. But that doesn't mean that these verbal attacks are acceptable behavior. Sounds like it's time for you to take a look at your organizational policies—does your organization have any policies about appropriate workplace conduct, and do these policies include information about appropriate and inappropriate workplace language? If not, it's time to develop some. Some organizations have established language codes that are separate and distinct from sexual harassment policies.[58] The behavior of these "equal opportunity harassers" may not be illegal, but they are still disrupting the workplace and interfering with employee performance. As the manager, you have a responsibility to make sure that the work environment doesn't interfere with employees' ability to work effectively on the job.

MANAGER'S KNOT 11.3

"I'm a mid-level manager in a small company, and we just started offering a training program designed to help employees recognize sexual harassment. All the managers went through the training, and then we ran the training within our individual units. After the training session in my unit, one of my employees came to see me. She told me about a series of incidents that have been going on the last few months. It's pretty serious—one coworker seems to be getting out of hand and beginning to become abusive toward some of the newer female employees. But the employee said she just wanted to 'vent' about the problem and asked me to keep her comments 'confidential.' What do I do?"

You need to let the employee know that you will do your best to conduct the investigation discreetly, and information will be released to other organizational members on a strict need-to-know basis. But you cannot ignore her comments. Once you become aware of the possibility of harassment in your organization, you have a legal duty to investigate. And that may mean that you need to identify the person bringing forward the complaint. If that's the case, you should remind both parties (the person bringing the complaint and the person accused) that retaliation is strictly prohibited.

ENDNOTES

1. U.S. Merit Systems Protection Board. (1981). *Sexual harassment in the federal workplace: Is it a problem?* Washington, DC: U.S. Government Printing Office; U.S. Merit Systems Protection Board. (1988). *Sexual harassment in the federal government: An update.* Washington, DC: U.S. Government Printing Office; Terpstra, D. E., & Baker, D. D. (1989). The identification and classification of reactions to sexual harassment. *Journal of Organizational Behavior, 10,* 1–14; Peirce, E. R., Rosen, B., & Hiller, T. B. (1997). Breaking the silence: Creating user-friendly sexual harassment policies. *Employee Responsibilities and Rights Journal, 10,* 225–242.

2. Hulin, C., Fitzgerald, L. F., & Drasgow, F. (1996). Organizational influences on sexual harassment. In M. S. Stockdale (Ed.), *Sexual harassment in the workplace: Perspectives, frontiers, and response strategies* (pp. 127–151). Thousand Oaks, CA: Sage; Pryor, J., LaVite, C., & Stoller, L. (1993). A social psychological analysis of sexual harassment: The person/situation interaction. *Journal of Vocational Behavior, 42,* 68–83; Timmerman, G., & Bajema, C. (2000). The impact of organizational culture on perceptions and experiences of sexual harassment. *Journal of Vocational Behavior, 57,* 188–205.

3. Welsh, S. (1999). Gender and sexual harassment. *Annual Review of Sociology, 25,* 169–190; Gutek, B. A., & Done, R. S. (2001). Sexual harassment. In R. K. Unger (Ed.), *Handbook of the psychology of women and gender* (pp. 367–387). New York: Wiley.

4. Crull, P. (1982). The stress effects of sexual harassment on the job. *American Journal of Orthopsychiatry, 52,* 539–543; Hamilton, J. A., Alagna, S. W., King, L. S., &

Lloyd, C. (1987). The emotional consequences of gender-based abuse in the workplace: New counseling programs for sex discrimination. *Women and Therapy, 6*, 155–182; Gutek, B. A., & Koss, M. P. (1993). Changed women and changed organizations: Consequences of coping with sexual harassment. *Journal of Vocational Behavior, 42*, 28–48.

5. U.S. Merit Systems Protection Board. (1981). *Sexual harassment in the federal workplace: Is it a problem?* Washington, DC: U.S. Government Printing Office; U.S. Merit Systems Protection Board. (1988). *Sexual harassment in the federal government: An update.* Washington, DC: U.S. Government Printing Office.

6. Schneider, K. T., Swan, S., & Fitzgerald, L. F. (1997). Job-related and psychological effects of sexual harassment in the workplace: Empirical evidence from two organizations. *Journal of Applied Psychology, 82*, 401–415.

7. Riger, S. (1991). Gender dilemmas in sexual harassment policies and procedures. *American Psychologist, 46*, 497–505; Gutek, B. A., & Koss, M. P. (1993). Changed women and changed organizations: Consequences of and coping with sexual harassment. *Journal of Vocational Behavior, 42*, 28–48.

8. Rudman, L. A., Borgida, E., & Robertson, B. A. (1995). Suffering in silence: Procedural injustice versus gender socialization issues in university sexual harassment grievance procedures. *Basic and Applied Psychology, 17*, 519–541; Gutek, B. A. (1985). *Sex and the workplace.* San Francisco: Jossey-Bass; Fitzgerald, L. F., Swan, S., & Fischer, C. (1995). Why didn't she just report him? The psychological and legal implications of women's responses to sexual harassment. *Journal of Social Issues, 51*, 117–138.

9. Sherwyn, D., Sturman, M. C., Eigen, Z. J., Heise, M., & Walwyn, J. (2001, June). The perversity of sexual harassment law: Effects of recent court rulings. *Cornell Hotel and Restaurant Administration Quarterly*, 46–56.

10. Johnson, M. A. (1999, October). Use anti-harassment training to shelter yourself from suits. *HR Magazine*, 76–81.

11. Abelson, R. (2001, June 10). Men, increasingly, are the ones claiming sex harassment by men. *New York Times*, sect. 1, p. 1.

12. Waldo, C. R., Berdahl, J. L., & Fitzgerald, L. F. (1998). Are men sexually harassed? If so, by whom? *Law and Human Behavior, 22*, 59–79.

13. U.S. Equal Employment Opportunity Commission. (1980, November 10). Final amendment to guidelines on discrimination because of sex under Title VII of the Civil Rights Act of 1964, as amended. 29 CFR Part 1604. *Federal Register, 45*, 74675–74677.

14. U.S. Equal Employment Opportunity Commission. (1990). Policy guidance on current issues of sexual harassment. Retrieved May 23, 2003, from http://www.eeoc.gov/docs/currentissues.html

15. Riger, S. (1991). Gender dilemmas in sexual harassment policies and procedures. *American Psychologist, 46*, 497–505.

16. MacKinnon, C. A. (2002). The logic of experience: Reflections on the development of sexual harassment law. *Georgetown Law Journal, 90*, 813–833; U.S. Equal Employment Opportunity Commission. (1990). Policy guidance on current issues of sexual harassment. Retrieved May 23, 2003, from http://www.eeoc.gov/docs/currentissues.html

17. *Harris vs. Forklift Systems, Inc.* (1993). 63 FEP 228.

18. Sherwyn, D., Sturman, M. C., Eigen, Z. J., Heise, M., & Walwyn, J. (2001, June). The perversity of sexual harassment law: Effects of recent court rulings. *Cornell Hotel and Restaurant Administration Quarterly*, 46–56.

19. Smiley-Marquez, C. (1999). Prevention vs. remediation: Anti-harassment training pays off. *Diversity Factor, 8*(1), 36–41.

20. *Lockard v. Pizza Hut Inc.* (1998). 162 F.3d 1062 (10th circuit).

21. Adler, R. S., & Peirce, E. R. (1993). The legal, ethical, and social implications of the "reasonable woman" standard in sexual harassment cases. *Fordham Law Review, 61*, 773–827; Kulik, C. T., Perry, E. L., & Pepper, M. B. (2003). Here comes the judge: The influence of judge personal characteristics on federal sexual harassment case outcomes. *Law and Human Behavior, 27*, 69–86.
22. Gutek, B. A. (1995). How subjective is sexual harassment? An examination of rater effects. *Basic and Applied Social Psychology, 17*, 447–467.
23. Blumenthal, J. A. (1998). The reasonable woman standard: A meta-analytic review of gender differences in perceptions of sexual harassment. *Law and Human Behavior, 22*, 33–57; Rotundo, M., Nguyen, D., & Sackett, P. R. (2001). A meta-analytic review of gender differences in perceptions of sexual harassment. *Journal of Applied Psychology, 86*, 914–922.
24. Rotundo, M., Nguyen, D., & Sackett, P. R. (2001). A meta-analytic review of gender differences in perceptions of sexual harassment. *Journal of Applied Psychology, 86*, 914–922; Gutek, B. A., Morasch, B., & Cohen, A. G. (1983). Interpreting social-sexual behavior in a work setting. *Journal of Vocational Behavior, 22*, 30–48; Jones, T. S., & Remland, M. S. (1992). Sources of variability in perceptions of and responses to sexual harassment. *Sex Roles, 27*, 121–142.
25. Janove, J. W. (2001, November). Sexual harassment and the three big surprises. *HRMagazine*, 123–130.
26. Gutek, B. A. (1995). How subjective is sexual harassment? An examination of rater effects. *Basic and Applied Social Psychology, 17*, 447–467; Pryor, J. B., & Day, J. D. (1988). Interpretations of sexual harassment: An attributional analysis. *Sex Roles, 18*, 405–417.
27. Grider, K., Wesely, N., Bailey, T., & Gee, K. (1992). The reasonable woman standard in hostile environment litigation. *Texas Bar Journal, 55*, 52–55; Perry, E. L., Kulik, C. T., & Bourhis, A. C. (2004). The reasonable woman standard: Effects on sexual harassment court decisions. *Law and Human Behavior, 28*, 9–27.
28. Rauch, J. (1997, June 23). Offices and gentlemen. *New Republic*, 22–28; Abelson, R. (2001, November 20). The disabled find a voice in the courts. *New York Times*, p. C1; Holzbauer, J. J., & Berven, N. L. (1996). Disability harassment: A new term for a long-standing problem. *Journal of Counseling and Development, 74*, 478–483; O'Blenes, C. (1999, June). Harassment grows more complex. *Management Review*, 49–51.
29. *Burlington Industries Inc. v. Ellerth.* (1998). 118 S. Ct. 2257; *Faragher v. City of Boca Raton.* (1998). 118 S. Ct. 2275.
30. Hogler, R. L., Frame, J. H., & Thornton, G. (2002). Workplace sexual harassment law: An empirical analysis of organizational justice and legal policy. *Journal of Managerial Issues, 14*(2), 234–250.
31. Hogler, R. L., Frame, J. H., & Thornton, G. (2002). Workplace sexual harassment law: An empirical analysis of organizational justice and legal policy. *Journal of Managerial Issues, 14*(2), 234–250.
32. Greengard, S. (1999, May). Zero tolerance: Making it work. *Workforce*, 28–34.
33. Kiley, D. (2002, October 21). Workplace woes almost eclipse Mitsubishi plan. *USA Today*, p. 1B.
34. Kosanovich, W. L., Rosenberg, J. L., & Swanson, L. (2002). Preventing and correcting sexual harassment: A guide to the Ellerth/Faragher affirmative defense. *Employee Relations Law Journal, 28*(1), 79–99; Bland, T. S., & Stalcup, S. S. (2001). Managing harassment. *Human Resource Management, 40*(1), 51–61.
35. Janove, J. W. (2001, November). Sexual harassment and the three big surprises. *HRMagazine*, 123–130.
36. Reddy, A. (2001, August 12). A training solution that clicks. *Washington Post*, p. H01.

37. Laabs, J. J. (1995, February). Sexual harassment: HR puts its questions on the line. *Personnel Journal*, 36–45.

38. Flynn, G. (1999). Dupont's formula for a harassment-free workplace. *Training and Management Development Methods, 13*, 9.01–9.04.

39. Canoni, J. D. (1999). Sexual harassment: The new liability. *Risk Management, 46*(1), 12–16.

40. Bland, T. S., & Stalcup, S. S. (2001). Managing harassment. *Human Resource Management, 40*(1), 51–61.

41. U.S. Equal Employment Opportunity Commission. (1999). Enforcement guidance: Vicarious employer liability for unlawful harassment by supervisors. Retrieved May 23, 3003, from http://www.eeoc.gov/docs/harassment.html

42. Gutek, B. A. (1997). Sexual harassment policy initiatives. In W. O'Donohue (Ed.), *Sexual harassment: Theory, research, and treatment* (pp. 185–198). Boston: Allyn & Bacon.

43. Perry, E. L., Kulik, C. T., & Schmidtke, J. M. (1998). Individual differences in the effectiveness of sexual harassment awareness training. *Journal of Applied Social Psychology, 28*, 698–723.

44. Buhler, P. M. (1999). The manager's role in preventing sexual harassment. *Supervision, 60*(4), 16–18.

45. Gravdal, K. (2000, May). Screening for harassment. *HR Magazine*, 115–124.

46. Meyer, A. (1992, July). Getting to the heart of sexual harassment. *HRMagazine*, 82–84.

47. Thacker, R. A. (1992). Preventing sexual harassment in the workplace. *Training and Development, 46*(2), 50–53; Bresler, S. J., & Thacker, R. (1993, May). Four-point plan helps solve harassment problem. *HRMagazine*, 117–124.

48. Johnson, M. A. (1999, October). Use anti-harassment training to shelter yourself from suits. *HRMagazine*, 77–81.

49. Buhler, P. M. (1999). The manager's role in preventing sexual harassment. *Supervision, 60*(4), 16–18; Johnson, M. A. (1999, October). Use anti-harassment training to shelter yourself from suits. *HRMagazine*, 77–81.

50. Maher, K. (2003, February 11). When office romance fizzles, the heartache can be double. Retrieved February 11, 2003, from http://online.wsj.com

51. Buhler, P. M. (1999). The manager's role in preventing sexual harassment. *Supervision, 60*(4), 16–18.

52. Schaefer, C. M., & Tudor, T. R. (2001, Summer). Managing workplace romances. *SAM Advanced Management Journal*, 4–10.

53. Massengill, D., & Peterson, D. J. (1995). Legal challenges to no fraternization rules. *Labor Law Journal, 46*, 429–435.

54. Schaner, D. J. (1994). Romance in the workplace: Should employers act as chaperones? *Employee Relations Law Journal, 20*(1), 47–71.

55. Williams, C. L., Giuffre, P. A., & Dellinger, K. (1999). Sexuality in the workplace: Organizational control, sexual harassment, and the pursuit of pleasure. *Annual Review of Sociology, 25*, 73–93.

56. Hymowitz, C., & Pollock, E. J. (1998, February 4). Corporate affairs. *Wall Street Journal*, pp. A1, A8.

57. Schaefer, C. M., & Tudor, T. R. (2001, Summer). Managing workplace romances. *SAM Advanced Management Journal*, 4–10.

58. Silverman, R. E. (2001, May 8). On-the-job cursing: Obscene talk is latest target of workplace ban. *Wall Street Journal*, p. B12.

CHAPTER

12

Managing Age in the Workplace

I n chapter 2, I gave you a brief thumbnail sketch describing the Age Discrimination in Employment Act (ADEA). I promised we'd return to the ADEA and explore the implications of this law for managing older workers. But this chapter isn't just about the older worker—it's about the role of age, and age differences, in the workplace. We'll start with an in-depth look at the ADEA and the legal requirements associated with it. But then we'll talk about some of the broader management issues associated with managing employees of different ages.

AGE DISCRIMINATION IN EMPLOYMENT ACT (1967)

You'll remember from chapter 2 that the ADEA prohibits discrimination in human resource management decisions (hiring, wages, promotions, hours worked, training, etc.) against people who are 40 years or older. That "40 years or older" is a big group of people, and it's getting bigger every day. By 2010, the median age of the U.S. workforce will be 40.6 years.[1] That means that about half your workforce will be protected by the ADEA.[2]

So, all job applicants and all employees that are age 40 or older are protected by the ADEA, right? Well, almost. There's one exception. Senior executives are not protected. An employee who is age 65 or older, who has spent 2 years in a policy-making position, can be required to retire. Lawmakers recognized that the success of a company is in the hands of its senior management, and they wanted to remove any legal impediments that would make it difficult to unseat executives whose poor performance was jeopardizing the organization's competitiveness.

Financially, age discrimination is very serious business. When plaintiffs win age discrimination cases, they win big. Age discrimination suits are among the most expensive discrimination suits an employer can face. The median court award in age discrimination suits is $269,000 as compared to $121,000 in race cases and just $100,000 in sex discrimination cases.[3] Why are age discrimination awards so high? First, under the ADEA, an organization may be liable for additional penalties if it is found guilty of willful misconduct; these penalties are not available for other types of discrimination. Second, the person who brings an age discrimination suit against an employer is more likely to be an employee than a job applicant. It's difficult for a lone job applicant to demonstrate age discrimination in hiring decisions. A job applicant rarely has detailed information about the other applicants in the hiring pool—including their qualifications or ages. As a result, only about 10% of age claims relate to hiring.[4] Instead, most age discrimination suits involve decisions made after the older worker is employed (e.g., discrimination in training or promotion opportunities, or discrimination in termination decisions). In these cases, plaintiffs can use their performance appraisal history, and their knowledge about how coworkers were treated, to buttress their claims that human resource management decisions were in fact influenced by age. When a judge or jury tries to estimate the costs a plaintiff incurred as a result of age discrimination, the plaintiff's contribution to the employment relationship (years of service) and the costs resulting from the discrimination (e.g., the lost wages associated with a termination or a promotion denial) may boost the size of the award.

An organization accused of age discrimination can try to defend itself in one of two ways. First, the organization might claim that age is a BFOQ for the job. Remember BFOQs from chapter 2? BFOQs are limited exceptions to EEO law, where the organization claims that essentially *all* members of a particular group are incapable of performing the job. Although BFOQs are rare, there tend to be more BFOQ exceptions with respect to age than other demographic characteristics, especially in situations where public safety is at stake. For example, it's legal for organizations to require bus drivers to be below a certain age, and to refuse to hire older applicants for bus driving positions. In jobs that involve public safety (e.g., police, firefighters, pilots), Congress also permits mandatory retirement. Employers can force employees in these jobs to retire (or transfer into other jobs) when they reach a certain age.[5]

Alternatively, the organization might argue that its decision was based on an RFOA. RFOA stands for a "reasonable factor other than age." An

RFOA applies to the situation where the organization has directly based its decision on a factor other than age, and that factor turns out to be associated with age. For example, if you're hiring people to do extremely detailed laboratory work, you might use a vision test as part of the selection criteria. Older applicants might perform more poorly on this test than younger ones and be less likely to be hired. But because visual acuity is a job requirement, a court might see this as a "reasonable" selection criterion despite the fact that it is associated with age. This RFOA defense causes some ambiguity in the application of the ADEA, as you'll see in a minute.

Under the ADEA, an individual clearly is protected against *disparate treatment* discrimination. Disparate treatment discrimination occurs when members of different groups receive unequal treatment or are evaluated by different standards. For example, an older job applicant might claim disparate treatment discrimination if she doesn't get a job even though she passed a selection test with a score of 95% and a younger job applicant was hired with a score of only 80%. Organizations that specify age ranges ("looking for a 20- to 30-year-old receptionist") or age-related characteristics ("looking for recent college graduates" or "looking to hire a young, energetic waitress") in their recruiting materials might also be viewed as engaging in disparate treatment discrimination (unless the organization can defend their age requirements as BFOQs) because they limit job opportunities to younger job applicants.

Adverse impact claims are a little trickier. Remember that in chapter 2, I explained that an adverse impact claim only has to show that organizational policies or decisions have a disproportionate impact on a particular group. These disproportionate effects are often observed in downsizing contexts. Even if an employer isn't basing downsizing decisions on age directly, other criteria (e.g., educational background, salary costs) may be associated with employee age and have a disproportionate impact on older employees. Courts once routinely gave the green light to adverse impact claims of age bias. Historically, courts have said that the ADEA is very similar to Title VII of the CRA, which prohibits *both* disparate treatment and adverse impact (see chap. 2). But a number of federal appeals courts are beginning to reject, or at least strongly question, the idea that plaintiffs can claim age bias just because an employer's actions have a harsher effect on older people. Instead, these courts insist that plaintiffs must show that their employer *intentionally* discriminated against them—simply showing adverse impact is not enough.[6] These courts argue that the ADEA is analogous to the Equal Pay Act (EPA). Under the EPA, employers can pay men and women differently as long as the differential is based on a reasonable factor other than sex (e.g., experience, skills). See the ambiguity caused by that RFOA defense? There are lots of criteria organizations use in downsizing (see chap. 10 for a discussion of these criteria). If courts see these criteria as "reasonable," it makes it difficult for plaintiffs to claim adverse impact discrimination, even if the downsizing has a statistically greater impact on older workers than younger ones.

There are some recent examples where an organization was able to defend itself against age discrimination claims by using RFOAs. The first example involves the Florida Power Corporation. A group of more than 100 former employees sued Florida Power when the company downsized. The plaintiffs argued that Florida Power's policies about who would be affected by the downsizing initiative were neutral in design, but unfairly impacted the company's older workers. In other words, the plaintiffs said that Florida Power's downsizing policies had an adverse impact on older workers. However, the 11th Circuit Court said that the adverse impact option wasn't available under the ADEA—and because the plaintiffs couldn't demonstrate that the decisions were based directly on age, they couldn't claim disparate treatment either.[7]

In another case, an employer based downsizing decisions on salary and terminated the workers associated with the highest payroll costs. Older workers at the company tended to have a longer employment history, occupy higher level positions, and earn higher salaries—so decisions to terminate employees based on salary had an adverse effect on older workers. However, the court was persuaded that there was no disparate treatment (both younger and older workers were terminated based on salary) and was unwilling to treat the adverse impact as age discrimination.[8]

These cases suggest that courts may be increasingly unwilling to accept statistical evidence of adverse impact *alone* as evidence of age discrimination. There has to be evidence that the organization intentionally used age in the decision-making process. The employer who decides to address financial problems by firing older workers because they have higher salaries is likely to be found guilty of age discrimination. But an employer who decides to resolve those financial problems by terminating higher salaried workers, many of whom are older, may *not* be guilty of age discrimination.[9] That's a subtle distinction, but one that is very important for organizations engaged in any kind of restructuring or downsizing effort that might have an adverse effect on older employees. Currently, the question of whether a judge will accept adverse impact statistics as evidence of age discrimination depends on the circuit in which the case is heard. The Supreme Court was supposed to hear the Florida Power Corporation case and resolve the controversy, but the court unexpectedly dismissed the Florida Power Corp. case without giving any explanation for its action.[10]

Despite the discrepancies across circuits, it's clear that employers need to avoid any implication that human resource decisions (hiring, promotion, firing, etc.) are based on an applicant's or an employee's

age. In situations (especially downsizing contexts) that have a disproportionate impact on older workers, nondiscriminatory criteria need to
be clearly specified and applied consistently to both older and younger
workers.

In downsizing situations, some organizations are asking exiting workers to waive their right to bring age discrimination suits. That's allowable
under the Older Workers Benefit Protection program, a 1990 amendment to the ADEA.[11] Under this act, companies can ask outgoing workers
to sign a promise not to sue for age discrimination. To be legal, companies offering these waivers must give older workers some kind of additional compensation, on top of the benefits and severance pay they would
have received from the downsizing.[12] Companies also must give employees information about the ages of people affected by the cutback (those
who have been terminated and those who have been retained) so that individuals can make informed decisions about whether they might want to
pursue an age discrimination suit.[13]

Manager's Checkpoint

The following questions might help you to ensure that
your human resource decisions are not discriminating
against older job applicants or employees:

- Have I examined my job advertisements, hiring practices, and
  human resource management policies to ensure that I am not
  using age as a basis for decisions? (For example, watch for job
  advertisements that explicitly mention a preferred age or age
  range. Unless the job involves public safety, it's probably inappropriate to use age as a decision criterion.)
- Are all organizational decision makers familiar with the requirements of the ADEA, and do they know not to use age as a factor
  in organizational decisions? (Even if your job advertisements and
  organizational policies are age neutral, individual decision makers may be using age as a decision criterion.)
- Am I basing my human resource decisions on clearly specified,
  job-related criteria that are applied consistently to applicants
  and employees of different ages? (Job-relevant criteria are
  more likely to be seen as "reasonable" and nondiscriminatory
  even if they have a disproportionate effect on older applicants
  or employees.)

MANAGING OLDER WORKERS

Now that you're familiar with the ADEA, let's take a step back and look at the broader issues associated with managing older workers. The ADEA is a little different from other EEO laws in that it only protects *older* workers and not younger ones. Why do older workers need legal protection in the workplace? Older people, and older workers in particular, tend to be associated with negative stereotypes. These stereotypes limit the opportunities that are available to older job applicants and older employees. Stereotypes can influence any human resource decision, but I'll focus on two areas that are particularly problematic for older people: hiring and training.

Older Job Applicants: Entry Issues

Consider Mary, a 50-something downsized manager back on the job market. Mary responded to an ad asking for managerial experience, and she's been called in for a face-to-face interview. What's going through the interviewer's mind? Let's listen in on his thoughts, and see how well the interviewer's impressions jive with the research findings on older workers.

The interviewer may be concerned about Mary's productivity potential. "After all," the interviewer thinks, "this is a job where the person we hire has to pull his or her own weight—a person of her age probably can't do it." Many managers expect older workers to be less productive than younger ones.[14] For example, management consultants Watson Wyatt Worldwide conducted a national poll of CEOs. Eighty-eight percent of the CEOs said that they thought age affects productivity—with most CEOs saying that productivity peaks around age 43.[15] Strike one! Negative beliefs about the relation between age and productivity are broad and sweeping—and often inaccurate. Across a wide range of jobs, there's a zero correlation between age and job performance.[16] That's right—*zero*. Knowing a person's age provides *no* information about how well the person is likely to perform. Manual labor tasks with intense speed or physical demands may sometimes place older workers at a disadvantage. However, the research suggests that, with increased experience, older workers develop effective work strategies that compensate for declines in speed, with no noticeable effect on overall productivity.[17] In many sales positions, older workers tend to outperform younger ones, partly because the older worker has accumulated more knowledge about the product and experience with customers. And for white-collar jobs, like the managerial position Mary is being considered for, experience is generally a better predictor of performance than chronological age.[18]

"Fine," thinks the interviewer. "But we need someone who is going to stay with the company a long time. A woman Mary's age, she's probably looking forward to retirement already. Either that, or she'll jump ship when another company offers her something closer to her previous employer's salary." Strike two! The interviewer's got it wrong again. Many older workers plan to continue working past the traditional retirement age of 65.[19] Once hired, older workers tend to be highly committed to their employers. The Bureau of Labor Statistics finds that only 3% of employees age 50 or over change jobs in any given year, compared with 10% of the entire labor force and 12% of workers age 25 to 34.[20]

"Well, there's another problem," thinks the interviewer. "We've got a big project coming up, and we need people working around the clock. Older people get sick all the time, and Mary will probably be taking a lot of time off." Strike three—you're out! Older people in the U.S. workforce are in very good health. More than three fourths rate their health as good or excellent, and most people in the United States can expect to reach age 65 without having health cause any major employment problems.[21] In fact, absenteeism rates for older workers tend to be *lower* than for younger workers.[22] And if you're concerned about older workers' on-the-job injuries, stop worrying—older workers make up 14% of the workforce, but they suffer only 10% of all workplace injuries.[23]

Inaccurate assumptions made by interviewers and other organizational decision makers make it difficult for older job applicants to get hired in the first place.[24] The older the job applicant, the fewer the interviews, and the longer the job search.[25] Older job applicants find it particularly difficult to overcome age stereotypes for jobs traditionally filled by younger workers (e.g., jobs in the fast food industry or jobs at amusement parks).[26] When organizational decision makers encounter an older job applicant for these "young" jobs, they can be skeptical about the older applicant's job fit and fail to seriously consider the applicant's qualifications. The ADEA demands that employers evaluate older workers individually, based on their individual capabilities and not on their age.[27] It's important to keep questioning your assumptions about older job applicants, and make sure that your hiring decisions are based on job qualifications, not on stereotypes about what older workers can or cannot do.

Some organizations recognize that older workers can be a valuable resource, and have gone out of their way to hire older workers. Box 12.1 describes some of these organizational success stories. But these organizations also offer some valuable lessons about how to manage older workers. In several cases, these organizations learned that managing older workers required some accommodations to help employees achieve their full potential. At Days Inn, for example, the company's incentive system had traditionally rewarded speed in reservation clerk performance. This system disadvantaged older workers, who tended to have a longer "talk time" with the customer—30 to 45 seconds longer, at least—than their

---

BOX 12.1
Proactive Efforts to Employ Older Workers

✖ Monsanto Co. brings back retirees as temps or part-timers to fill gaps and save money. In one year alone, the Retiree Resource Corps saved Monsanto some $600,000, primarily in overhead from agency fees.[28]

✖ Younger workers in Days Inn's reservation call center were staying only one year. When older workers were hired for those jobs, the retention rate grew to 3 years. Plus, the older workers cost 64% less to train and recruit than the younger ones.[29]

✖ Bonne Bell, a family-owned cosmetics firm, launched a seniors-only cosmetics production department 5 years ago. During that time, the group has handled work that used to be outsourced—saving the company more than $1 million. Now, seniors account for close to 20% of a total workforce of 500 and there is a waiting list for each shift.[30]

✖ MITRE Corp., a 5,000 employee company providing technology research and development, enables older employees to stay in the workforce by offering phased retirement, part-time work, and a program called "Reserves at the Ready." This program allows employees with at least 10 years of company service to become part-time on-call employees staffing projects throughout the corporation.[31]

✖ Vita Needle Co., a manufacturer of stainless-steel tubes and hypodermic needles, boasts that it has never asked anyone to retire in its 70-year history. The average age of its workforce is in the low 70s.[32]

✖ Deloitte Consulting designed their Senior Leaders Program to retain aging talent in an industry that frequently suffers from early burnout. The program gives Deloitte's best senior partners the opportunity to work anywhere in the world, doing whatever they want, whenever they want.[33]

---

younger counterparts. Is that a problem? No. Older workers were engaging customers in personal conversations and collecting important sales information—and booking more rooms along the way.[34] At Bonne Bell, the company found that their older machines, running at a slower pace, were a good fit to the members of their senior production team. If the machines ran too fast, new employees became frustrated and quit. Is the slower machine pace a problem? No. Shipping goals are set and met on the seniors' production line, just like the others.[35]

Older Workers: Training and Development Issues

Try a thought experiment. You come in to work one day and in your inbox you find two memos. One memo is from Stan, a 30-year-old engineer re-

questing that you send him to an intensive training session on new hydrau-
lic techniques. The second memo is from Joe, a 53-year-old engineer
requesting the same training. Unfortunately, the budget only allows you to
send one employee. Who would you choose?

Research suggests that the older worker is more likely to be denied the
training opportunity than the younger worker.[36] In fact, the Department of
Labor found that 55- to 64-year-olds were only one third as likely to receive
training as 35- to 44-year-olds.[37] Older workers may also be discouraged
from participating in informal developmental opportunities, such as job ro-
tation or project assignments.[38] It's that same stereotype problem again. In
one survey of human resource executives, employees 50 years and older
were described by respondents as inflexible, averse to change, and resis-
tant to learning and understanding new technologies.[39] You see how it
works: Managers think older workers won't learn anything from the training, so they allocate their training dollars to younger workers instead. But
now the cycle begins anew: Older workers who don't have the opportunity
to maintain or develop their skills inevitably fall behind, confirming the
managers' negative stereotypes about older workers, and making managers even less likely to send older workers for additional training. This cycle
may be especially vicious in high-tech environments where technology
changes rapidly and skills quickly become obsolete. Corporate bosses believe that the performance of scientists and engineers peaks in the early
30s and then declines gradually over the rest of the career.[40] However, one
of the most important factors influencing the productivity of scientists and
engineers over age 50 is whether they work in productive climates characterized by frequent contact with colleagues, a diversity of work activities,
and a cohesive working group.[41] In other words, the decline bosses are seeing isn't driven by chronological age at all, but by the way companies structure the work environment of their older tech workers.

What are the facts about training older workers? Younger and older
workers both benefit from training. Older workers are just as interested in
skill development and new technology as young people,[42] and the ability to
learn continues well into old age.[43] However, people do learn differently as
they age, and your organization's training programs may need some modifications to accommodate the needs of older workers. An older person
learns better in self-paced or self-directed pressure-free learning environments,[44] and in contexts that emphasize active learning.[45] If your company
training still relies on passive lecture formats where the instructor crams a
lot of material into a short time period, it may be time to reevaluate the
training program—to the benefit of older *and* younger trainees.

One innovative approach that organizations are taking to developing
older workers is through reverse mentoring programs, where it's the younger workers who are asked to help develop the older ones—particularly in

areas involving technical expertise.[46] GE, for example, started a reverse-mentoring program to help senior managers get involved in electronic commerce. The protégés in the program ranged in age from the late 30s to nearly 60; mentors were no older than early 30s.[47] This kind of one-on-one coaching may be an effective way to accommodate different learning styles and personalize the training to the older worker's individual needs.

 Manager's Checkpoint

The following questions might help you to ensure that you are not missing out on the potential of your older job applicants or employees:

- Are stereotypes about older workers influencing my decisions about older job applicants? (Before deciding not to hire an older job applicant, ask yourself whether you'd make the same decision if the applicant were younger. This can encourage you to focus on objective criteria rather than assumptions based on age.)
- Are training and development opportunities available to employees of all ages? What criteria am I using to approve or deny training requests? (Establishing policies about training opportunities, and educating employees about those policies, can help to ensure that older workers are not missing out on developmental opportunities available to younger workers.)
- How is training delivered in my organization? Are instructors sensitive to the training needs of different ages? (Training programs that are self-paced and actively involve the trainee in the learning process are likely to be more effective for older trainees.)

MANAGING ACROSS THE GENERATIONS

So far we've talked only about "older" workers. "Older," as defined by the ADEA, is that portion of the workforce age 40 and older. But what about the rest of the workforce? In the U.S. population, people are living longer, *and* they are staying in the workplace longer. The people you manage are likely to span four distinct generations. Let's take a look at these generations, and the challenges age diversity brings to today's managers. Table 12.1 summarizes the generations comprising today's workforce.

The oldest group in the workforce is the *Traditionalist* generation (also known as Matures or Veterans). Born before 1945, most members of this group have already retired. However, the youngest Traditionalists are only

TABLE 12.1

Workforce Generations[48]

Generation Nickname	Birthdates	Proportion of Workforce	Career Stage
Traditionalists (also called Matures or Veterans)	1900–1945	About 12% (17 million)	Transitioning into retirement
Baby Boomers	1946–1964	About 49% (68 million)	Mid- and late-career
Generation X	1965–1975	About 23% (32 million)	Early- and mid-career
Generation Y (also called Millennials or Echo Boomers or Nexters)	1976–1995	About 16% (23 million)	Early-career

in their early 60s and still actively engaged in their careers. The next group is the *Baby Boomers*. You met the Baby Boomers in chapter 8, when we discussed careers. Now in their 40s and 50s, Baby Boomers fill the bulk of middle management positions in today's organizations. Members of the Baby Boomer generation tended to delay having children until later in life, and they had fewer children than members of previous generations, so the Baby Boomers' progeny, *Generation X*, is a much smaller proportion of the population. Members of Generation X are beginning to establish themselves in their careers. The newest members of the workforce, *Generation Y* (also known as Millennials, Echo Boomers, or Nexters), are just starting their careers. Born in 1976 or later, the oldest members of Generation Y are the students you are recruiting from college and graduate programs.

Trying to bracket the generations within specific birth years may seem like a futile exercise. After all, how different is a Baby Boomer born in 1964 from a Generation Xer born in 1965? However, the generations are defined not just by these (somewhat arbitrary) year ranges, but also by the economic and historical context that shaped their attitudes and expectations about work and careers.[49] The Traditionalists grew up in the shadow of the Great Depression. Their parents taught them that just getting a job was a lucky break and holding onto that job was a matter of individual persistence and dedication. Many Traditionalists had the same employer their entire career. Baby Boomers entered the workforce during an era of relative prosperity and enjoyed rapid advancement up the corporate ladder. But many members of Generation X saw their Boomer parents lose jobs as a result of organizational downsizing and mergers. Generation Xers started their careers in high-flying Internet startups—and watched the startups fizzle a few years later.[50] Given these different experiences, it's probably not too surprising that members of different generations define "job security" differently and have different expectations about the likelihood of long-term employment at any one company.[51]

What does this age diversity mean for managers? Consider two major challenges.

Challenge One: Managerial Succession

The distribution of generations poses a particular challenge in terms of managerial succession. Traditionalists have been leaving the working world at relatively young ages, and a large number of Boomers will become eligible to retire over the next few years. However, the Generation X pool is small (see Table 12.1), and Generation Y is still a decade or two away from filling management gaps.[52] The result is that businesses trying to maintain full staffing levels will have to simultaneously retain Traditionalists and Baby Boomers, and recruit and develop Generations X and Y.

The popular press has been trying to pin down what members of these different generations want from their employers. Traditionalists are described as wanting big salaries and important titles, outward manifestations of success that are of little importance to Baby Boomers.[53] Both Baby Boomers and Generation Xers are supposed to care more about the job content, and doing work that "matters,"[54] but some authors report that Generation Xers are more concerned with money than are the Boomers.[55] Generation Y individuals are described as uninterested in climbing the corporate ladder—but at the same time, they are very comfortable negotiating material outcomes like high salaries and signing bonuses.[56] Trying to keep all these different preferences straight is enough to make a manager's head spin!

Efforts to get an exact fix on the specific expectations of members of different generations may be misguided. Researchers are finding that there's a great deal of diversity within each generation, and the values that an individual brings to the workplace can be very different from the values expected based on generation membership.[57] And the differences that are observed across the generations may be more a function of career stages (see chap. 8) than generational cohort. For example, it's not unusual to see people's preferences for organizational benefits influenced by their age, their career stage, and their level of responsibility for family members other than themselves.[58] However, there is a general trend of which you should be aware: Researchers suggest that, in general, members of later generations are less likely to feel that work is, or should be, a central part of life.[59] Members of later generations are more likely to value opportunities to balance work and personal goals.

Keeping that general trend in mind can help you to design effective re-cruitment and retention strategies that appeal to members of different generations, albeit for different reasons. Flexible work arrangements (part-time jobs, flexible work hours, job sharing, telecommuting) might help you to hold on to experienced Boomers as they transition into retirement and simultaneously recruit new employees from Generations X and Y.[60]

Challenge Two: Status Incongruence

The second challenge is tougher. You also have to get members of these different generations to work together. Age differences themselves aren't necessarily the problem. Even fairly large age differences between supervisors and subordinates seem to have little effect on how much supervisors like their subordinates or how positively they evaluate subordinate performance.[61] But age gaps are harder to manage if the gap is accompanied by organizational roles and responsibilities that run counter to expectations. Given today's turbulent marketplace, many of your new hires may be experienced individuals downsized from another organization or embarking on a second career. At the same time, you may have been promoting younger employees to fill gaps in the managerial hierarchy. As a result, 20- and 30-something bosses may be supervising workers in their 50s or 60s or even older, inverting the usual expectation that older employees supervise younger ones. A supervisor who is younger than his or her subordinate is violating social norms that suggest older and more experienced employees should supervise younger ones. Researchers call this phenomenon *status incongruence*—the situation where a person's organizational status (their position in the organizational hierarchy) is inconsistent with their social status (e.g., their age).[62] Status incongruence makes both the younger supervisor and the older employee uncomfortable. We've been taught to respect our elders. That can make it hard for a younger manager to provide negative feedback, or to assign humdrum tasks, to an older employee.[63] Older employees may dislike taking orders from a manager young enough to be their child.[64]

Research on the status incongruence phenomenon suggests that it is especially problematic when there are clear hierarchical differences between the supervisor and the subordinate. One study, for example, investigated status incongruence between employees and their team leaders, and between those same employees and a higher level supervisor. Employees who were older than their team leaders responded positively to the age difference. They were absent less frequently and they engaged in more helpful behavior not formally required by the job. But employees who were older than their formal supervisors responded negatively, including trying to learn more about other jobs so they could transfer.[65]

These findings suggest that organizations may be able to overcome status incongruence problems by minimizing the status differences within workgroups (e.g., by using informal team leaders or facilitators rather than formal supervisors). In addition, status incongruence effects are less likely when employees of different ages can identify characteristics (e.g., hobbies, sports, or other outside interests) that they have in common. Employees of similar ages tend to have common nonwork-related experiences (e.g., shared historical experiences, common family stages). Nonwork-related conversations about these common experiences ease the way for more effective work-related communications.[66] When these nonwork-related conversations do not spontaneously arise (e.g., when the supervisor and subordinate are of very different ages), employees may need help in developing and identifying common interests.

WHAT'S NEXT?

In this chapter, I explained how the challenges associated with managing older workers go beyond the legal requirements of the ADEA. In the next chapter, we'll turn to another law, the ADA, and the challenges (and opportunities) associated with employing people with disabilities.

FOR FURTHER READING

Barrier, M. (2002, March). An age-old problem. *HRMagazine*, 34–37.
Maurer, T. J., & Rafuse, N. E. (2001). Learning, not litigating: Managing employee development and avoiding claims of age discrimination. *Academy of Management Executive, 15*(4), 110–121.
Reingold, J., & Brady, D. (1999, September 20). Brain drain. *Fortune*, 112–126.
Wellner, A. S. (2002, March). Tapping a silver mine. *HRMagazine*, 26–31.

MANAGER'S KNOT 12.1

"I've been interviewing candidates for an entry-level management position. The strongest candidate is a woman in her mid-50s who lost her former job during a downsizing initiative. She's good, and she's got a wealth of experience, but really, she's overqualified for this position. She's used to a big staff and a big budget—we're just a small startup operation. If I hire her, I'm afraid that she'll be dissatisfied and not stick around very long."

Careful—it sounds like you're making a lot of assumptions here. Have you clearly explained the job's responsibilities to the applicant? Many older workers who are "starting over" after being downsized by a former employer know that they are unlikely to get a new job at the same level as the one they left. Your position may offer this applicant other kinds of challenges and opportunities—the opportunity to work in a growth area, the opportunity to learn about a new customer base, or the opportunity to develop a new product from scratch. In addition to losing a valuable candidate, denying this woman the job on the grounds that she is "overqualified" could be seen as discriminatory. Some courts have suggested that "overqualified" is just a code word for "too old."[67]

MANAGER'S KNOT 12.2

"I manage a local radio station, and we're considering a change in our programming format. We'd like to move from the easy-listening, soft-rock format we have now to one that's more contemporary. This isn't a super-big change—it's not like we're suddenly going to start playing rap and punk. But we would like the characteristics of our DJs to reflect the demographics of the audience we're trying to reach. Is it a problem if we replace our 50-something DJs with new employees in their 40s?"

Yes, it's a problem. You're violating the ADEA whenever you use age as a basis for human resource decisions and those decisions have a negative impact on workers 40 years old or above. In similar cases, courts have said that it is irrelevant whether replacement workers (new hires) are *also* protected by the ADEA; the only thing that matters is that terminated workers lost their jobs because of their age.[68] You'd have to convince the court that being in your 40s is a BFOQ for the job—a tough argument to make, because people in their 40s and 50s can both be knowledgeable about "contemporary" music and spin the appropriate records.

MANAGER'S KNOT 12.3

"I supervise a group of tellers at a branch bank. The bank is going to introduce a new computer system, and we've been encouraging the tellers to start attending training sessions. The system won't come online for a while, but it helps us to manage the absences if we can stagger the training over several months. When I talked with my tellers about the training, the younger ones jumped at the chance to attend the training course, but the older ones held back. What gives? I thought you said that older and younger workers are equally interested in training and skill development. Now that I think about it, I've noticed that the older tellers haven't been signing on for any of the optional training we offer, either."

Yes, research does indicate that both older and younger workers say that they value training opportunities.[69] However, remember that the type and style of training also makes a difference. If your branch's training programs use a traditional training style that emphasizes lectures and rote memorization, the training program may not be a good fit to the learning needs of the older tellers. Ask your older tellers about their experiences with training in the past—what worked, what didn't? This information might help you to design a training program that appeals to the older tellers as well as the younger ones.

ENDNOTES

1. Barrier, M. (2002, March). An age-old problem. *HRMagazine*, 34–37.
2. Himmelberg, M. (1999, March 3). Workforce is aging, shrinking. *Arizona Republic*, pp. A1, A10.
3. Carnahan, I. (2002, August 12). Removing the scarlet A. *Forbes*, 78.
4. Carnahan, I. (2002, August 12). Removing the scarlet A. *Forbes*, 78.
5. Moss, M. (1997, June 17). Gray area: For older employees, on-the-job injuries are more often deadly. *Wall Street Journal*, pp. A1, A10.
6. McMorris, F. A. (1997, February 20). Age-bias suits may become harder to prove. *Wall Street Journal*, pp. B1, B10; Barrier, M. (2002, March). An age-old problem. *HRMagazine*, 34–37.
7. *Adams v. Florida Power Corp.* (2001). 255 F.3d 1322 (11th Cir.).
8. *Marks v. Loral Corp.* (1997). 66 Cal. Reptr. 2d 1 (Cal. App. 4 Dist.); Bass, S. L., & Roukis, G. S. (1999). Age discrimination in employment: Will employers focus on business necessities and the "ROFTA" defense? *Commercial Law Journal, 104*, 229–239.
9. Gregory, R. F. (2001). *Age discrimination in the American workplace: Old at a young age.* New Brunswick, NJ: Rutgers University Press.
10. Chemerinsky, E. (2002, May). Can plaintiffs make disparate impact claims in age discrimination cases? *Trial*, 72–73; Siniscalco, G. R., Rahm, R. H., & Quinn, S. M. (2002). Adverse impact liability for age discrimination. *Employee Relations Law Journal, 28*(3), 75–104.
11. Barrier, M. (2002, March). An age-old problem. *HRMagazine*, 34–37.
12. Carnahan, I. (2002, August 12). Removing the scarlet A. *Forbes*, 78.
13. Woo, J. (1992, December 8). Ex-workers hit back with age-bias suits. *Wall Street Journal*, pp. B1, B14; McMorris, F. A. (1998, June 8). EEOC issues clarification of rule on termination of older workers. *Wall Street Journal*, p. B2.
14. Crew, J. C. (1984). Age stereotypes as a function of race. *Academy of Management Journal, 27*, 431–435.
15. Work week. (1998, March 24). *Wall Street Journal*, p. A1.
16. Hansson, R. O., DeKoekkoek, P. D., Neece, W. M., & Patterson, D. W. (1997). Successful aging at work: Annual review, 1992–1996: The older worker and transitions to retirement. *Journal of Vocational Behavior, 51*, 202–223; Warr, P. (1994). Age and employment. In H. C. Triandis, M. D. Dunnette, & L. M. Hough (Eds.), *Handbook of industrial and organizational psychology* (2nd ed., Vol. 4, pp. 485–550). Palo Alto, CA: Consulting Psychologists Press; Waldman, D. A., & Avolio, B. J. (1986). A meta-analysis of age differences in job performance. *Journal of Applied Psychology, 71*, 33–38.
17. Czaja, S. J. (1995). Aging and work performance. *Review of Public Personnel Administration, 15*(2), 46–61; Czaja, S. J., & Sharit, J. (1993). Age differences in the

performance of computer based work as a function of pacing and task complexity. *Psychology and Aging, 8*, 59–67; Giniger, S., Despenszieri, A., & Eisenberg, J. (1983). Age, experience, and performance on speed and skill jobs in an applied setting. *Journal of Applied Psychology, 68*, 469–475; Bosman, E. A. (1993). Age-related differences in the motoric aspects of transcription typing skill. *Psychology and Aging, 8*, 87–102.

18. Avolio, B. J., Waldman, D. A., & McDaniel, M. A. (1990). Age and work performance in non-managerial jobs: The effects of experience and occupational type. *Academy of Management Journal, 33*, 497–422.

19. Wellner, A. S. (2002, March). Tapping a silver mine. *HRMagazine*, 26–31.

20. Fisher, A. (1996, September 30). Wanted: Aging baby boomers. *Fortune*, 204.

21. Paul, R. J., & Townsend, J. B. (1993). Managing the older worker—don't just rinse away the gray. *Academy of Management Executive, 7*(3), 67–74.

22. Martocchio, J. J. (1989). Age related differences in employee absenteeism: A meta-analysis. *Psychology and Aging, 4*, 409–414.

23. Fisher, A. (1996, September 30). Wanted: Aging baby boomers. *Fortune*, 204.

24. Finkelstein, L. M., Burke, M. J., & Raju, N. S. (1995). Age discrimination in simulated employment contexts: An integrative analysis. *Journal of Applied Psychology, 80*, 652–663.

25. The job-huntin' blues. (1998, December 14). *Business Week*, 8.

26. Perry, E. L. (1997). A cognitive approach to understanding discrimination: A closer look at applicant gender and age. *Research in Personnel and Human Resources Management, 15*, 175–240.

27. Gregory, R. F. (2001). *Age discrimination in the American workplace: Old at a young age.* New Brunswick, NJ: Rutgers University Press.

28. Reingold, J., & Brady, D. (1999, September 20). Brain drain. *Fortune*, 112–126.

29. Fusaro, R. (2001, July-August). Needed: Experienced workers. *Harvard Business Review*, 20–21; Kirkland, R. I., Jr. (1994, February 21). Why we will live longer … and what it will mean. *Fortune*, 66–77.

30. Ansberry, C. (2001, February 5). The gray team: Averaging age 70, staff in this cosmetics plant retires old stereotypes. *Wall Street Journal*, pp. A1, A15.

31. Wellner, A. S. (2002, March). Tapping a silver mine. *HRMagazine*, 26–31.

32. Work week. (1998, March 24). *Wall Street Journal*, p. A1.

33. Reingold, J., & Brady, D. (1999, September 20). Brain drain. *Fortune*, 112–126.

34. Machan, D. (1989, September 4). Cultivating the gray. *Forbes*, 126–128; Fusaro, R. (2001, July/August). Needed: Experienced workers. *Harvard Business Review*, 20–21.

35. Ansberry, C. (2001, February 5). The gray team: Averaging age 70, staff in this cosmetics plant retires old stereotypes. *Wall Street Journal*, pp. A1, A15.

36. Rosen, B., & Jerdee, T. (1976). The influence of age stereotypes on managerial decisions. *Journal of Applied Psychology, 61*, 428–432; Rosen, B., & Jerdee, T. (1977). Too old or not too old. *Harvard Business Review, 55*, 97–105.

37. Simon, R. (1996). Too damn old. *Money, 25*(7), 118–126; Warr, P. (1994). Training for older managers. *Human Resource Management Journal, 4*, 22–38.

38. Maurer, T. J., & Rafuse, N. E. (2001). Learning, not litigating: Managing employee development and avoiding claims of age discrimination. *Academy of Management Executive, 15*(4), 110–121.

39. AARP. (2000). *American business and older employees survey.* Washington, DC: American Association of Retired Persons.

40. Work week. (1995, April 13). *Wall Street Journal*, p. A1; Farris, G. F., DiTomaso, N., & Cordero, R. (1995, August). *Over the hill and losing it? The senior scientist and engineer.* Paper presented at meetings of the Academy of Management, Vancouver.

41. Farris, G. F., DiTomaso, N., & Cordero, R. (1995, August). *Over the hill and losing it? The senior scientist and engineer*. Paper presented at meetings of the Academy of Management, Vancouver.

42. Simpson, P. A., Greller, M. M., & Stroh, L. K. (2002). Variations in human capital investment activity by age. *Journal of Vocational Behavior, 61,* 109–138; Czaja, S. J., & Sharit, J. (1998). Age differences in attitudes toward computers. *Journal of Gerontology: Psychological Sciences,* 329–340; Huuhtanen, P., & Leino, T. (1992). The impact of new technology by occupation and age on work in financial firms: A 2-year follow-up. *International Journal of Human-Computer Interaction, 4,* 123–142.

43. Adler, T. (1991, May). Not all cognitive skills affected by age. *APA Monitor,* 16; Wellner, A. S. (2002, March). Tapping a silver mine. *HRMagazine,* 26–31.

44. Rosen, B., & Jerdee, T. H. (1988). Managing older workers' careers. *Research in Personnel and Human Resources Management, 6,* 37–74; Hendrix, C. C. (2000, March/April). Computer use among elderly people. *Computers in Nursing, 18*(2), 62–68.

45. Azar, B. (1998, July). Older workers need not be left behind by technology. *APA Monitor,* 24; Hendrix, C. C. (2000, March/April). Computer use among elderly people. *Computers in Nursing, 18*(2), 62–68.

46. Greengard, S. (2002, March). Moving forward with reverse mentoring. *Workforce,* 15.

47. Murray, M. (2000, February 15). GE mentoring program turns underlings into teachers of the web. *Wall Street Journal,* pp. B1, B18.

48. U.S. Department of Labor. (2002). *Civilian labor force.* Retrieved February 2, 2003, from http://www.bls.gov/emp/emplab1.htm

49. Smola, K. W., & Sutton, C. D. (2002). Generational differences: Revisiting generational work values for the new millennium. *Journal of Organizational Behavior, 23,* 363–382.

50. Watson, N. (2002, October 14). Generation wrecked. *Fortune,* 183–190.

51. Lancaster, L. C., & Stillman, D. (2002). *When generations collide.* New York: HarperBusiness.

52. Lancaster, L. C., & Stillman, D. (2002). *When generations collide.* New York: HarperBusiness.

53. Robinson, K. (2002, December). Get ready to mediate among generations, speakers advise. *HR News,* 6–7.

54. Cohen, J. (2002). I/Os in the know offer insights on Generation X workers. *APA Monitor, 33*(2), 66–67.

55. Hornblower, M. (1997, June 9). Great expectations. *Time,* 58–68.

56. Wallace, J. (2001, April). After X comes Y. *HRMagazine,* 192.

57. Mulvey, P. W., Ledford, G. E., Jr., & LeBlanc, P. V. (2000, Third Quarter). Rewards of work: How they drive performance, retention and satisfaction. *WorldatWork,* 6–18.

58. Mulvey, P. W., Ledford, G. E., Jr., & LeBlanc, P. V. (2000, Third Quarter). Rewards of work: How they drive performance, retention and satisfaction. *WorldatWork,* 6–18; Jurkiewicz, C. L., & Brown, R. G. (1998, Fall). GenXers vs. boomers vs. matures. *Review of Public Personnel Administration,* 18–37.

59. Smola, K. W., & Sutton, C. D. (2002). Generational differences: Revisiting generational work values for the new millennium. *Journal of Organizational Behavior, 23,* 363–382.

60. Flynn, G. (1996, November). Xers vs. boomers: Teamwork or trouble? *Personnel Journal,* 86–89.

61. Tsui, A. S., & O'Reilly, C. A. (1989). Beyond simple demographic effects: The importance of relational demography in superior–subordinate dyads. *Academy of Management Journal, 32,* 402–423.

62. Bacharach, S. B., Bamberger, P., & Mundell, B. (1993). Status inconsistency in organizations: From social hierarchy to stress. *Journal of Organizational Behavior, 14*, 21–36.
63. Hymowitz, C. (1998, July 21). Young managers learn how to bridge the gap with older employees. *Wall Street Journal*, p. B1.
64. Shellenbarger, S., & Hymowitz, C. (1994, June 13). Over the hill? *Wall Street Journal*, pp. A1, A8.
65. Perry, E. L., Kulik, C. T., & Zhou, J. (1999). A closer look at the effects of subordinate–supervisor age differences. *Journal of Organizational Behavior, 20*, 341–357.
66. Zenger, T. R., & Lawrence, B. S. (1989). Organizational demography: The differential effects of age and tenure distributions on technical communication. *Academy of Management Journal, 32*, 353–376.
67. *Taggart v. Time, Inc.* (1991). 924 F.2d 43 (2nd Cir.)
68. Greenberg, J. C. (1996, April 2). Ruling backs age bias lawsuit. *Chicago Tribune*, pp. 1, back page.
69. Simpson, P. A., Greller, M. M., & Stroh, L. K. (2002). Variations in human capital investment activity by age. *Journal of Vocational Behavior, 61*, 109–138.

13

Managing Employees
With Disabilities

P eople with disabilities represent a huge underutilized resource for American businesses. There are 54 million Americans who have some kind of disability. But two out of three disabled people who are capable of working are unemployed, making this the demographic group with the highest unemployment rate.[1] Want more sobering statistics? Even in the late 1990s, when most employers were scrambling to find enough qualified workers, 70% of blind Americans who wanted a job couldn't find one. Among the employed blind, 30% are underemployed relative to their qualifications.[2]

In chapter 2, I gave you a quick overview of the Americans with Disabilities Act (ADA). I promised we'd return to the ADA and get into the topic in more depth. In this chapter, I'll tell you more about the ADA and explain what the law requires managers to do (and not do) in order to avoid discriminating against people with disabilities.

However, creating a positive environment for employees with disabilities takes more than just staying inside the law—it takes questioning your own stereotypes about people with disabilities, and examining how your organization may be unintentionally limiting opportunities for people with disabilities to succeed. One survey found that 43% of HR managers working for federal employers and 22% of those working for private employers described the negative attitudes of supervisors and coworkers as a continuing barrier to the employment and career advancement of people with disabilities.[3] That's bad news for both the employer and the disabled employee or job applicant, because these negative attitudes are often based on misperceptions and misinformation.[4] Employers who take proactive steps to hire people with disabilities find that their experience refutes negative expectations about disabled employees. For example, a 30-year study at DuPont revealed that employees with disabilities displayed job performance equal to or better than their coworkers without disabilities. And the employees with disabilities had safety and attendance records far above the norm.[5] DuPont's experience is far from unique. Box 13.1 describes some of the success experiences companies have had when they employ people with disabilities.

BOX 13.1
Proactive Efforts to Employ People with Disabilities

× IBM's Project Able program focuses on hiring and retaining workers with disabilities. Since 1999, the company has hired more than 200 people with disabilities.[6]

× About 750,000 airplane components are manufactured, machined, or assembled for Boeing Company at the Seattle Lighthouse for the Blind. A Boeing spokesperson says that the parts have an "exceptionally low" rejection rate of one per thousand.[7]

× Pizza Hut has employed thousands of individuals with disabilities over the last 15 years, and turnover among them is approximately 100% less than turnover among other new hires. Pizza Hut has saved millions of dollars from this lower turnover. In addition, it has received millions of dollars in federal tax credits for hiring job candidates with disabilities.[498]

× Sears Roebuck found that the average cost of accommodating employees with disabilities—raising or lowering a desk, putting in a ramp, altering a dress code—was less than $50.[9]

AMERICANS WITH DISABILITIES ACT (1990)

You'll remember from chapter 2 that the ADA prohibits discrimination against people with physical or mental *disabilities*. Employers are required to make a *reasonable accommodation* for applicants and employees with disabilities who are capable of performing the *essential functions* of the job. Employers do not need to make accommodations that would cause *undue hardship*. Those few sentences contain a lot of terms that need clarification. I've provided a summary of the ADA terms in Table 13.1. You might also consult the EEOC's guidelines on disabilities (available at eeoc.gov) for more information about the ADA.

What's a Disability?

"Disability" is defined as a physical or mental impairment that substantially limits one or more major life activities, such as walking, talking, seeing, hearing, or working. That definition is intentionally broad. Congress' goal in drafting the ADA was to develop a definition that would encompass most of the physical and mental conditions that people think of as disabilities. But, at the same time, Congress wanted to make sure that the definition would exclude basic physical characteristics (e.g., eye color) or trivial medical conditions (e.g., an infected finger).[10] There are certain conditions that are explicitly excluded from coverage under the ADA. These conditions include pedophilia, compulsive gambling, kleptomania, and pyromania.

Now that we've clarified what is *not* a disability under the ADA, let's see if we can figure out what *is*. Employees who bring discrimination claims under the ADA have to first establish that their conditions qualify as disabilities in order to demonstrate that they are protected by the law. Some conditions clearly meet the definition of a disability: A visual impairment such as blindness interferes with the life activity of seeing, so blindness is a disability under the ADA. A hearing impairment such as deafness interferes with the life activity of hearing, so deafness is a disability under the ADA. But that leaves a lot of conditions in a gray area. In this gray area, the decision about

TABLE 13.1

Components of the Americans with Disabilities Act (1990)

Term	Definition
Disability	A physical or mental impairment that substantially limits one or more major life activities
Essential functions	The primary duties associated with a job; duties that are critical to job performance
Reasonable accommodation	Modifications of the job or the work environment that allow a person with a disability to perform a job's essential functions
Undue hardship	Financial and nonfinancial costs that make an accommodation unreasonable for an employer to provide; depends on the type and cost of the accommodation needed, the size of the employer's business, the financial assets available to the employer, and any disruption caused by the accommodation

whether the condition qualifies as a disability under the ADA has to be made on a case-by-case basis. For one person, a physical condition like "arthritis" might be severe enough to substantially limit his or her ability to walk or work (and therefore meet the ADA criterion for a disability); for another, "arthritis" might not qualify. The critical issue in determining whether a person has a disability as defined by the ADA is not whether the person *has* a medical impairment, but the *effect* of that impairment on the person's daily life.[11]

Given the ADA's broad definition of a disability, it's probably not surprising that employers and people with medical impairments often disagree on whether the impairment constitutes a disability under the law, and several of these disagreements have now made their way through the court system. In general, these cases indicate that the courts are defining a disability very narrowly.[12]

In one case, twin sisters had applied for jobs as pilots at United Airlines. Both sisters had worked as commercial jet pilots and had extensive flight experience. They had uncorrected vision of 20/200 and corrected vision of 20/20. However, United required pilots to have *uncorrected* vision of 20/100. There's no disputing the fact that the sisters had visual impairments. However, the U.S. Supreme Court said that the sisters were not disabled as defined by the ADA. Why? Because their conditions were correctable (through the wearing of eyeglasses or contact lenses). As a result, the sisters' visual impairments did not "substantially limit" their life activities.

A similar logic was used in another case involving a UPS mechanic who was required to drive heavy vehicles as part of his job. He was terminated because of hypertension (high blood pressure), although he controlled his condition with medication. Again, the U.S. Supreme Court decided that the employee's condition did not qualify as a disability under the ADA. Why? Because the condition was controllable through medication. As long as the employee took his medication, the condition did not "substantially limit" his life activities.

And, in a third case, a former assembly line worker developed carpal tunnel syndrome and tendonitis, conditions that caused severe pain to her arms and hands. Again, the Supreme Court ruled that this employee's condition did not meet the definition of a disability under the ADA. Her condition prevented her from performing some of the manual activities associated with assembly line work, but she was still able to perform many manual tasks, including those associated with her personal hygiene.[13] Therefore, the court decided that her impairment did not substantially limit any *major* life activities.[14]

So what's the bottom line? This series of Supreme Court rulings provides some guidelines about when an applicant's or an employee's impairment is likely to be recognized as a disability. In general, the impairment has to be ongoing and noncorrectable. That eliminates a lot of conditions from ADA coverage, such as eyesight problems that can be improved by eyeglasses, or ailments, such as high blood pressure or diabetes, that can be controlled with medication.[15] In addition, the impairment has to prevent or severely restrict those life activities that are of central importance to daily life.[16] This might involve demonstrating, for example, that the impairment restricts the individual's ability to see, hear, walk, or talk outside of the workplace. It's not enough for an employee or job applicant to demonstrate that his or her impairment made it difficult or impossible to perform a particular job. In order for an employee or job applicant to be substantially limited in the major life activity of working, the impairment has to affect the individual's ability to perform a wide range of jobs.

Who Is Protected?

Now that you know the basic definition of "disability," we need to complicate it a little further. Three distinct groups of people are protected by the ADA. The first group includes those people who are *currently disabled*. This group includes those people who have a physical or mental condition that is currently limiting their life activities. You can't discriminate against someone because of his or her current medical condition.

The second group includes people who were *previously disabled*. This group includes people who previously experienced an impairment, but are not currently limited in their life activities by that impairment. For example, suppose one of your employees learns that he has a cancerous tumor. The employee has surgery and follow-up medical treatment and is currently cancer-free. This employee is still covered by the ADA. You can't discriminate against someone because of his or her medical history.

The third group includes people who are *regarded as disabled*. Take an employee who is HIV-positive but has not yet developed any symptoms associated with AIDS. This employee is not a member of either of the two previous categories of ADA coverage—she is not currently experiencing any impairment of her life activities, and she hasn't experienced those impairments in the past. But, if the organization treats her as disabled (i.e., if managers make assumptions about her capabilities as a result of her positive HIV status), it would be discrimination under the ADA. You can't discriminate against someone based on myths, fears, or stereotypes about his or her medical condition.

This last group (people who are regarded as disabled) also encompasses people who are associated with or who are related to people with disabilities. The ADA prohibits discrimination against people who are associated with a disabled person—as a caregiver, a family member, or a friend. For example, parents of a child with a disability or employees who volunteer time at an AIDS hospice are protected under the ADA. People who serve as caregivers to family members with disabilities say that managers often are reluctant to hire or promote them, because the managers assume that the caregivers won't be able to handle the workload.[17] According to the ADA, you can't discriminate against someone based on their caregiving status, or based on assumptions you are making about their ability to balance their work and nonwork responsibilities. The ADA does not explicitly require that you accommodate caregivers with time off or schedule changes (but the FMLA might require such accommodation—see chap. 2).

What's an Essential Function?

Do you play golf? Even if you don't golf yourself, you're probably familiar with the general structure of the game. Think about the game of golf, and answer this question: How essential is it that a player walk between shots? In other words, if a player makes a shot, and then rides a golf cart to the ball before playing the next shot, is that person still playing golf? Think about it, and we'll come back to the question in just a minute.

Every job has essential and nonessential functions. *Essential functions* are the primary duties—the responsibilities that are absolutely critical to job performance. A truck driver must be able to drive a truck. A typist must be able to type. *Nonessential functions* are the peripheral activities—activities that might be nice to have the jobholder perform, but not essential. Under the ADA, managers making decisions about employees or applicants with disabilities are only supposed to consider whether the person with a disability can perform the *essential functions* of the job—not the nonessential ones.

What does the ADA have to do with my question about golf? Well, in 2001, the Supreme Court had to decide whether walking between shots was an essential function of the game of golf. Casey Martin is a professional golfer who suffers from Klippel–Trenaunay–Weber Syndrome in his right leg, severely restricting his ability to walk a golf course. He wanted to ride a golf cart between shots when he competed in major tournaments. The issue was hotly debated: The PGA argued that walking between shots *is* an essential function because it adds an element of "fatigue" to golf events. Professional golfers may walk 20 miles or more during a typical 4-day, 72-hole PGA tournament.[18] However, the Supreme Court disagreed, saying that "shot-making" was the essential component in a golf competition, not walking.[19]

Just like the Casey Martin case, deciding whether a particular task is an essential or nonessential function is a judgment call. Suppose you're hiring a mailroom employee. One of the applicants has a back injury that prevents him from lifting heavy objects. Most of the time, mailroom employees sort letters, but sometimes a heavy package comes in that needs to be delivered to the addressee. Is "lifting 40-pound packages" an essential function of the job? How do you decide? One factor to consider is the amount of time spent on the task; a task that is performed only once in a while, for a brief period, probably is not an essential function. If 40-pound packages come in daily, lifting them might be an essential function. But, if 40-pound packages only get delivered a couple of times a year, lifting them probably isn't an essential function. You should also consider how much of a problem it would be if that particular task didn't get done—nonessential functions, by definition, are not very critical. For example, would it be a disaster if the 40-pound package wasn't delivered until the next shift so someone other than the employee with the back injury could handle it?

Remember, you can only base decisions about people with disabilities on their ability to perform the essential functions of the job. That means you can't discriminate against people with disabilities based on nonessential elements like appearance or customer reactions. Let's say you have a job applicant who is obese. The applicant's weight causes difficulty walking and breathing, so the applicant clearly meets the definition of having a "disability." Now what? Do you have to hire the applicant? It depends on the essential functions. If you are hiring a construction worker, and the applicant's weight makes it impossible for him to climb the scaffolding and carry the necessary equipment, he cannot perform the essential functions of the job and should not be hired. But if you are hiring a secretary, your decision to not hire the job applicant might be discriminatory if it is based on the applicant's weight.[20] Answering phones, typing letters, and filing correspondence are essential functions associated with a secretarial job, and the applicant's obesity probably does not interfere with those tasks.

Even if a person with a disability can perform the essential functions of a job, employers can refuse to employ individuals if their performance of a job would pose a threat to either their own health and safety, or the health and safety of others. For example, in one case, the Supreme Court okayed a refinery's decision to not employ a worker whose liver disease made it dangerous for him to work in the chemical-laden atmosphere of the refinery.[21]

What's an Accommodation?

Accommodations, in general, modify the job or the work environment so that a person with a disability can perform the essential functions. Depending on the disability, accommodations might include acquiring new equipment, changing work schedules, redistributing tasks and responsibilities, changing the physical environment, putting things into smaller loads, or providing qualified readers or interpreters.

In many cases, accommodations are surprisingly low tech. An accommodation for a paraplegic employee might be as simple as propping a desk up on blocks so a wheelchair can slide under it. Some disabilities can be easily accommodated through the use of standard office equipment such as headsets, paper stands, electric hole punchers and staplers, or tape recorders.[22] At the high tech end, equipment is available to accommodate a huge variety of disabilities in many jobs. Employees with visual impairments can benefit from the use of speech recognition systems on office PCs or screen magnifiers. Telecommunications products are available that allow deaf employees to read what is spoken on the other end of a telephone line. Even paralyzed individuals can use a computer through the assistance of programs that are controlled by eye movements.[23] Pitney Bowes has developed a copy machine that can be operated by almost anyone. The Universal Access Copier is outfitted with speech recognition and has selector buttons that can be controlled with a mouse, fingers, or pointing stick. And for wheelchair users, the copier is designed to be lower to the ground than conventional machines.[24]

Often, the job applicant or the employee is the best source for identifying a reasonable accommodation. People with disabilities may be able to clearly describe the kinds of changes and adjustments that would benefit them. However, other sources of information are also available. For example, the Job Accommodation Network (JAN) is a free consulting service sponsored by the Department of Labor's Office of Disability Employment Policy (www.jan.wvu.edu, 800-526-7234). JAN gives advice to employers about hiring and accommodating people with disabilities and its Web site offers many suggestions on how to accommodate specific disabilities.

What's Undue Hardship?

All that talk about using technology to accommodate employees with disabilities can sometimes make dollar signs start flashing in managers' heads, but providing reasonable accommodations doesn't need to break the bank. In fact, most accommodations are not expensive at all. Studies by JAN have shown that 15% of accommodations cost absolutely nothing, and only 22% cost more than $1,000.[25] Sometimes employees provide their own accommodations in the form of assistive devices or equipment. If these accommodations are used outside of the workplace, they are the employee's responsibility to provide, not yours. Funding for accommodations may be available from tax deductions or state rehabilitation agencies. The EEOC Web site (eeoc.gov) contains information about federal tax incentives designed to encourage the employment of people with disabilities and to promote the accessibility of public accommodations.

The ADA requires only that employers provide *reasonable* accommodation, not the best or most technologically advanced accommodation available. You don't have to hire a full-time sign language interpreter if the employee's hearing disability can be accommodated by passing notes to clarify the spoken words. In addition, you don't need to provide any accommodation that would impose an *undue hardship* on your business.

Undue hardship is another one of those judgment calls. An assessment of undue hardship is based on a consideration of the financial and nonfinancial costs associated with providing an accommodation. In determining whether an accommodation imposed an undue hardship on an employer, a court would consider the type and cost of the accommodation needed, the size of the employer's business, and the financial assets available to the employer. Buying and installing voice recognition software might impose an undue hardship on a struggling mom-and-pop business; the same accommodation is unlikely to constitute an undue hardship for a Fortune 500 corporation. Accommodations that disrupt the work of other employees or interfere with the normal course of business might also constitute an undue hardship, but the disruption has to directly result from the accommodation. Disruptions that result from fear or prejudice are unlikely to be considered as undue hardship.

The ADA in Practice

The ADA was a very popular law when it was first enacted. It seemed like a win–win proposition. The ADA was expected to benefit people with physical impairments by reducing discriminatory practices that exclude them from productive employment. At the same time, the ADA would benefit employers by encouraging them to ease labor shortages by taking advantage of this underutilized labor pool. Initially, it was expected that most complaints brought under the ADA would deal with hiring discrimination against employees with visual or auditory impairments—people who have historically been underemployed in the U.S. workforce.

More than 10 years after enactment, it's interesting to see how the ADA has actually been applied. There are two surprises. First, relatively few complaints to the EEOC are claiming discrimination resulting from disabilities like blindness and deafness. In fact, the two most common categories of complaints are mental disabilities and back problems![26] Second, most cases don't involve hiring discrimination, they involve discrimination in termination decisions. More than one half of the claims filed with the EEOC are from people claiming that they were wrongfully terminated due to their disability status.[27] In other words, the people filing disability discrimination claims are usually *employees*, not job applicants. As a practicing manager, two of the biggest disability-related challenges you are likely to face are accommodating employees with mental disabilities and accommodating employees who develop a disability during their employment.

Accommodating Mental Disabilities.   The ADA prohibits discrimination against people with either physical or mental impairments that limit their life activities. Individuals with mental impairments covered by the ADA include employees who suffer from bipolar disorder, severe phobias, clinical depression, or other psychological conditions. There's a high likelihood that you will be managing employees who have these or other mental disabilities. In a typical office of 20 people, chances are as many as 4 coworkers will suffer from a mental illness in a given year.[28] Depression is one of the most common mental illnesses. Each year, clinical depression alone causes a loss of some 200 million working days in the United States.[29] And depressive episodes are most likely to occur when people are in their 20s, 30s, and 40s—years in which people are likely to be hitting their stride in their chosen careers.[30]

Like people with physical impairments, employees with mental impairments have to cope with discrimination in the workplace that is often based on inaccurate information about their disabilities.[31] However, discrimination against people with mental or psychological disabilities can be even harder to identify and manage than discrimination against people with physical disabilities. On the employee side, people with these disabilities often have learned to hide their conditions for fear of damaging their careers, making it more difficult to identify situations in which accommodation is needed.[32] And on the employer side, many managers are uncertain about how employees with nonphysical disabilities should be accommodated. It's one thing to accommodate an employee in a wheelchair by making physical changes to the workplace. It's less clear how to accommodate an employee coping with the emotional issues associated with a psychological condition.

The good news is that, in many cases, accommodating employees with mental disabilities can be accomplished using the same strategies as accommodating employees with physical disabilities.[33] Employees with mental disabilities often require accommodations in the form of time off for medical treatment or reduced work hours—similar to the accommodations needed by employees coping with physical impairments. Employees who are taking medication to manage their illnesses may require an adjustment in their work schedules so that more difficult tasks can be performed while the medication is at full effect. Other employees might require modifications to their workspaces (e.g., working in a less crowded area, or introducing white noise) in order to effectively manage the amount of visual or auditory stimulation they receive from their physical environment.

Managers sometimes are reluctant to accommodate employees with mental illnesses. They fear that they will be forced to retain employees who are difficult to work with or employees who use their illness as an excuse for shoddy work or special treatment.[34] However, the same ADA requirements, as well as their limits, apply to mental and physical disabilities. The goal of the ADA is to ensure that qualified employees with disabilities (employees who can perform a job's essential functions) are not discriminated against in the workplace. You *are* required to accommodate employees with mental disabilities who are capable of performing the job's essential functions. But you should *not* lower work standards, tolerate misconduct, or give someone a make-work job as part of the accommodation.[35]

Accommodating Employees with Disabilities.   Managers who are familiar with the ADA sometimes think the law only applies when new employees are hired. However, the ADA also requires that you accommodate employees who develop a disability during the course of their employment. Be on the alert for requests for accommodation from current employees. Employees who need accommodation may not mention the ADA directly or use a legal term like "reasonable accommodation." They may simply ask for some kind of help or point out obstacles they are experiencing in their jobs. These informal statements still constitute requests for reasonable accommodation under the ADA, and they require your attention.[36]

In general, the law requires employers to make greater efforts to accommodate a current employee who becomes disabled than a job applicant with a disability. Accommodating employees' disabilities might require some creative thinking. In addition to the accommodations discussed earlier, reasonable accommodations for employees who develop a disability might include the opportunity to work from home or to be transferred to a different job.[37] In addition, the ADA requires managers to be sensitive to the needs of employees who are injured on the job. Historically, injured workers were sent home and didn't return to work until they were 100% capable of performing their old jobs the same way they had always been performed. But under the ADA, you (the employer) are required to bring back to work anyone you can reasonably accommodate. Many organizations now have return-to-work programs designed to accommodate employees who are recovering from injuries. These employees might return to work on a reduced work schedule or do light-duty work during the recovery period.[38]

Finally, be attentive to the long-term career needs of employees with disabilities. Some research finds that people with disabilities, once hired, have limited opportunities for advancement in their organizations. People with disabilities are viewed as dependable and productive in lower level positions, but tend to be overlooked when managerial positions become available.[39] Don't let an employee's disability blind you to the contributions he or she could make by assuming greater responsibilities in the organization.

MANAGING THE HIRING PROCESS

Now that you know the basic elements of the ADA, let's think about how you would apply the law to your own management context. Under the ADA, part of your responsibility is to modify the job application and hiring process so that employees with disabilities can be considered for employment. A close look at your application process might identify ways that the process screens out people with disabilities who are able to perform the essential functions of the job. For example, a classified ad that requires making a telephone inquiry might prevent people from applying if they have a hearing disability that limits their ability to use the phone. If the essential functions of the job do not include phone skills, this application process might be discriminatory. Can the application process be expanded to include in-person inquiries or inquiries by letter? A hiring process that requires applicants to take a paper-and-pencil test might prevent people from being considered if they have certain physical disabilities (e.g., limited motor skills or a visual impairment). If these physical requirements are not essential functions associated with the job, this hiring process may be discriminatory. Can an applicant take the test in other ways—for example, by having the questions read out loud and offering verbal answers?

It's good management practice to consistently describe to prospective applicants the requirements of the hiring process and ask whether any accommodations will be needed.[40] Is there a written test? Will applicants participate in a work simulation? Does the office location require climbing a flight of stairs? This information helps applicants to prepare and bring any adaptive equipment (e.g., eyeglasses, hearing aids, canes) that they need for the screening procedure.[41]

Once you've ensured that the application process can accommodate people with various disabilities, the next thing to consider is the employment interview. As we discussed in chapter 5, most hiring decisions involve a face-to-face interview. So it's a good idea to think about how you would interview someone with a disability now—before it happens. Look around your office and the building in which it is located. Could someone access it using a wheelchair? How would someone with a visual disability learn where your office is located? If an applicant arrives with an assistant or a sign language interpreter, can your interviewing space accommodate an additional person?

It's during the interview that you are most likely to learn that an applicant has a disability. In addition, the interview context is where you and the applicant are most likely to discuss any accommodations that might be required if the applicant is hired. The ADA does not permit employers to directly ask questions about an applicant's current health or past medical history. For example, asking an applicant "Do you have asthma?" would be clearly inappropriate. In addition, the ADA specifies that job applicants cannot be asked to take a medical exam until a job offer has been extended. (You can make job offers conditional on the results of a postoffer medical exam—but only if the exam is required of all new employees and any postoffer decisions are based on medical issues that are directly job related.)

So, if you can't come right out and ask applicants if they have a disability, how are you supposed to learn whether a job applicant has a disability that might require accommodation? There are three possibilities: (a) The disability might be apparent (e.g., the applicant arrives at the interview in a wheelchair or accompanied by a guide dog); (b) during the interview, the applicant might initiate a discussion about a disability that is otherwise not apparent; (c) during the interview, you ask a question about job performance that prompts a discussion about a nonapparent disability. Regardless of how you learn about an applicant's disability, you are responsible for accommodating an applicant who can perform the essential functions of a job.

In the first situation, your job is easy. If the disability is apparent, you can directly ask someone to describe or demonstrate how they would perform job-related tasks. The other two situations are more difficult. Remember that the applicant with a disability is balancing on a tightrope. If the applicant and the prospective employer can have a frank, candid discussion about the disability and needed accommodations, both sides benefit. But an applicant who discloses a disability and requests an accommodation risks having opportunities denied because of discrimination or misperceptions.[42] That's why your interviewing style is so important—you want to make sure that the job applicant knows enough about the job's requirements to be able to recognize whether their disability is likely to be an issue. Of course, that's no surprise to you. After reading chapter 5, you already know how valuable job interviews can be in providing realistic job previews to prospective employees.

You can create opportunities for applicants to describe their disabilities and accommodation needs by clearly describing the job's essential functions (this job requires working on Saturday; this job requires lifting 50-pound boxes; this job requires travel on short notice) and asking *all* applicants if anything would prevent them from performing those functions. It's perfectly reasonable to ask applicants, point-blank, behavioral questions (remember those from chap. 5?) about barriers and support that they've experienced in the past: "Describe a barrier or obstacle that you encountered in a previous job. How did you overcome that barrier or obstacle?" or "Is there any technology or equipment that you used in previous jobs that made you a better performer?"[43] Notice that these questions can be asked of every applicant and can open up a frank communication about what the applicant needs to succeed in your work environment—without making any assumptions about disabilities.[44] Describing the job's psychological demands (e.g., situations that require a fast decision based on incomplete information, situations that require multitasking), and asking employees how they would manage those demands, can also help employees to understand the nonphysical demands of the job. Forewarning applicants about a job's psychological demands may be especially important for applicants with mental disabilities. Applicants with insufficient coping skills for the job conditions can screen themselves out or request appropriate accommodation.[45]

Manager's Checkpoint

Use the following questions to make sure you are prepared to interview job applicants with disabilities:

- Have I reviewed the application process to ensure that qualified people with disabilities can apply for the job? (Pay special attention to parts of the application process that can only be done in one way—e.g., by using a phone, or by taking a paper-and-pencil test. Unless these procedures directly mimic essential functions of the job, the application process may be preventing people with disabilities from applying.)
- Have I made sure that the physical space in which I conduct interviews is accessible to employees with disabilities? (Be on the alert for interview rooms that are too small to accommodate interpreters, seeing eye dogs, or wheelchairs. Also watch for interview rooms that are only accessible by stairs or have doorways too narrow to allow wheelchair access.)
- Am I familiar with the job's essential functions? (Remember that decisions about applicants with disabilities can only be based on the essential functions. Review job descriptions and clarify which requirements are essential, and which are nonessential. Talk with current job incumbents and coworkers about the relative importance of different job activities. Consider the consequences that would result if some activities were not performed by a new hire.)
- Have I developed behavioral interview questions that focus on the job's essential functions? (Behavioral questions will help the

applicant to identify situations in which accommodations may be necessary, and open the door to a frank discussion about how the applicant can best perform the job.)

MANAGING COWORKERS OF PEOPLE WITH DISABILITIES

Now, let's address some practical issues. You know the law, and you want to make sure that your organization makes every effort to accommodate employees with disabilities. Imagine yourself in this situation. You're a store manager, and one of your employees, Amy, is being treated for a serious illness. The treatment appears to be successful, but it has unfortunate side effects—nausea and diarrhea. Amy has asked to be allowed to use the rest room whenever need arises. This is a no brainer, right? Amy has suggested an accommodation that is absolutely free, so you readily agree to the accommodation.

Now, fast forward 2 weeks. Several of Amy's coworkers have noticed her slipping off to the rest room. These coworkers resent the way Amy flaunts the rules. Store employees are usually asked to limit rest room visits to their regularly scheduled breaks, to ensure that there are always enough employees available on the floor to respond to customers. Rumors are starting to spread regarding favoritism.

What's the point of this example? The point is that you don't just manage an employee with a disability—you manage that employee as well as all of his or her coworkers. Accommodations can raise issues about unfair treatment, especially when coworkers are not privy to all of the underlying information.

Let's be clear about what you *don't* do in this situation. You *don't* call a storewide meeting and tell everyone about Amy's condition and the accommodation you've arranged. Under the ADA, an employer has a responsibility to preserve confidentiality about employees' medical information, which includes information about the disability itself, and information about any accommodations. Information should be shared only on a need-to-know basis.

So, what *can* you do? The EEOC suggests that managers respond to coworkers' questions in general terms. When Amy's coworkers complain about favoritism, you might say that you are following the company's policy of assisting any employee encountering workplace difficulties. Or you might say that you are responding to a personal issue and respect the employee's privacy—and would show the same respect for any employee.[46] These responses stop short of sharing any personal information about Amy's condition, and let you address coworker complaints without violating the confidentiality requirement of the ADA.

But that doesn't solve the broader problem. Next week, another employee with a different disability will ask for a different accommodation, and a new set of rumors will start. A better long-term solution is to educate all your employees about the ADA. Do your employees know about the ADA and its requirements? A general education seminar might help to make employees more sensitive not just to coworkers' needs but to the needs of customers with disabilities as well.[47] Ideally, this kind of seminar would be conducted before any employee requests an accommodation. A seminar on the ADA can help coworkers to understand that what looks like unfair treatment may actually be an effort to accommodate an employee's disability. And most employees can understand why a coworker wouldn't want personal information about a medical condition or its side effects to be shared.

This kind of educational effort becomes even more important when coworkers are directly affected by the organization's efforts to accommodate a disabled employee.[48] For example, hiring an employee with a hearing disability may impose some additional requirements on coworkers. Let's say that you run a gift basket business, where customer orders come in by phone, by mail, and by fax. You've hired a hearing impaired employee who can handle the mail and fax orders, but not the phone orders. Coworkers need to be ready to step in when the phone rings. One survey found that a majority of U.S. employees (52%) believe it's fair to have their own work schedules or job duties changed to accommodate coworkers with disabilities. But the survey also found that workers don't consider many conditions to be qualified disabilities—including cancer, diabetes, or AIDS.[49] Again, these findings point to the importance of educating your entire workforce about the ADA—including explaining the range of medical conditions that may be disabilities.

In addition to education, you may want to explicitly reward coworker behavior that facilitates the integration of people with disabilities into the workplace.[50] These rewards may be tangible or intangible. For example, the performance appraisal system may directly consider the extent to which coworkers work effectively with their teammates—including teammates with disabilities. More important, however, may be the social rewards associated with management approval. By explicitly recognizing and encouraging employees who mentor or support coworkers with disabilities, you can encourage these behaviors.

Manager's Checkpoint

Use the following questions to anticipate and manage the concerns of coworkers who work with an employee with a disability:

- Am I familiar with the ADA requirements regarding confidentiality? Who is in a "need to know" position? (The ADA requires that you share information about an employee's disability and any accommodations with supervisors and coworkers only on a need to know basis.)
- Have I educated my workforce about the ADA and its requirements? Do employees know the broad range of disabilities that are covered by the ADA, and the kinds of accommodations that might be made? (These educational efforts should emphasize that disabilities may sometimes be invisible to coworkers, but nonetheless require accommodation.)
- Do my employees understand the importance of "pitching in" to help coworkers perform their jobs—including coworkers with a disability? Am I prepared to evaluate and reward these behaviors? (Your performance evaluation system is a valuable tool in situations where coworkers must assist in the accommodation effort. Make sure that employees understand that accommodating coworkers is part of their own job responsibilities—and that these responsibilities will be recognized and valued by the organization.)

WHAT'S NEXT?

We've come to the end of the line. In these 13 chapters, we've covered the basics of human resource management. And, in the last few chapters, we've focused on some important challenges resulting from the demographics of today's workforce. Your managerial toolkit is now fully stocked. Good luck in your future human resource management efforts!

FOR FURTHER READING

Cohen, S. (2002, October). High-tech tools lower barriers for disabled. *HRMagazine*, 60–65.

Rodriguez, A., & Prezant, F. (2002, August). Better interviews for people with disabilities. *Workforce*, 38–42.

Segal, J. A. (2001, February). I'm depressed—accommodate me! *HRMagazine*, 139–148.

Wells, S. J. (April, 2001). Is the ADA working? *HRMagazine*, 38–46.

MANAGER'S KNOT 13.1

"I recently hired a computer programmer with multiple sclerosis. She's terrific. The only problem is that, because of her muscular weakness, she can't maintain an erect sitting position for more than about thirty minutes. Every half hour, somebody will need to help her get repositioned so that she can breathe properly and continue working. Is that my responsibility? Can I assign the responsibility to one of the employee's coworkers?"

Accommodating people with disabilities in the workplace often requires the cooperation of coworkers. First, make sure that the employees who will be working with the programmer know the basics of the ADA and its requirements. Emphasize the wide range of disabilities that are covered by the law—and the ways that hiring and retaining people with disabilities can benefit organizations. Then explain the needs of the new hire. Many of your employees may be unfamiliar with multiple sclerosis and its effects. If they respond negatively to the new hire, it's likely to be because of their own fears or misunderstandings about the condition. Before the new hire arrives on site, make sure that coworkers have had the opportunity to air their concerns and get their questions answered. If your employees understand the needs of their new coworker, and the ways that she will be contributing to your group, they are more likely to be willing to assist in the accommodation effort.

MANAGER'S KNOT 13.2

"One of my employees has a drinking problem, and it's beginning to affect his job performance. Can I fire this employee, or is he protected under the ADA?"

Alcoholism may, in some situations, constitute a "disability" under the ADA. If your employee is currently receiving treatment for his condition, you may be required to provide reasonable accommodation (e.g., time off to attend Alcoholics Anonymous meetings). However, all employees, whether or not they have disabilities, are subject to the same organizational performance and conduct standards. If this employee is not meeting performance standards, you should take the same disciplinary action you would take with any employee. And if the employee is violating organizational rules or policies (e.g., by drinking on the job), you can take disciplinary action.

MANAGER'S KNOT 13.3

"I recently hired a new employee to work on a big new project with a pressing deadline. Her job offer was conditional on passing a medical exam. Well, the exam identified a problem. It's not life-threatening, but the treatment will require her to miss several days of work every week—it'll be impossible for her to contribute to this project on a full-time basis. Can I rescind the offer? Meeting the project deadline requires a 24/7 commitment over the next few months."

The answer to your question hinges on whether regular attendance until the project deadline constitutes an "essential job function." If attendance is an essential job function, and there is no reasonable accommodation that would allow the employee to fulfill that function, she is not qualified, and the offer can be rescinded. But rescinding the offer is not a decision you should make lightly. Review the project requirements and the consequences of not meeting the project deadline so that you can clearly demonstrate that regular attendance over the next few months would constitute an essential job function.

ENDNOTES

1. Cohen, S. (2002, October). High-tech tools lower barriers for disabled. *HRMagazine*, 60–65.
2. Johnston, L. (1999, July 4). Blind left out of America's economic prosperity. *Arizona Republic*, p. A23.
3. Dutton, G. (2000, December). The ADA at 10. *Workforce*, 41–46.
4. Fichten, C. S., & Amsel, R. (1986). Trait attributions about college students with a physical disability: Circumplex analyses and methodological issues. *Journal of Applied Social Psychology, 16*, 410–427; Fuqua, D. R., Rathbun, M., & Gade, E. M. (1984). A comparison of employer attitudes toward the worker problems of eight types of disabled workers. *Journal of Applied Rehabilitation Counseling, 15*, 40–43; Gouvier, W. D., Steiner, D. D., Jackson, W. T., Schlater, D., & Rain, J. S. (1991). Employment discrimination against handicapped job candidates: An analog study of the effects of neurological causation, visibility of handicap, and public contact. *Rehabilitation Psychology, 36*, 121–129; Ravaud, J. F., Madiot, B., & Ville, I. (1992). Discrimination towards disabled people seeking employment. *Social Science and Medicine, 35*, 951–958.
5. Conlin, M. (2000, March 20). The new workforce. *Business Week*, 64–68.
6. Cohen, S. (2002, October). High-tech tools lower barriers for disabled. *HRMagazine*, 60–65.
7. Work week. (2000, February 15). *Wall Street Journal*, p. B1.
8. Raphael, T. (2002, August). Disabling some old stereotypes. *Workforce*, 88.
9. Hunt, A. R. (1999, March 11). The disabilities act is creating a better society. *Wall Street Journal*, p. A23.
10. Lee, B. A. (2001). The implications of ADA litigation for employers: A review of federal appellate court decisions. *Human Resource Management, 40*(1), 35–50.

11. Lee, B. A. (2001). The implications of ADA litigation for employers: A review of federal appellate court decisions. *Human Resource Management, 40*(1), 35–50.

12. *Murphy v. United Parcel Service.* (1999). 119 S.Ct. 1331; *Sutton v. United Air Lines.* (1999). WL 407488 (No. 97-1943); *Toyota Motor Manufacturing Kentucky, Inc. v. Williams.* (2002). 122 S. Ct. 681.

13. Mook, J. R. (2002). Toyota v. Williams: The disability analysis continues. *Employee Relations Law Journal, 28,* 25–46.

14. Barrier, M. (2002, July). A line in the sand. *HRMagazine,* 35–42; Work week. (2002, January 15). *Wall Street Journal,* p. A1; Gearan, A. (2001, November 8). Supreme Court urged to expand disability law. *Arizona Republic,* p. D5.

15. Greenberger, R. S. (1999, June 23). Supreme court narrows scope of disability act. *Wall Street Journal,* pp. B1, B4; Garland, S. B. (1999, April 26). Protecting the disabled won't cripple business. *Business Week,* 71–73.

16. Mook, J. R. (2002). Toyota v. Williams: The disability analysis continues. *Employee Relations Law Journal, 28,* 25–46.

17. Shellenbarger, S. (2000, September 13). Employees complain bosses don't recognize roles as caregivers. *Wall Street Journal,* p. B1.

18. Greenberger, R. S. (2001, January 18). High court hears arguments on disabled professional golfer. *Wall Street Journal,* p. B3; Murphy, K. (1998, February 12). Ticket to ride. *Arizona Republic,* pp. A1, A12.

19. Robb, R. (2001, June 30). PGA case puts all sport and all rules in jeopardy. *Arizona Republic,* V5.

20. Work week. (1999, August 24). *Wall Street Journal,* p. A1; Lambert, W. (1993, November 23). U.S. Court ruling bars hiring bias against the obese. *Wall Street Journal,* p. B12.

21. Greenhouse, L. (2002, June 11). Employers, in 9-0 ruling by justices, extend winning streak in disabilities-act cases. *New York Times,* p. A24.

22. Rodriguez, A., & Prezant, F. (2002, August). Better interviews for people with disabilities. *Workforce,* 38–42.

23. Williams, J. (2000, March 20). Enabling technologies. *Business Week,* 68–70.

24. Williams, J. (2000, March 20). Enabling technologies. *Business Week,* 68–70.

25. Cohen, S. (2002, October). High-tech tools lower barriers for disabled. *HRMagazine,* 60–65.

26. Work week. (1999, January 5). *Wall Street Journal,* p. A1; Santiago, F. (2000, July 5). ADA complaints full of pains in the back. *USA Today,* p. 5A; Curtis, K. (1999, May 20). Bias against employees with mental ills lingers. *Arizona Republic,* pp. D1, D3.

27. Armour, S. (1998, September 25). Disabilities act abused? *USA Today,* p. 1B; Wells, S. J. (2001, April). Is the ADA working? *HRMagazine,* 38–46.

28. Tanouye, E. (2001, June 13). Mental illness: A rising workplace cost. *Wall Street Journal,* pp. B1, B6.

29. Forster, J. (2000, October 30). When workers just can't cope. *BusinessWeek,* 100–102.

30. Tanouye, E. (2001, June 13). Mental illness: A rising workplace cost. *Wall Street Journal,* pp. B1, B6.

31. Tringo, J. L. (1970). The hierarchy of preference toward disability groups. *Journal of Special Education, 4,* 295–306; Schneider, C. R., & Anderson, Z. (1980). Attitudes toward the stigmatized: Some insights for recent research. *Rehabilitation Counseling Bulletin, 23,* 299–313; Bordieri, J. E., Drehmer, D. E., & Taylor, D. W. (1997). Work life for employees with disabilities: Recommendations for promotion. *Rehabilitation Counseling Bulletin, 40*(3), 181–191.

32. Tanouye, E. (2001, June 13). Mental illness: A rising workplace cost. *Wall Street Journal,* pp. B1, B6.

33. Sonnenberg, S. P. (2000, June). Mental disabilities in the workplace. *Workforce*, 142–146.
34. Stone, D. L., & Colella, A. (1996). A model of factors affecting the treatment of disabled individuals in organizations. *Academy of Management Review, 21*, 352–401.
35. Forster, J. (2000, October 30). When workers just can't cope. *BusinessWeek*, 100–102.
36. O'Blenes, C. (1999, September). ADA lessons from the front lines. *Management Review*, 58–60.
37. Podlas, K. (2001, September/October). Reasonable accommodation or special privilege? Flex-time, telecommuting, and the ADA. *Business Horizons*, 61–65.
38. Jeffrey, N. A. (1996, October 28). Employers aggressively attack disability costs. *Wall Street Journal*, pp. B1, B6.
39. Bordieri, J. E., Drehmer, D. E., & Taylor, D. W. (1997). Work life for employees with disabilities: Recommendations for promotion. *Rehabilitation Counseling Bulletin, 40*(3), 181–191; Bolton, B., & Roessler, R. (1985). After the interview: How employers rate handicapped employees. *Personnel*, 38–41; Freedman, S., & Keller, R (1981). The handicapped in the workforce. *Academy of Management Review, 6*, 449–458.
40. Woodward, N H. (1999, January). Interviewing people with disabilities. *HRMagazine Focus*, 13–20.
41. Rodriguez, A., & Prezant, F. (2002, August). Better interviews for people with disabilities. *Workforce*, 38–42.
42. Florey, A. T., & Harrison, D. A. (2000). Responses to informal accommodation requests from employees with disabilities: Multistudy evidence on willingness to comply. *Academy of Management Journal, 43*, 224–233; Cleveland, J. N., Barnes-Farrell, J., & Ratz, J. M. (1997). Accommodation in the workplace. *Human Resource Management Review, 7*, 77–108; Baldridge, D. C., & Veiga, J. F. (2001). Toward a greater understanding of the willingness to request an accommodation: Can requesters' beliefs disable the Americans with Disabilities Act? *Academy of Management Review, 26*, 85–99.
43. Rodriguez, A., & Prezant, F. (2002, August). Better interviews for people with disabilities. *Workforce*, 38–42; Sonnenberg, S. (2002, August). Can HR legally ask the questions that applicants with disabilities want to be asked? *Workforce*, 42–44.
44. Cohen, S. (2002, October). High-tech tools lower barriers for disabled. *HRMagazine*, 60–65.
45. Segal, J. A. (2001, February). I'm depressed—accommodate me! *HRMagazine*, 139–148.
46. Petesch, P. J. (2000 November). Popping the disability-related question. *HRMagazine*, 161–172.
47. Frierson, J. G. (1992, May). An employer's dilemma: The ADA's provisions on reasonable accommodation and confidentiality. *Labor Law Journal*, 308–312.
48. Colella, A. (2001). Coworker distributive fairness judgments of the workplace accommodation of employees with disabilities. *Academy of Management Review, 26*, 100–116.
49. Smith, B. (1992, July). That was then, this is now: Workers are willing to accommodate coworkers with disabilities. *HR Focus, 69*, 3–5.
50. Stone, D. L., & Colella, A. (1996). A model of factors affecting the treatment of disabled individuals in organizations. *Academy of Management Review, 21*, 352–401.

Author Index

Note: *b* indicates box, n indicates endnote

A

Abelson, R., 102, *113*n16, 205, *220*n11, *221*n28
Adler, R. S., 207, *221*n21
Adler, S., 54, *67*n14
Adler, T., 231, *240*n43
Aeppel, T., 40*b*, *48*n32
Alagna, S. W., 204, *219*n4
Alder, G. S., 175, *182*n53
Alexander, K., 187, *199*n13
Aley, J., 44, *49*n54
Ambrose, M. L., 175, *182*n53
Amsel, R., 243, *260*n4
Anderson, Z., 251, *261*n31
Ansberry, C., 230, 230*b*, *239*n30, *239*n35
Antonioni, D., 92, 93, *113*n5, *113*n9
Armour, S., 60, *68*n45, 126, *134*n24, 172, *181*n32, 189, *199*n25, 250, *261*n27
Armstrong, L., 174, *181*n41, *181*n44
Arndt, M., 127, *135*n29
Arnold, D. W., 55, *67*n20
Arthur, D., 11, 12, 21, 22, *25*n8, *25*n9, *25*n18, *26*n37, *26*n38
Arthur, M. B., 142, *156*n15
Ash, R. A., 148, *157*n40
Atwater, L. E., 164, *180*n4

Avolio, B. J., 228, *238*n16, *239*n18
Azar, B., 231, *240*n45

B

Bacharach, S. B., 235, *241*n62
Bahls, J. E., 171, *181*n30
Baig, E. C., 97, *113*n13
Bailey, T., *221*n27
Bajema, C., 204, *219*n2
Baker, D. D., 203, *219*n1
Baldridge, D. C., 254, *262*n42
Balu, R., 125, *134*n22
Bamberger, P., 235, *241*n62
Barada, P. W., *67*n17
Barbee, A. P., 61, *68*n54
Barnes-Farrell, J., 254, *262*n42
Barrett, R. S., 109, *114*n35
Barrick, M. R., 59, *67*n34, *67*n35, *69*n56
Barrier, M., 223, 225, 227, *238*n1, *238*n6, *238*n11, 245, *261*n14
Baskin, M., 163, *180*n3
Bass, S. L., 226, *238*n8
Bassett, G. A., 109, *114*n35
Bauer, T. N., 45, *49*n57
Bedeian, A. G., 109, *114*n33, *114*n35
Behling, O., 57*b*, *67*n29
Bemus, C., 32, *47*n7

263

Subject Index

Note: *b* indicates box, *f* indicates figure, *t* indicates table

CPSIA information can be obtained at www.ICGtesting.com
Printed in the USA
LVOW04s0159260215

428366LV00009B/116/P